D0272378

CHARLIE MAGRI
CHAMPAGNE CHARLIE

Foreword by Jim McDonnell

First published in hardback 2007
by Pennant Books

Edited by James McDonnell

British Library Cataloguing-in-Publication Data:
A catalogue record for this book is available from
The British Library

ISBN 978-1-906015-09-1

Design & Typeset by Envy Design Ltd

Printed and bound in Great Britain by William Clowes Ltd, Beccles, Suffolk

Pictures reproduced with kind permission of Ricky Manners, PA Photos, Lawrence Lustig, Frank Tewkesbury, John Dawes Pictures.

Pennant Books
A division of Pennant Publishing Ltd
PO Box 5675
London W1A 3FB
www.pennantbooks.com

Contents

Foreword

Charlie Magri, I call the alphabet man! All-action, brilliant, composed, determined, energetic, fast, great, hungry, inspirational, jolting, kind, lovely, mighty, nimble, open, proud, quality, ready, strong, terrific, unbelievable, vicious, winner, x-rated fighter, yours truly … Z – the end of the line.

Charlie is a man who reached the end of his journey by becoming the Flyweight Champion of the World! The above is what Charlie was and is, as a fighter and as a person. Charlie was, I believe, a freak of nature. When I first met him, it was 1983, at the Royal Oak gymnasium, the Terry Lawless fight factory, as we used to call it. I was in awe of the man to be honest with you. I looked up to him and admired him as a 16-year-old amateur boxer when he ruled the amateur game along with Pat Cowdell. I was now 22 years old and ABA Champion and Commonwealth Games silver medallist, and found myself in the same gym as one of my boxing heroes, having just turned professional with Terry.

I can remember punching the heavy bag alongside Charlie and, as I was three divisions above my flyweight compatriot, fighting at lightweight at the time, I should have been the more powerful puncher, but I can remember Charlie was rocking the bag all over the place, and, to my amazement and slight embarrassment, I couldn't match his amazing intensity as he hit the bag, even though I tried in vain! It confirmed the fact that he was something truly special, a pocket rocket, a power-punching machine, and a future World Champion.

The next step was swapping punches with Charlie for the first time in sparring. My apprehension was well founded and I was not disappointed when I got in the ring with this little powerhouse of a man! I felt privileged (sort of!) to be able to spar with a man I had looked up to and idolised as an amateur pugilist! This was the first of many long sparring sessions between me and Charlie, and the greatest learning curve any young professional could wish for. I really mean that. My confidence rocketed knowing I was working with the very best in the business, and I was always keen for advice from Charlie, which was always gladly forthcoming. In fact, it was Charlie who advised me to come down from lightweight to featherweight, where I became the undefeated European Featherweight Champion! Cheers, mate!

Jimmy McDonnell, former European Featherweight Champion, now a trainer.

CHAPTER 1

From Tunisia to Mile End

My name's Charlie Magri. Former British, European and WBC World Flyweight Champion, East End boy from Stepney Green. Well, that's what most people think of when they hear the name Charlie Magri at any rate.

In fact, the truth is a little bit stranger than that. I was born on 20 July 1956 to Andre and Rose Magri, but not in the East End. Although I'm well known as an East End fighter, I wasn't born in London, not even in England. In fact, I was born in Tunis, the capital of Tunisia in North Africa.

Both my parents were born in Tunisia, and their families were from there too. Apparently, they both had French-Maltese grandparents, though more on my dad's side I think. If you look up the surname Magri, it's quite a popular name in Malta, and there's more Magris in Malta than anywhere else outside of Italy. Magri supposedly comes from the Greek word *Makri*, which means tall – though, of course, not in my case, seeing as I'm only five-foot-three. My mother's name was Rose, or Rosa, but her friends called her Julia, which was a sort of nickname, because it was her middle name. Her family were apparently originally from Marseille somewhere way back, but nobody seems to know quite where. It's all tangled up somewhere in the history of the family.

My dad's side were a French-Maltese family too. Dad had two sisters and a brother; he had some family that had moved to London from Tunisia too, and there were others who had moved to Paris. The family on my dad's side had a business link with Tunisia way back in their history, nobody is sure just how far back it goes because it was so long ago, but, because of that, my great-grandparents had emigrated there from Malta and had eventually settled in Tunisia. Really, when you look at it, my family were all over the place, French, Maltese, Italian, Tunisian; everything but English in fact.

The reason we ended up moving to England was that things started changing in Tunisia when my mum and dad were still there. Tunisia was a French colony at that time, but the Tunisians had decided they'd had enough of that, and they separated from France. Now, like a lot of other people who lived there who had French in their family, my parents didn't much fancy what might happen to them now that the Tunisians had taken control, and they left. So, in 1958, when I was only 18 months old, my mum and dad came to England, crossing the Mediterranean on a long boat journey with a load of kids in tow – me, Walter, Georgie, Tony, Joey and my sister Rita. My youngest sister Mary was the only one of us who was actually born here.

It's funny, isn't it? Most people think of me as being English, an East Ender and a British World Champion but, if you look at my family, I'm a bit of a cross-breed really. But, as far as I was concerned, as I came here at 18 months old, and as all I ever really knew was England, that was it, I was English.

CHAPTER 2

So, What's in a Name?

Now that I've cleared up the myth about my East End roots, I have another confession. My real name isn't Charlie at all, or at least it wasn't to start with, because the thing is, like where I was born, there's a bit more to that than meets the eye. I was actually christened Carmel Magri by my mum and dad.

When I was about five years old, we were living right opposite the brewery on Sidney Street, and then we moved to Burdett Road, and to the Burdett Estate. That was one of my earliest memories as a young kid, of all our stuff being packed up and us moving from our old house to our new one. I was only about three or four years old, but I can remember being confused about what was going on because I couldn't really understand what all the commotion was about.

At that point, I'd only been to school for six months at St Mary and St Michael's School in Commercial Road. When we moved house, there was a school on the estate itself called Stebbon School, and so I moved there from St Mary and St Michael's. Anyway, when I joined that school, my real name, Carmel, was on my birth certificate, so I was registered at the school as Carmel Magri. At the other school I'd just been called Charlie. You see, the French-Maltese use Carmel as the same name as Charlie in English, so in England, Carmel is Charlie.

So, that first day at Stebbon School, I was down on the school register as Carmel, and I heard my name called out at registration: 'Carmel.' Compared to all the other names on the register – normal English names like George, John, David – it sounded a bit strange, and stood out compared to theirs. From then on, every time I heard that name, it frightened me because it stood out, and, not only did I have a strange name, but I was also very small. I was one of the smallest boys in the school; in fact, I was bloody tiny! To give you an idea of just how small I was as a kid, when I had my first proper amateur bout at the age of 11, I was 4 stone 6, only 62 pounds in weight! My own son, when he was the same age was over eight stone in weight, almost twice as heavy! In a funny way, though, being so small forced me to toughen up really, gave me a fighting spirit, and made me into what I became, a fighter.

When you're that small, people tend to think they can take liberties with you, and people started on me at school quite a bit, taking the piss out of my name, or trying to push me around. They would take the mickey, and that would be it, I'd just go for them. I had a really bad temper on me when I was a kid, and I would fancy my chances with anyone, despite being much smaller than everyone else, or maybe because of it. You could say I had a bit of a chip on my shoulder, I suppose. I was very small and I had that name to deal with, and I guess in a way those sorts of things make you want to stand up for yourself. And, after a while, people stopped taking the mickey, because I'd have a go, no matter how big they were. I was pretty fearless.

A few years later, when I started boxing as an amateur I changed my name. When I was with the Arbour Youth Boxing Club, the club secretary Jimmy Graham wrote to the ABA for me, and asked them to change my name to Charlie Magri, and that was that. I never did it by deed poll or anything like that, I just contacted the ABA and they did the rest. So I guess, in fact, officially my real name is still Carmel, but, well, everyone calls me Charlie. I spoke to my father and told him that I was going to go to the ABA so I could box under the name Charlie Magri instead of Carmel, and he understood.

He said, 'Change it, go ahead and do it.'

I was 11 years old at the time. I guess like most people I just wanted to fit in and have what sounded like a normal English name, something that didn't stand out. Jimmy contacted the ABA and saw to it for me and that was that. I went from Carmel Magri, born in Tunisia, to Charlie Magri, East End boy and amateur boxer.

CHAPTER 3

Life at the Burdett

The Burdett Estate was, as it turned out, my home from then until I was about 20 years old. It was only then that I finally moved and got a place of my own, and even then that was my own flat on the same estate! So the Burdett Estate was really my home for all the years I was growing up. The Burdett was brilliant, I really loved it there. It was a real community back then, and everyone knew each other. I guess you could say it was a tough place, and there were a lot of hard men there, but my dad, God rest his soul, was the sort of bloke who didn't take any shit off of anyone; he didn't mess around, and he was well respected by the people in the area. Like a lot of people in the East End at that time, he was a tough proud man, who worked hard to provide for his family, and, in his case, he had a lot to contend with, with five boys in the family, and two girls as well, nine people in all, all living in the same place! It was like a madhouse sometimes, especially with so many young boys in the house.

Yeah, I suppose you could say the Burdett Estate was a bit rough. There were little gangs associated with different areas of the Burdett, and if you crossed into their territory people would have a go. It was nothing serious, not like now when people are shooting each other all over the place. It was just kids giving each other a bit of ear'ole and the occasional clump, but it made you scared to walk across from one block to another sometimes in case you'd get it. I had quite a few mates on the estate who would go down to the Arbour Youth with me; Martin McGowan, Kieran McGowan, Johnny Fuller and David George were all my mates down the club. One of them, David George lived on the edge of Burdett Road and, when I'd call for him to go to boxing, I had to sort of cross the estate to get to him. Now, because of my boxing, I never really got involved in any of the little gangs on the estate as such, but there was this one kid called Quinn, who always gave me a bit of ear'ole as I walked through the estate to meet up with David. This Quinn was only a little bloke, like me, but he'd shout out to me, 'Where you going? Boxing again, are ya, Magri?' Every day he used to heckle me on the way to the boxing club, until one day I decided I'd had enough, and I jumped over the fence and gave him a clump and shut him up.

There was always a bit of fighting between kids in those days, and I guess I got a lot of practice fighting before I ever started boxing. Having so many brothers, I had plenty of sparring partners, as all of us, except for Joey, were forever scrapping with each other, always sodding about. I can remember once the lot of us were all messing about in my parents' bedroom, and there was this old flimsy wardrobe in there. We were all laying into each other and suddenly there was this loud crash and we looked round and we'd totally destroyed the wardrobe, we'd gone right through it! There was this great bloody noise, and just then we heard my dad coming back from work. We were all terrified! Luckily for us, my mum got in before he got there, and she just started laughing! When my dad came in, he had this look on his face, and it didn't look like the face of a man who was too happy, but Mum turned around to him, and she just said, 'Boys will be boys, Andre,' and he saw the funny side, thank God. We were lucky she was there to make him see that funny side.

Our house was always packed and always lively. Joey was the quiet one of the family and he was the only one who had his own room. He was the sort who liked to keep himself to himself, and, in a way, he still does. He even had a telly in his own room, which none of the rest of us was allowed, because he spent so much time in his room, in his own little world. He was like the peacemaker of the family between the boys. When we were always scrapping and arguing, Joey would try to sort things out; he was almost like the second dad of the family, as he was the oldest and the most sensible, and the rest of us looked up to him and listened to him when he told us to shut up or calm it down. Thank God he was there, because the rest of us were always at it.

It was only a four-bed flat, bear in mind, and there were nine of us in that house when I was growing up! Mum and Dad's room was on the landing on the left-hand side as you came in the front door, and me, Georgie, Tony and Walter all shared a room. Then there were my sisters Rita and Mary, who shared their room. As you can imagine, there wasn't a lot of peace and quiet to be had in that house, because you were hardly ever on your own. Me, George, Tony and Walter were always in the sitting room watching telly, but Joey was pretty much on his own, and my sisters used to play together in their own room.

I wonder sometimes how my mum and dad coped with us five boys in the family. Walter was the scrappiest of the lot of us. I always thought that Walter had all the tools to have been a bloody brilliant boxer. He had fast hands like you wouldn't believe. When he would get in a fight, cor! He couldn't half handle himself. He was totally fearless as well, he didn't care if there was one or a hundred, he would fight absolutely anyone. I can remember him coming back home once covered in blood, and him telling me he'd got into a fight with three geezers on the train because they'd said something to him he didn't like. But, in boxing, you need to have the temperament to go along with it, and I don't know that Walter could have controlled his temper enough to have boxed, but he was a really hard man. He's calmed down a lot now as he's got older, but back then he was a right handful.

Tony was the joker of the family – always was and always will be. He was absolutely mental, he could have me in stitches just like that, because he had such a mad sense of humour. My sister Rita was another one with a mad sense of humour. Georgie was really talented, and he was mad about his football. When there are five boys in a family, well, everyone is going to give you a bit of respect because there's safety in numbers; you've always got back-up if things go a bit wrong. All the brothers looked out for each other. I was the youngest, Walter was five years older, Georgie was six years older, Tony was eight years older, and Joey was nine years older than me. We were like a little clan there were so many of us. With my mum and dad, my brothers, my sisters and me, there were nine of us in total, almost enough for our own football team!

My dad got a job as soon as he came over here; he worked at a butchers shop in Stratford, called Passinghams, and my mum stayed home. I guess, in a lot of ways, it was a very traditional family set-up. My mum was a devout Catholic, and she stayed at home most of the time looking after the house and us. She certainly had her hands full anyway with so many of us round her all the time. She probably needed to pray to cope with it all. One of the things I really remember about Mum was that she was forever burning candles; she was always praying, especially later when I was fighting for a living. I tell you, if there'd been a blackout in our house, we would've never had to worry, because Mum always had a job lot in the house of those little thin church candles. Dad worked hard to provide for us, and she was a housewife, and that was the way it worked back then. My dad used to go down to Whitechapel sometimes at the weekends, because there was a little Maltese community around there, but Mum didn't go out and about much. I think that really my mum was a very shy woman; she felt comfortable around her family and in the house, but she wasn't someone who liked being in a lot of company, as she would get embarrassed.

Like I said, I didn't move out of that flat until I was about 20, when my boxing was going well, and I was with my girlfriend. I had a mate at the council – I won't mention his name in case he still works there, you never know! He told me he could get me a place on the Burdett Estate of my own, but that someone had died in it recently, which apparently was putting people off taking it. It didn't bother me really, so I took it and just did the place up. The flat was literally opposite my parents' flat; I was just over the road, so it's not like I was going far, but it meant I could get a bit of peace and quiet, because, when you're training all the time, well, you want a bit of time to yourself, don't you?

In fact, right now, I live less than a half a mile from Burdett Road, so I'm still close to where I lived all those years ago, in the area I knew growing up. It's funny, I've travelled all over the world fighting, but, at the end of the day, I've always come back home to the East End, Mile End, Stepney Green; the areas where I was brought up, the East End of London. I guess a place gets into your blood, and I'm still living in the streets that I know so well, even though the place has changed a lot since I was a kid. I'm an East Ender through and through at the end of the day.

CHAPTER 4

Getting the Boxing Bug

Most people, when they think of a fighter, they imagine someone who from the first time they watched a boxing match on television thought to themselves, 'I want to be one of those!' Then they go rushing down to the local gym with their kit and ask to join up. Well, this might surprise you, given that I'm a former fighter, but, until I actually started boxing, I wasn't really much of a boxing fan. People expect you to have been a huge boxing fan from day one, like you were born with a boxing glove in your head or something, but for me it wasn't like that. Funnily enough, my mum's dad had done a bit of boxing when he was young, and her cousin was a middleweight boxer, by the name of Gratien Tonna. He was a really good fighter, and he beat Alan Minter and Kevin Finnegan, was French Middleweight Champion, and fought for the middleweight title against Rodrigo Valdez and Carlos Monzon, so I guess the boxing side of me was in my mum's blood!

When I was young, I didn't watch much boxing, aside from watching Muhammad Ali like everyone did at that time, but I'd never been to a live fight in my life. I must have been about 12 years old when I first saw Ali, and I'd never seen anything like him. Ali absolutely made boxing what it is today, and everyone in boxing should be thankful that Ali came along when he did. Like anyone growing up in the 1960s, to me he was a real star; he was bigger than boxing, bigger than anything, and I idolised the man. There was, of course, a lot of boxing on the TV and people like Henry Cooper were well known in this country, and you'd catch boxing on the television all the time, but I didn't really follow it with that much interest.

My first love, like a lot of young lads in the East End of London, was football. I'd followed my brother Georgie into football, because he was really good as a youngster; in fact, he was good enough to have turned professional, and had trials for some professional football teams. George had an offer at one point to play for Luton Town; they wanted to sign him, but he was seeing a girl from Limehouse in London, and she didn't want to move to Luton, and his career fizzled out. Because Georgie was a few years older than me, and he was doing so well at football, when I was about seven years old, I joined a local football team, at Loxley Estate. It was just a midweek league.

Now, like I said, as a youngster, boxing wasn't really the sport I followed or wanted to get into, it was football, but, in a funny way, it was football which led me into boxing. I was a good little footballer as a young kid, very fit and competitive. I realised I was good at football, because I was good on the ball and I could run all day, but I knew that being so small it was going to be difficult; all the other lads were so much bigger than me and that made things harder.

There was a mate of mine, Kevin Sullivan, who played for a youth team in East London, at the Isle of Dogs. One day Kevin told me that he had a trial for Millwall Football Club youth team, and I said I would go along with him, sort of for good luck. I wasn't really planning on playing for them or anything, but I had my kit with me in case I had a bit of a kickabout later on. So, when I got there, they must have thought I'd come for the trial day, and they asked me if I wanted to have a trial for the team. I ran on, played a bit, and they told me I could play for the team if I wanted to. I thought, 'Brilliant! Suddenly I'm in the Millwall youth team!'

At that time, the captain of the youth team was a guy by the name of Jimmy Batten. If you don't know who Jimmy is, he was a right good footballer who went on to become a right good fighter. Jimmy really was a fantastic footballer, he was good enough to have turned professional, I reckon, and but for the boxing he probably would have done, but he turned out to be such a good fighter that football came off second best in the end. Jimmy was about 11 at the time, only a few months older than me, but he'd already been boxing for quite a while by that age, and he was already a top schoolboy amateur fighter when he was captain of the Millwall Football Club youth team. To be honest with you, I think that Jimmy was one of those blokes who was just all around good at sport; he could probably have turned his hand to anything if he wanted to and I'm sure that if he hadn't followed boxing he would have ended up doing just as well, if not better, at the football.

Jimmy went on to be a great amateur and professional, winning the British light middleweight title as a professional, but, back then, as a schoolboy amateur, he was absolutely unbeatable; he was tearing through them as an amateur, absolutely mullering his opposition. As a schoolboy-level boxer, he was beating everyone, and he won the Junior ABAs, but then he turned pro early at 18, a good four years before I did. Jimmy had a good professional career, but I always thought that he could have gone even further than he did had he stayed amateur for a while longer, but he had a wife and kids when he was still young, and so he had to turn professional to put food on the table, and maybe burned himself out a bit too young. What I do know is that Jimmy was one of the most talented fighters I ever saw, and he was a genuinely tough man in and out of the ring.

Because Jimmy was doing so well at the boxing, I'd heard loads about him before, from around the area, as he was fighting for the Poplar Club, another East London amateur gym. I guess I sort of looked up to him, because he was a winner, and he was getting right up there in the rankings. He was about 8–10 months older than me, and he had that little start before me; I was impressed by what he'd done as a boxer, and all the trophies he was winning.

So, when I'd been playing for the Millwall youth team for a while, I asked Jimmy one day, 'Jim, what's it like, the boxing?'

He said, 'Brilliant, it's great. You're on your own, you get a trophy yourself, you win it yourself; you don't have a team with you, you do it all by yourself.'

I thought, 'That sounds great, my own trophy, I fancy that.'

To me, the winning is what it was all about, getting those trophies, and knowing you'd beaten other boys, being good at what you did, and being a winner, something there were no guarantees of in the football; you weren't in charge of your own destiny.

You see, one of the things I didn't like about the football was that you weren't the guv'nor in there. When I was playing, I used to think that the coaches were picking on me sometimes because of my size, because I was the smallest in the squad by a long way, and I reckon that made me stand out. If I did anything wrong, they would notice it more because I was the smallest. I would be playing well, and suddenly, boom, they'd pull me off and I'd get substituted. It didn't feel fair, because I felt like I was playing well. Maybe they had their reasons, but I used to play inside right and I thought I was pretty good in that position, but, just when I'd be getting into it, all of a sudden they'd substitute me, and someone else would be on. What can you do about that? That annoyed me, because I wanted to be on the pitch playing, not sitting on the sidelines watching the bloody game; it used to drive me completely mental. I was so competitive that the idea of not getting to play would really get to me.

The idea of boxing sort of caught my imagination, because with boxing I could do it all myself, just me, the gloves, the vest, the gumshield and the boots, and nobody putting me on the bench. I wanted to be a winner, and I thought I had a better chance doing it at something where it was one-on-one than a team game where I had to wait to be picked or hope the rest of the team would get a result, and so I thought I'd try my hand at boxing. I suppose that moment right there was the beginning of my obsession with boxing, my boxing bug, which I was to have for 20 years, the start of something that was going to take over my whole life, and change it, and me, forever.

CHAPTER 5
Early Fights

Although there were five boys in the family, we didn't all go to the same school, so, if I would get bullied at school, I didn't have them to back me up, and, because of the age gap, by the time I got to secondary school, some of my brothers had already left because they were so much older than me, so I was on my own.

So it was my first day at my secondary school, Cardinal Griffin, and it was play-time. I was in the school playground, and I could see this black lad, and someone had got a sticker out of a book, a picture of a monkey, and stuck it on his back. He was walking around with a monkey's head on his back! Everyone was pointing and laughing at him. I didn't even know who he was at that time, but I pulled it off his back and gave it to him, and he went, 'Who done that, who done that?'

I said, 'I done it. What are you going to do about it?'

Now, to this day, if you asked me why I did that, I couldn't tell you, except for the fact that he seemed pissed off about it and I saw that as a red rag to a bull. I guess that's just the way I was back then; if someone fronted me, I was just ready to give it back to them.

So then he came charging over towards me, and we had a little fight. It wasn't anything much really, just a bit of pushing and shoving, and then it was broken up by one of the teachers who came over and pulled us apart.

The kid said to me, 'I'm going to have you for sticking that on my back.'

The teacher said, 'Did you do that, son?' He didn't even know my name because it was my first day at the school.

'No. I never done it,' I said. 'I just said I did.'

He said, 'What on earth did you do that for? Come on, you two, into the office.' He took us into the office and the teacher was taking the mickey out of me for saying I did it.

The kid said, 'You shouldn't have stuck this on my back.'

I said, 'I did say I done it, but I never stuck it on your back.'

I thought that was the end of it; I left it like that with the fight being broken up, and thinking I wouldn't hear any more about it, and off I went to my classes. It was my first day at school after all and I wasn't that keen to have a load of aggro, so I wasn't going to go following it up if he didn't. So, later that day, I found out which classes I was in, and, of course, who was in one of my classes? The same kid!

He came up to me in the class and said, 'After school, you and me.'

Now, after chatting to some of the other kids in my year, it turned out that this kid I'd had the barney with, who was called Benny, his brother was the best fighter in the second year, and Benny was supposed to be the best fighter in the first year. Great! He was going to have me after school, and apparently he's going to have his brother there as well, double trouble! I didn't fancy those odds much, so, as I was getting ready to leave school, I said to a mate of mine from the estate who was at the school, 'Do me a favour, go run over the bridge and get my brothers.'

As it happens, there were only two of my brothers at home by the time he got there, but they came running down to this big fight. My brothers were a good few years older, too old for Benny and his brother to have a fight with. My brothers had a talk with the two of them and, in the end, they got me and Benny to shake hands and call it a day. I ended up becoming this kid's mate after all that! We didn't even have a fight! I reckon I was lucky we didn't fight. After that, though, I got a little bit of respect because I had nearly had a fight with Benny and his brother who was the best fighter in the second year. No one really came near me much after that … well, almost nobody.

One thing I never liked was bullies. There was this one guy at school, a right big bully, a big, tall geezer. Anyway, I was going to the toilet one day, and he was there and he wanted me to give him some money. I don't like that, I don't give no one anything. As a young lad, I had a chip on my shoulder; I'd fight anyone. So he was in the toilet and he said to me, 'I want two bob off you.'

I said, 'You ain't getting anything off me, mate.'

He was holding his hand out for the money, so I took hold of his fingers and I bent them right back. He was going, 'Aaaarrggh!'

I said, 'You want money, do you? You ain't getting my money, mate.' I bent his fingers back so far that I broke one of them.

He came out of the toilet screaming in pain, and he fell down on the floor. I walked out of the toilet and there were all these kids out there waiting to find out what happened and I said, 'Go and pick him up.'

He had to go to hospital to have a splint put on his finger. I might have been small, but I didn't give anything to anybody. I guess even then I had it in me to be a fighter, because I wouldn't back down from anyone, even if I thought I was going to get a hiding.

There's one other fight at school that really stands out in my mind as well, this was a few years later, but thinking about fights at school it reminded me. There was this one teacher at my secondary school, Cardinal Griffin, who was a right bully, a real bastard he was. He used to like throwing his weight around with the kids at school, and slap them about. We were all on the coach one day, going somewhere, probably to games, and he came over because of the noise and tried it on with me, tried to rough me up. I think I was almost 15 because it was the year before my first Junior ABA. I stood up to him and he put his hand on me and started roughing me up. He slapped me right in the face and I lost the plot and smacked him one right in the face. I proper clumped him, and I almost knocked him off his feet and he backed off quickly, all shaken up. I think it was the first time anyone had stood up to him, because he was a grown man in his thirties. I ran into him a few years back funnily enough near where I am now, and I saw him in this pub in the area called Galloway's. He came over to me and said hello, and I told him straight, 'I'm a man now, and what you did was bang out of order. You ought to be ashamed of yourself, slapping little kids around like that. I'm glad I did what I did to you, because you were a horrible bastard.'

CHAPTER 6

First Time at the Arbour

So, anyway, after speaking to my pal Jimmy Batten, I decided in my own mind to try my hand at boxing, and in the East End in those days there were loads of good amateur clubs. One of the nearest, though, was in Stepney Green, where I'd first lived as a kid, and it was called the Arbour Youth Club. I used to pass the Arbour Youth all the time, and so a few weeks later, as I was walking through Stepney Green with my brother Walter, I figured we might as well go and have a look and see what this boxing lark was all about. As Walter was always getting into scraps with people, I figured he would be up for it, so I asked him if he fancied going along to the boxing club with me and joining up. He was well up for the idea and said, 'Yeah, I'll join with you.'

The front door was wide open when we got there, so me and Walter just strolled into the club and had a look around. I walked right over to the heavy bag, because there was nobody on it, and me and Walter started belting it around. The next thing I know, this trainer came over and shouted, 'Oi, oi, oi, what you doing? Stop. You can't do that, you've got to join the club.'

I said, 'I want to join.'

He said, 'OK, then, why do you want to box?'

I said, 'I want to box because I want to be my own winner. I play football at the moment and there's 12- and 13-years-olds and I'm in the subs all the time, and all that. I want to be on my own.'

'You think you can fight, do you?'

'Yeah, I think I can.'

'Tell you what I'll do then, son,' he said. 'If you come back in two weeks' time, we'll have a look at you.'

Now, I didn't know at the time, but that was my first introduction to Tommy Adams. I guess, looking back on it, you would say he was my first trainer really. I was better known when I was being trained by Jimmy Graham, because I was winning ABA titles and all that by then, but my first trainer really when I started boxing was Tommy Adams. Tommy trained me until I was about 14, then Jimmy Graham took over, because Jimmy was the senior trainer and Tommy trained the juniors.

Anyway, I realise now that the two-week wait was Tommy's little trick to see how keen I was; it was a little try-out to see if I'd come back. He didn't used to say come back next week or tomorrow, because he wanted to see if you were really keen or if you just fancied yourself as being a bit of a hard nut. Me? I was so keen I came right back the next day! I'd come down on my own this time, because Walter was too impatient to wait two weeks, and so he hadn't bothered coming back.

Tommy saw me and said, 'I told you to come back in two weeks' time, son.'

I said, 'No, can't I join now?' I had a little plastic bag with my plimsolls and kit in it, and I was ready to go right then and there.

He said, 'I told you no. Come back in two weeks.'

'I want to start now. Please let me start now!'

'No, come back in two weeks' time.'

So I walked out the door in a right huff! I was desperate to get in there and start walloping something, to start learning all about boxing. I just couldn't wait.

I got about 20 steps up the road and I thought, 'I'm going to go back and ask him again if I can do it. I've got my kit. He shouldn't turn me away.'

So straight back in I went, and walked straight over to Tommy.

'Christ almighty!' he said. 'I've told you, haven't I? How many times have I told you? Come back in two weeks' time!'

I was ten years old, and I only weighed four-and-a-half stone, but I wanted to stay and have a go. So, I said, 'Can't I just watch?'

'Bloody hell!' Tommy said. 'All right then, just sit down over there and watch – and keep your mouth shut!'

So I sat there watching some of the other lads training and sparring, but I soon started getting bored. I really wanted to have a go, so I went over to Tommy again and I said, 'Excuse me, I've got my kit.'

He was getting frustrated, and I could see by his face that he was getting pissed off with me. 'I told you two weeks' time. Don't you ever bloody listen?'

But he must have seen how desperate I was, because, finally, he looked at me and he said, 'You really want to start, don't you? Go on then, go and get your kit on.'

So, I put my kit on, but, of course, now all I wanted to do was get in the ring! First day an' all!

'Can't I get in the ring?'

Tommy went to me, 'No, you flippin' well can't! I told you two weeks' time, now you want to get in the ring!'

I kept going, 'Let me get in the ring please, let me get in the ring.' But, of course, this time he didn't give in!

The next time I went down there, a couple of days later, Tommy showed me some shadow boxing, and got me joining in with the other lads on some training drills. He showed me how to move, circle left and right, do shuttles backwards and forwards, how to step across and move from side to side in the ring, and how to close the gap; we drilled it over and over again.

From day one, I wanted to learn how to fight, so I watched really closely and, once I'd got the hang of something, I'd practise over and over and over again. The week after that, Tommy showed me the punch bag, and how to hit it with a jab correctly, and follow it with a right cross, and how to stand properly to get power into it. Tommy would say things like, 'Your legs are going back too far, try to get your distance right, Charlie, get your distance. Stand off the bag a bit.'

Gradually, he let me into more and more of the secrets of boxing, and I loved it. He started showing me how to skip, and jump the rope properly and get my timing right. Learning to skip takes ages, but I was on it every single day, trying to get it right. It's hard to work out how to get your co-ordination right so you can skip properly and you have to be really fit to keep doing it for a long time, but I wanted to do it right from day one.

A week or so later, some of the other boys in the gym were sparring. I asked Tommy loads of questions about what was going on in the ring, and he could see that I was really interested in the boxing, and wanted to learn. Even when I was really young, I was mad on training and wanted to do everything I could, right from the start, to be the best that I could. I was obsessed with it right from the word go, and I think even at that stage Tommy could see that I wanted it really badly and so he took the time out to show me things before he really wanted to.

So I was sitting near Tommy, and I was asking him loads of questions about the sparring, and he said to me, 'Cor, you're right keen, aren't you? You've been here every day and I've been watching you, Charlie, you've been training like a maniac every single day in here. You really want to learn, don't you?'

'Yeah, Tommy, I do,' I said to him. 'I just want a chance. Tommy. Let me get in that ring and have a spar with someone.'

'All right, son,' he said. 'We'll see what we can do for you next week then. How's that?'

'Brilliant!' I said. 'Lovely, Tommy, that's great!'

CHAPTER 7

Getting Stuck In!

So, one day the following week, I was at the club, skipping and watching some of the lads sparring at the same time. Tommy came over to me, and said, 'You ain't half taking a lot of notice, aren't you? You're bloody keen, aren't you? Do you want to get in there with them?'

I said, 'Yeah, go on then, lovely.'

I had no idea what I was letting myself in for at all. I'd been in fights before, of course, scraps at school and on the estate and that, but this was different, getting up in the ring in front of the whole club, and having to spar with gloves against someone who knew what they were doing. It's one thing having a scrap in the street, when two people don't know how to punch, but in a ring it's completely different. Some fighters might tell you that the first time they ever sparred they felt right at home, and, from that first time they put the gloves on and had a go, they felt they'd found the sport for them. Well, let me tell you right now, *my* first spar wasn't anything like that at all!

There was this boy there, whose name I don't remember now,

but he was a little bit older and a bit of a bully; he always went hard in sparring with the smaller boys. Tommy's only gone and called him over! 'You, get your gloves on. You're getting in with Magri,' Tommy said and he stuck me in with him!

This kid was older and taller than me, and quite a bit heavier than me as well, so, all in all, it wasn't looking too great for me in there. I went in there all confident, though. Well, I was loving it, wasn't I? I was finally getting the chance to get in there and have a go.

All of a sudden, the bell went. 'Ding ding!' Round one!

Well, you should have seen me. I went flying in there with my head down, with my arms flying around like two windmills, trying to stop myself getting hit in the face, while this kid was jabbing me in the mush, and making me feel a bit silly.

Tommy was shouting, 'Keep your head up, keep your head up.'

I had my head down because I didn't want to get hit in the face, so I was swinging away like a maniac. I couldn't really land a thing on this other kid, because he'd been going a while and knew what he was doing, and it was quite embarrassing standing there getting hit with my hands whizzing around. It was a lot harder than I thought. Cor! You should have seen me. I grabbed hold of the kid, and I was wrestling him and everything. Tommy couldn't stop laughing.

Afterwards, Tommy came up to me and said, 'See, I told you. It ain't as easy as you think, is it?'

I said, 'No, it ain't.'

But it didn't put me off going. I still wanted to go back and learn more, and so I kept turning up week after week to practise, doing all the training – but, after that first session, well, I wasn't so bloody keen on sparring again. To be honest, it had frightened me a bit getting clumped like that, and it put me off. I kept doing the training but I was wary of getting back in the ring. I just kept my head down and didn't mention sparring to Tommy after that.

Now, Tommy Adams was a canny feller, and he must have noticed, because a week or two later he came up to me and said,

'Do you want to have another go at sparring sometime, Charlie?'

'Yeah,' I said, 'I'd like to have another go sometime.' I wasn't too sure really, but I said it anyway.

'Right then, get in the ring, and get your gloves on.'

'What!' I said. 'Nah, I can't, Tommy, not now. I need to practise more. I'm not ready for it.'

But Tommy wasn't having any of it; he knew that first sparring session had made me a bit frightened, and I guess he wanted to see how I'd cope with having another go. At some point, you've got to find out if someone's got the bottle or not, and this was my turn to see if I really had the bottle to box.

To make it even more of a test, he put me in with the same kid I'd sparred with the first time. This time, though, after having a couple of weeks' more practice, learning the moves and how to throw my punches properly, I gave as good as I got and gave him a bit of a clump, and he didn't like it. It taught me that with the right practice you could beat anyone, because now that I'd been going for a while and had learned some of the tricks, I could stand there and fight him on even terms and I'd also overcome my first bogeyman. I'd overcome my first hurdle, and after that whenever I sparred with that kid he didn't try to go hard with me any more, because he knew he would get it right back at him.

If you put the work in, you get the results out and, if you work hard enough, you can achieve whatever it is you put your mind to. You've got to have belief, but you've also got to work bloody hard. I learned that very early on at the Arbour Youth, and it was a lesson which stayed with me for the rest of my boxing career.

CHAPTER 8

My First Bout

Now, if you ask anyone who trained with me, or anyone who knew me when I was fighting as a professional, they'll tell you the same thing. I always trained like an absolute madman. Some fighters have to be dragged kicking and screaming into the gym, but you had to drag me *out* of the gym I was so obsessed with training. It was something which was in some ways good and in some ways not so good for me later on in my career. Even as an amateur, I used to train seven days a week, twice or even three times a day at the weekends. I was never out of the gym.

I would go for a run about four times a week as an amateur, not every day, because you don't concentrate on roadwork so much as a young amateur – that comes later as a professional – and I preferred the gym work to the running anyway. I would get down the Arbour Youth about 6.30 in the evening. We used to start about seven in the evening, but I liked to get there a half-hour early and get a little bit of extra time in. I'd usually be the first there. Then, first off, I'd do some stretching exercises, and loosen right up, and then do some skipping, maybe half-an-hour. Then

I'd do some sparring. I'd spar with all the young kids, everyone. I'd usually have about 20 rounds of sparring a week. I'd practise all my moves out on everyone that was at the gym. I learned so much in those early days sparring with all the boys at the club. Some of the other lads weren't that keen on sparring, but, once I got over my fear of it, I bloody loved it. It was a chance to get in there and try out all those moves from practice for real. I used to do loads and loads of sparring; the other lads would do a minute, jump in and jump out, but I'd do three minutes all the time.

It was great because, as an amateur, you'd come across all different styles with so many sparring partners to choose from. It was especially good for me as a flyweight, because there aren't usually so many flyweights as a pro, but there were loads of young lads who were around my weight or near enough that I could spar with them. Later as a pro, it was a lot harder to find different sparring partners, and I'd have to fight bigger men most of the time, which can be a problem as you're always in with bigger punchers, so you have to be careful and you can't go hard with them. I figured the more I got in that gym and trained, which was every single day, the more I'd be prepared when that first fight came along, and I just couldn't wait to get in there and try out all the moves I'd learned for real. I was dying to fight.

I'd been going down to the club for about three months, training like a madman, and I was probably there more often than any of the boys at the club. I'd had ton of sparring against all the younger lads down there, but no fights, and I was desperate to get in the ring for real and have an amateur bout. I really wanted to get my hands on one of those trophies that Jimmy Batten had been on about, and I could already picture it up there on my mantelpiece. But, when you'd only been there a few months, they didn't usually let you fight; they wanted to teach you to defend yourself properly in sparring, where people were pulling their punches, before they'd let you get in the ring with someone who was trying to knock your head off and win the fight! And, of course, if you do that too early, it can discourage a young kid from boxing. As usual, though, *I* wasn't going to just wait around until someone asked me to fight, and the first chance I got I was going to be up there in front of everyone in the ring.

Then, one day, suddenly, I got the chance I was looking for. They announced to us that there was a show coming up the next month, and they were taking a team down to take on the Poplar Amateur Boxing Club. It was a club show, where one club would invite another along to send their boys in against their lads, and they were holding it at Poplar Baths. As soon as I heard that, I was off on one straight away! There was no way I was going to let it go. I went on and on about being given a chance to go up against their boys, and I kept on moaning at Tommy, 'Let me on it, let me go.'

It was 1968 and I was 11 years old, and I couldn't bear the thought of not getting to fight on this show. To make it even worse, a couple of my mates had also joined. They'd got on the show, so now I *really* wanted to go, and in the end they let me. Poor old Tommy, I think in the end he got sick and tired of listening to me moan and whinge at him, and in the end it was easier for him and his ear'oles to just let me go rather than say no.

So we went down to this show at Poplar Baths, and I was all excited. I'd told my whole family – who by now had figured out where I was going every evening after school! – that I was going to have my first fight, and I invited them along to the show. Then I heard the bad news: the boy I was supposed to fight hadn't turned up! I was devastated, because it was all such a big deal in my mind, and now suddenly I wasn't going to fight.

Then I found out from some lads at the Poplar club that there was a lad down there that hadn't got anyone to fight, because there was nobody else his size, and I figured I could fight him instead. He was an Asian boy from Orpington in Kent, called Chris Genkin. He was my weight but he'd already had about five or six fights.

Tommy Adams said to me, 'No bloody way, Charlie! I don't

want to let you fight him, he's too good for you, and he'll give you a bloody hiding.

'You can't fight this lad from Orpington; no way are you going to fight him. He's too good for you; he's had five fights, won four, lost one.'

But I said, 'I'll fight him.' And I kept on and on and on.

Poor old Tommy, he must have got sick of listening to me going on sometimes.

So he said, 'You're so bloody keen, you bloody well fight him then!'

Tommy could see just how much it meant for me to fight, and I guess that's why he let me do it against his better judgement, because on paper I shouldn't have been fighting the kid at all.

I just had to fight. I knew that my dad and my brothers were going to be there, and I was meant to be boxing, wasn't I? I'd announced to my whole family that I was fighting and it was my big day, so I was all keyed up. I'd been training for about three to four months and sparring. You wouldn't believe how badly I wanted to fight, and in the end, well, they caved in.

Well, to cut a long story short, I boxed the kid and I got beaten on points. I held my own against him in parts, but he'd had too many fights for me and, although it was close, he got the nod he deserved, and my first bout turned out to be a loss. I was absolutely devastated! I was someone who always hated losing, I think you've got to hate losing to be any good at any sport; it's got to be like life and death, and it was to me from day one in boxing. I wanted to fight and beat everyone put in front of me, and my first fight was no different. I was pig sick that I'd lost my first fight.

To make matters worse, when I got out of the ring, my brother Joey started taking the right piss and he said, 'You might as well pack it in, Charlie.'

So I was really upset now, because not only had I lost, but, to make it worse, all the other boys from Arbour Youth Club had won. I was the only loser in my first fight. Some bloody start! So

I've gone 'boom', that's it. I ain't standing for no more of that. I was back down the gym, training like a complete maniac, desperate to get back in there and win one. The next time I went down to Arbour Youth, the main trainer, Jimmy Graham, called me over. He took me into his office and said he wanted to talk to me.

Jimmy said, 'Look, you done well, son; you done really well against that boy. That boy was too good for you, simple as that. You nearly beat him, it was a majority decision and it was close. You should be proud, he was more experienced than you, and you still nearly beat him in your first fight. That's something to be proud of. Don't be so hard on yourself.'

I guess Jimmy could see how upset I was about losing, and appreciated how much I wanted to win, but he wanted me to know there was no shame in losing to a better fighter and someone with more experience. If you're training fighters, like I did years later, you want people who hate losing, but you've got to help them overcome a loss and find a way to win next time out.

I might have come close to winning it, but I didn't win it, did I? To make it worse, my brother took the piss out of me. I was so upset; I hated losing, always did. I made my mind up then and there that, the next time I bloody well fought, I was going home the winner, not the loser.

CHAPTER 9

The Winning Trail

A few weeks later, there was another show on, in Tottenham this time, and I was going down as a spare. Now, when you're a spare, it means that you go down there, but your name isn't on the programme. You turn up and, if there's someone your weight, size and age, and if they accept it, you can have a fight. Being a light flyweight, which I was then, and all of about four-and-a-half stone, it wasn't always easy to find fights against boys around my own age. They aren't going to put you in with a kid much younger than you because it's not fair, and most boys my age were bigger than me. It's different when you're fighting in championships, but at club shows, as long as everyone agreed to the fight, both the clubs and the boys, you could fight someone who was around your weight. But, with me, I was always giving weight away because I was so small.

That evening, I got down to Tottenham where all the other Arbour Youth boys were on the show, and there was a boy there from Tottenham called Michael Pomorsky, who was near my weight. Tommy Adams told me, 'Yeah, he's about three or four pounds heavier than you; he's had one fight, he lost it. You've had one fight, you lost it.'

So it looked like a fair match-up this time.

They told me he was Polish, and he did have a Polish name, and my mind ran away with itself and I got to thinking he was actually from Poland. Of course, he was from Tottenham really, but in my mind I'm fighting this Eastern European, and that made me worried, as Eastern European fighters were really feared back then in amateur boxing, pretty much like they are now. And I thought I'd got one of them in my second contest! I went around telling all the other lads that I had to fight this Polish guy!

Anyway, Tommy and Jimmy went to his club and they made the match, and I thought to myself, 'I ain't going to lose this time.'

I'll tell you what; I went in there like an absolute lunatic. I was punching him left, right and centre. What my brother said after my first fight came back to me, and the embarrassment of losing in front of my family, and I went at him like my life was on the line. I was all over him, and they stopped it in the second round because he couldn't defend himself, and I got a nice big trophy for it. I'd won my very first trophy and that meant a lot to me, that I had something to show for it. I liked the feeling, it felt really good winning something all by myself. And that was it, I'd got the bug, the winning bug.

The next time I lost was – you guessed it – when my family were watching me again. I hadn't lost since that first fight and had won about 20 bouts by then. I was boxing at a show at the York Hall in Bethnal Green, and I didn't know it, but a couple of my uncles had come over from France and, along with my brother Joey, they'd all sneaked in. As far as I was aware, they didn't know I was boxing. I hadn't told them, but they read about it in the local paper, the *East London Advertiser*.

I was boxing a big tall flipping slim bloke from West Ham called Mickey Street. He was one of those types that are always dancing round in the ring. I got stuck in right from the first bell. It was a really good fight, hard and close fought as it happens, but in the end he won it with a majority of 3–2. He got the decision and I was so upset. I thought, 'Oh no, my family are here again and I've lost again.' I'd won all the other fights when there was nobody there watching me, but, as soon as they turn up, I lost!

I beat Mickey three times after that, once in a tournament just after that first fight, and then twice more over the next two years, but, unfortunately, not that night when I wanted to show my family what I could do.

It felt like it was some sort of jinx at first, but, after that, my family started following me and they got to see me winning regularly. I started winning loads of fights. They saw me beat Mickey Street in the Essex Championships, and I beat a kid called Jimmy Coleman from Brixton in the North East divs. I won about four fights and I got to the semi-finals of the Schoolboy Championships where I lost to a good kid by the name of Ricky Beaumont, who went on to be a right good fighter, good enough to win an ABA title later on, and almost get as far as the British title at lightweight as a professional.

After that, I went on a bit of a run. I had another fight a week later; I won that one, then another, then another, until eventually I kept winning bouts all the time, and I made the local paper, the *East London Advertiser*. There was an article saying, 'MAGRI ON A ROLL', and my brother Joey came back home with the paper, saying, 'What's all this then, Charlie?'

In the summer, the Arbour Youth Club used to take all the lads to box in Surrey and we used to go on a little sort of tour around the amateur clubs round that way. They'd go to Hillcrest, Camberley, Rosehill, and all these places. We had an arrangement with a lot of the clubs around that area. What I didn't know was that my family had been in touch with the Arbour Youth and they'd found out where we were going to be one night when we were fighting at Hillcrest, so they could come and watch. My mum and dad were there, and so was one of my brothers, and they came into the dressing room while I was getting ready. I saw them walk in and I thought, 'Oh no!' The last time they all turned up unannounced I'd lost the fight, and now they were here again. I told them I didn't really want them there, because last time they came and watched me, I'd lost.

But, this time, even my mum had turned up! She hadn't come before because she didn't want to see me get hurt, but, now I was on a bit of a run, she wanted to come and see how I was doing. As it turned out, it was the last time she came to see me fight.

I was boxing this kid called Stevie Ellis from the Hillcrest Club. So the fight started, and my mum was sitting at ringside, and, as soon as the bell went, Stevie Ellis's mum went berserk! She started screaming and shouting: 'Kill him, Stevie, go on, kill him!'

My mum heard this and that was it – she walked straight out of the hall and stood outside. I boxed really well as it happens, and I beat him on points, but my mum never saw me win that fight because she was outside for the whole thing. My dad was there, though, and he was well pleased.

After the fight, my mum told me, 'I don't want to come no more, Charlie, to hear people like that woman screaming for him to kill you. I'm not ever coming again.'

My poor mum was sitting right next to the woman when she was screaming and she couldn't bear it. From that day until I retired, she never came to any of my fights. Every time I fought, my mum must have burned about 20 of those little church candles on a sort of shrine she had; she was worried sick about me every time I got in that ring, bless her. I'm glad she didn't come to watch me fight after that, because it would probably have killed her seeing me getting hit in the ring.

That turned out to be a great summer for me, it was my first big winning streak, and I never lost on our little tour of Surrey. I felt like a real little champion, having gone that whole season without losing a fight after those first couple of setbacks, and I was getting to like being a winner. Now, funnily enough, I've heard there's a guy called Malcolm Herbert who claims that he beat me that summer. He was a good fighter, schoolboy finalist and all that, but I know for a fact he never beat me, because *nobody* beat me that summer. So, if you're reading this, Malcolm, I'm telling you, you never beat me!

For the first time that year, I'd got into the schoolboy finals, which was a good result. It was my first year as a competitive amateur. I'd got through all my local divisions, and lost in the semi-final of the competition to Ricky Beaumont who was a lot more experienced than me; it was further than anyone had expected me to get. All in all, it was a great year for me; I was on a winning streak, had won a lot more than I lost, and I could already see a future for me in boxing ... but the best was yet to come by a long way.

CHAPTER 10
Magri the Matchmaker

Now, one thing that you've got to understand that's different between now and the days when I was a young amateur fighter is that there were loads of great fighters around when I was fighting at amateur, and so many fighters from that era went on to become top professionals, people like Alan Minter, John Conteh, Clinton McKenzie, Pat Cowdell, Terry Marsh, Colin Jones, all top amateurs, and the list goes on and on. Part of the reason, I think, is that, back in those days, fighters didn't wear headguards as amateurs – that didn't come into effect until a few years later – and fights weren't stopped as soon as someone got a slight nosebleed or took a solid shot. The amateur fights were a lot harder, a lot more like the professional game, and because of that the fights were exciting, and people used to turn out in droves to watch young lads fighting in the amateurs. The ABA finals were held at Wembley, and even the schoolboy finals were shown on television, that's how big it was, even the national schoolboy finals were on television! Amateur boxers could become stars back then, even before they turned professional. Nowadays, it's rare for that to happen – you have to go and win an Olympic medal to make a name for yourself these days, but, back then, winning the ABA title was a really big deal. Winning your local divisional and the London competition was hard, let alone the ABA title! Everyone knew who you were even if they weren't mad on boxing because amateur championships were really big news.

The truth is, I think, there were just a lot more people boxing in those days. There were loads of amateur boxing clubs, and they'd organise their own shows all the time and invite other clubs down. They'd send a list out to loads of other clubs listing all their fighters to see if they could get opponents for them. It was all done like that, not like now when everything has to be done through the ABA. They'd find a local venue, hire it out and put a show on, simple as that.

There aren't as many of those club shows any more. These days it's all sit-down dinner shows, because there's more money in it for the clubs; they don't really advertise them to the public, but all the people involved in the clubs go along and put the word about. It's easier for them to do that because they can hire the hall for nothing, charge say 40 quid for a ticket, and then the venue take a cut on the drinks, and the local club makes the money on the meal.

When I was growing up in the East End, there were loads of boxing clubs in the area and they all had fighters: Poplar, St George's, Arbour Youth, Repton, Peacock, Globe Town, Dagenham, to name just a few of them. The likes of Repton are still going strong, but my old club Arbour Youth, for instance, although it's still there, hasn't really got many fighters; it just teaches fitness training to young kids. Things have changed a whole lot and only a few of the amateur clubs turn out good fighters. Even then, with the exception of people like Amir Khan, the public don't have a clue who most of them are until they turn professional, which most of the best ones do too young, before they've really learned their trade.

I can remember when I was a kid, boxing was even something

which would be used to sort out trouble at school. If there was a fight in the playground between a couple of the boys, sometimes a teacher would bring the boxing gloves out and take them into the PE hall to sort it out, and the other boys would all come and watch. You'd never get away with that these days, a teacher putting on an unofficial little boxing match to sort out a bit of bother in the playground! Can you imagine doing that now? There'd be absolute bloody murder! The teacher would get sued and the school would probably close down.

I can remember once, I was having a little scuffle at Cardinal Griffin and a teacher pulled the two of us up. He said, 'Right, you two, come with me. Let's go and sort this out. Think you can bloody well fight, do you?'

So, he took us to the hall and gave us a set of boxing gloves each.

The thing he didn't know was that I *could* fight. I was 13, and I'd already had a lot of amateur bouts by then. Now, even though the teacher didn't know I could box, the other kid bloody well knew it.

'Sir, this isn't fair, Charlie's a boxer, sir, he boxes, for the Arbour Youth Club.'

'Shut up, get the gloves on and fight.'

The teacher was a bit of a sadistic bastard, he didn't give a toss. This poor kid, he got a right battering. I was dancing around him, jabbing his head off, smacking him in the body. He might have had a chance in a street fight, but, with gloves and boxing rules, there was only going to be one result for the lad, a right kicking. In the end, the teacher could see which way it was heading, and he pulled us apart and that was that; the poor kid's face was a right mess. I suppose it was a bit out of order me giving him a hiding like that, but, well, it was the teacher's idea, not mine.

Anyway, like I said, there were loads of really well-known amateurs about in those days, and two of the best known in the North of England were the Feeney brothers, George and John. They would both go on to be British Champions at their weights as professionals years later, George at lightweight, and John at bantamweight. They were from Hartlepool and they were big names even as amateurs, I guess because of their hard fighting styles which they kept all the way through their careers.

Well, because of George Feeney, you could say I got into the matchmaking business. George Feeney's trainer from his boxing club, Hartlepool Catholic Boys' Club, took out an advert in the *Boxing News*, asking for fights for Feeney, because he couldn't get any opponents at his own weight. He was boxing at light flyweight and, like me, he had trouble sometimes finding opponents. Most amateurs if they were that weight would grow out of it really quickly as they got older. I was about 6 stone 2 at the time, and Feeney was fighting at about 6 stone 10. Neither of us could get fights. There weren't enough people around that weight at my age, because I was about 14 at this time.

So I went to Jimmy Graham and said, 'Jimmy, I want to fight George Feeney. I've seen the advert and I want to fight him.'

Jimmy said, 'No way, Charlie, he's too heavy for you; he's 6 stone 10 and you're only just over six stone.'

I said, 'Well, it's only a few pounds. I can fight him.'

Now, eight pounds might not sound like a lot, but, when you only weigh just over six stone, it's a hell of a lot of weight, and especially in boxing! Jimmy knew this, and he said to me, 'It might not sound like a lot, Charlie, but you'll see just how much it is when you get in the ring and he starts hitting you.'

Well, as usual, I went on and on and on at him to let me fight, begging him, pleading with him, and generally doing his head in and telling poor old Jimmy how I could beat this kid despite him weighing more than me.

In the end, just as Tommy used to, Jimmy got sick of listening to me, and he threw his hands in the air and said, 'I tell you what, if you want to fight him that badly, *you* can make the phone call, because I'm not doing it.'

With that, Jimmy walked off in a bit of a huff and left me to it.

Now, I guess Jimmy thought that would be the end of it. I doubt he thought I would phone them myself, but I had other ideas. I really wanted to fight him. Truth was, I wanted to fight *everyone* in those days. If there was someone out there I could prove myself against, I wanted to get out there and fight them. So I found the number for Feeney's club, Hartlepool Catholic Boys' Club, and I called them from the phone in the Arbour Youth office.

'Hello, is that Hartlepool Catholic Boys' Club?'

'Yes.'

'I've seen the advert in the *Boxing News*, and I've heard you can't get an opponent for Feeney for your next show. Well, I'll fight him.'

'Who the bloody hell are you? You're not meant to be making fights for yourself! Get your club secretary on the phone, will you? I can't make the fight with you.'

'No, no, my club secretary said I should call. I want to come to Hartlepool and fight Feeney.'

I didn't even know where Hartlepool was. I had no idea how far away it was, or how I'd get there, but I knew I wanted to fight George Feeney.

Jimmy overheard me on the phone, and realised he had to step in and talk to the bloke, because he was getting pissed off. So Jimmy Graham got on the phone and said, 'Look, I'm sorry about all this, he's a right monkey this boy. I can't talk him out of it; he wants to make the fight himself. He really wants to fight.'

The two of them had a right laugh about it between themselves, this young kid trying to arrange his own fights, but in the end the fight was made. It was agreed that I would appear on a show up there, and then George Feeney would come down and appear on one of our club shows for a return fight. When I think about it now, it was a bit mental of me, organising my own fight and travelling the length of the country to take on George Feeney, without even knowing where Hartlepool was! I just knew that there was someone near my weight who wanted to fight, and that was good enough for me.

So, after all the training, the day of the fight came, and I got the train up there with Jimmy Graham and Danny Scur. (Danny used to volunteer to help out at the club, lovely bloke he was. He used to carry the kit bags and help out in the corner and all that.) We were on the train, and Danny had brought a cooked chicken and a flask full of tea that he'd made at home, and we had that on the train on the way there. It wasn't glamorous in those days! There was no lottery funding to go round back then, you just got on and did the business; you had to try to scrape by. I'll tell you what, though, they were great days, honestly, some of the best times of my life, and you won't hear me complaining about it. Travelling the country as a young lad with Jimmy, Danny and Tommy to all these shows was fantastic. I was doing it all just for fun and for the buzz of competing, of taking on all these other fighters and proving I was up there with the best of them.

So we arrived for the fight on George Feeney's home turf in Hartlepool and, I tell you what, it wasn't the warmest of receptions. In fact, it was one of the scariest atmospheres I've ever come across in all my years of boxing, amateur and professional. The people in Hartlepool weren't exactly welcoming, and everywhere I went they were calling me all sorts of names; people were trying to beat me up and they were spitting at me and effing and blinding on the way to the arena. The police even had to escort me into the building. There'd been a bit of noise in the local papers about me coming up, and the locals weren't exactly keen on some cocky lad from London coming up to take on their local hero. Feeney was a popular lad up there, as was his brother, and I can remember looking in the crowd and seeing all these big mad-looking blokes with skinheads. I thought I was going to get skinned alive in there. I honestly thought I might not even make it as far as the start of the fight.

In the end, after a right hard fight, I beat him. Everyone was going mad after the fight; there were loads of skinheads there, and they were all kicking off. It looked really bad, until George Feeney took it on himself to sort the trouble out. George Feeney was a lovely lad. He got up in the ring and started shouting at everyone to stop it, because he knew them all there; he was only a kid, but he was up there shouting, even at the older people in the crowd who wanted my blood. I thought I was going to get throttled. Feeney helped escort me out. I had to have a police escort with me because it was so bad, but I made it home in one piece, and it was arranged that a week later he would come down to London, and box me on an Arbour Youth show.

Now, here's a funny thing which I never found out about until years later. When we had the return match, George Feeney got a lift down with someone to get to the fight, but what I never knew before the fight – because George and his people weren't about to tell me of course – was that, on the way down, they got about 10 miles away from the arena when the car packed in! They had to push the bloody thing miles before they could get the car working again, and then he had to get in the ring and have a fight with me! Imagine having to get in the ring after something like that! The poor lad must have been knackered by the time he got there. The result was that I beat him again, and now I held two wins over one of the famous Feeney brothers!

A while ago, I'd heard that George's brother John, who I'd also fought as an amateur, wasn't doing too well and that his health wasn't great, and it's never nice to hear that about someone you've fought. I respected Feeney because he was a hard fighter. So I was pleased when I saw an issue of *Boxing News* recently and there he was, with his red cheeks looking healthy, smiling back at me from the page. He seemed happy with his life, and it said in the magazine that he still went out for regular runs. John Feeney always was a fit lad, who would fight like a demon from bell to bell, and I can imagine him still out running like that. It's funny, but in boxing you always have a strange kind of feeling about people you've fought. Unless there's some really bad blood between you, which is rare, then normally, once that bell goes and the fight is over, there's a little link that stays between you for ever; this thing that the two of you have with each other that nobody else in the world has or, unless they've been a fighter, can really understand. I wish John and George Feeney well; they were good opponents and tough lads, and I hope John is as well as he looked in the pages of that magazine.

CHAPTER 11

Danny Scur's Big Night

Now, as I mentioned, Danny Scur was one of the other people who helped out down the Arbour Youth. He wasn't one of my trainers, but he was someone who was always at the club, and who I spent a lot of time around as an amateur learning to box. He was a great feller Danny, quite an old feller, and I think he worked as a dustman during the day and was a volunteer for the club in the evenings. He was what they called a kit man or a bucket man, and he would be there in the corner along with Jimmy or Tommy Adams during the fights. Danny was really clever with his hands, and he used to make all the skipping ropes for the Arbour Youth by hand. He used to get the leather for the ropes from old sewing machines; he'd take the belts off and split them, and then make wooden handles for the ropes from old broom handles, trim it all up, and tie the leather on to hooks which he screwed into the handles. The club didn't need to spend money on skipping ropes, as every single one was made by hand by Danny.

Danny and his wife used to let me go around to their house after I finished training. Arbour Youth was at Stepney Green, and just near it was John Cass School on Stepney Way, and then down the side of the school there were these little houses where Danny lived with his wife. After training on a Saturday sometimes, they'd let me come around and they'd give me a cup of tea and some biscuits, and I'd just sit and chat to Danny about boxing. Danny loved his boxing, and me and him would sit there for hours chatting about people like Ruben Olivares who I absolutely idolised as a young amateur.

Now, like I said, Danny wasn't one of my trainers, but, by chance, one day Danny had to take a step up from the bucket man to become my sole corner man for the evening. There was this mixed-race kid called Kelvin Lavinya from West Ham, who was a right tasty little fighter, but I'd heard he couldn't get any fights, just like George Feeney, so I reckoned I'd have some of that. I was about 14 at the time, and I volunteered to go down to his club and fight him in a show at Poplar Baths, which was right near to me. So Jimmy phoned the club and made arrangements, and that was it, the fight was set.

I arranged to meet Jimmy at the Arbour Youth, and then we'd make our way down to Poplar for the fight.

Now, the most important thing in my life at that moment was to have Jimmy Graham, my trainer, in my corner. The kid I was fighting against, Kelvin Lavinya, was Schoolboys Champion at his weight that year, and I needed Jimmy in my corner.

So, the night of the fight came, and I made my way to the club to meet Jimmy and Danny. I was waiting at the club but there was no sign of Jimmy. I waited and waited and still he didn't show. In the end, they sent someone down to Jimmy's house to find out what was going on, and, when they came back, it was terrible news. 'Jimmy's been taken ill, Charlie. He's got ill and he's had to be rushed to the hospital.'

I was devastated! I was worried for Jimmy, of course, but I was also worried for myself. I was about to have the biggest fight of my life, and my trainer wasn't going to be there in my corner! I thought, 'What the bloody hell am I going to do?'

So I said to Danny, 'Listen, Danny, I can't not turn up now; I'm going to look stupid. You've got to take me down there, Danny, please.'

'What?' he said. 'I can't take you down there, Charlie. I don't know what to tell you to do, do I? I'm only the bucket man. What am I going to say to you when you're fighting?'

'I don't care, Danny, I'll fight him on me own, and you don't need to tell me anything, just take me down there.'

Well, when we got down there for the fight, Danny was more nervous than I was! I was really nervous, but Danny was all over the place, hopping about, telling me all sorts of things, and getting all worked up, and he was making me more and more bloody edgy! I was getting right narked, and I told him to shut up. I was being so rude to him because he was making me all worked up the way he was carrying on.

All he kept saying was: 'What am I going to tell you? What am I going to say?'

'Don't say anything, Danny, just put me bloody gumshield in, will you?' I said.

He was sweating buckets before we got into the ring, and I said to him, 'What's the matter with you, Danny? You're sweating like a madman.'

'I don't know what to say, Charlie; I don't know what the hell I'm doing.'

I looked across the ring at this kid, with a massive afro, looking like one of the Jackson Five. He was really flash, you could tell even before the fight started; he was bouncing about all over the place, shadow boxing and skipping around the ring.

Now Jimmy Graham had always told me when I was fighting a slick boxer like that to come out and try to hurt them as quick as possible in the first round, and, once you've got them hurt, just keep them moving backwards and stay on them, so they can't be effective. The first round, I couldn't really get close to him, as he was just bouncing around all over the place and I was struggling to get hold of him.

After the first round, Danny's face was a picture. He was so nervous he couldn't think of what to say, so I just thought about what Jimmy always told me, and told Danny to calm down and just be quiet.

'Shut up, will you, Danny, for God's sake! You're making me nervous,' I said. 'Just take my gumshield out between rounds and rub me down and I'll do the rest.'

I suppose I was being a bit rude to him really; he was a grown man after all, and I was just a kid, but the way he was carrying on was making me so bloody nervous I couldn't think straight.

I went out there and a few seconds into the second round, I caught him with a lovely right hand right on the point of the chin. His big afro went flying everywhere, and he was really shaking down to his boots. He grabbed hold of me straight away to try to clear his head, and then I heard him spit his gumshield out of his mouth. I felt the gumshield go down the back of my vest, and the next thing I knew there was this burning pain coming from my neck. I grabbed my neck and I could feel this massive pain, and I realised that the bastard had bitten me! I went mental, and I started effing and blinding.

I said to the referee, 'Oi, the little bastard just fucking bit me!'

The referee came over and he went, 'I'm warning you, Magri, no more of that, you'd better stop swearing.'

'Stop swearing!' he's telling me. The kid's just bitten me right in the bloody neck like Dracula, and I'm getting a warning for effing and blinding!

That made me even more angry than I would have been, and after that I went mental. I chased this kid all over the ring like a lunatic trying to take his head off, and I could see he was really scared; he was just trying to stay away from me.

I came back to the corner and Danny went to me, 'This is brilliant, isn't it?'

'Brilliant?' I thought. 'I've got a trainer who's so nervous he doesn't know what to say, and I'm being eaten alive in the ring!'

In the end, though, I absolutely battered this kid. I did him up in the third round.

That was the one and only time that Danny was my corner man, and thank God for that, because I think the fright would have killed him if he'd done it again!

CHAPTER 12

The Merthyr Matchstick

One of the interesting things when you look back at your career as an amateur fighter is the names you fought against; some fighters who may have gone on to make a big name for themselves and become famous in their sport, and others you remembered because you thought they would go on to big things and they didn't. Other times, you look back with a bit of sadness, and think of fighters whose careers and lives didn't quite work out. It's a very funny feeling to think of these fighters, people who you saw in their prime, at their best, full of life. You don't know at the time what's going to happen to them, they're just another fighter you got in the ring with as an amateur, just another good boy you wanted to meet and beat to make a name for yourself.

For me, one of those that I came across was Johnny Owen, the 'Merthyr Matchstick', as he was known. Johnny got his nickname because he looked like someone had glued him together out of matchsticks. He was tall and gangly, and all bone and skin; in fact, he looked pretty sickly to be honest with you. He didn't really look like a fighter at all, but, let me tell you, nobody who fought Johnny ever thought he couldn't fight. Johnny Owen's name will always be linked with his death after his shot at the WBC world bantamweight title in 1980, when he fought Lupe Pintor, the great Mexican bantamweight World Champion. Sadly, he slipped into a coma after the fight, and never came round. It was all over the newspapers and on television. What a sad few weeks that was for everyone involved in boxing in this country, and a bad day all round for the sport, but of course it was tragic for Johnny's family.

That night Johnny gave Pintor a rough fight, but the problem was that, even though he was outlanding Pintor five to one at times, every shot Pintor landed was hurting him badly, and snapping his head back. Johnny was such a brave boy, though, and he took so much punishment in the ring that night, and paid the price for it. When they examined him after the fight, it turned out that Johnny had an unusually thin skull and a thicker-than-average jaw. The injury that killed him could have happened at any time apparently, because his jaw could take a blow that would have broken another man's, but the force of it was so dangerous because of his thin skull.

My first meeting with Johnny came on 20 December 1972 when I was boxing on a show between Tower Hamlets and Cardiff, and a team of us had travelled up to Cardiff. Johnny at that time was a top Welsh amateur at my weight, who was my opponent on the show. I've still got the little yellow flyer that they handed out for the show that night in my collection of memorabilia, and it feels strange looking at his name on that piece of paper.

The night of the show, on the way up to Cardiff, I can remember I started to feel really terrible on the coach. I was so travel sick that I didn't want to fight at all when I arrived because of it; I was practically green when I got off the coach. I turned to Eamonn Cole, who was the Tower Hamlets trainer, and I said, 'I'm telling you, Eamonn, there's no way I can fight anyone. I feel like I'm going to be sick everywhere.'

He could see that I wasn't well, but he just told me to calm down and said to wait a couple of hours and see how I felt then. And, sure enough, after a couple of hours the travel sickness was gone, and I felt fine to fight.

So that night, I was fighting Johnny. Even though Johnny went on to win the British, Commonwealth and European titles at bantamweight, back then as a 16-year-old he wasn't even a proper flyweight! When we both got on the scales that night before the show to check our weights, I was bloody well amazed how big and tall he was when I stood next to him. I can remember asking Eamonn, 'Are you sure this geezer's the same weight as me? He might be skinny, but he ain't half bloody tall!'

I couldn't believe that this great big five-foot-eight guy was fighting in the same weight class as me. But, when we got on the scales, he wasn't just in the same weight class; he was actually two pounds lighter than me! It shows just how skinny he was that he could come in that light.

On the night, I won the fight, which was no mean feat, let me tell you, because Johnny Owen was a bloody good amateur fighter. He had 120 amateur fights, and won 106 of them, and he went on to represent Wales 17 times in all, so a win over Johnny Owen was a bloody good result now that I look back on it, especially as I got the stoppage.

Johnny and his family were such lovely people. Despite the fact that I'd beaten their son, and stopped him as well, Johnny's mum and dad came up to me after the fight and invited me back to their house for a cup of tea! That was the sort of people Johnny and his family were, lovely people. They were so nice to me after that fight, even though I won the bout, and they took me into their house and made me feel welcome. A lot of other parents were nowhere near as understanding when I was an amateur, like McDermott's mum, who actually gave me a slapping for beating her boy in the Junior ABA finals – but more of that later!

Even though I won that fight easily, the thing I remember was that he was a harder puncher than his shape suggested. Johnny had a devastating jab, and I can remember it being rammed into my face over and over again and thinking how hard it was. Luckily, I managed to work my way underneath the jab, and got up and under, as they say, to go to the ribs, and then worked my way up to that chin, way up there in the air, and caught him and put him over. The referee stopped the fight and I got the result.

I kept in touch with Johnny, and I used to see him here and there at shows over the years. As a professional, Johnny fought a lot of the people I'd beaten as amateurs, like John Feeney, Dave Larmour and George Sutton. We also both beat Dave Smith and Neil McLaughlin as professionals. Our careers were going along pretty similar paths too, with both of us winning the British and European titles and looking like we were heading for world honours.

Now something that isn't widely known is that me and Johnny came close to fighting against each other as professionals. Me and Johnny boxed on the same bill one night in 1980, when Alan Minter was boxing Vito Antuofermo for his middleweight title. Johnny had just beaten John Feeney for the British bantamweight title, and I had won on the same bill later that night defending my European title against Giovanni Camptaro. I was sitting in the dressing room after the fight, and Johnny came in to congratulate me on the win.

He said, 'You and me, Charlie, we should fight, we're both popular fighters; we could make a right cracking show of it like.'

I thought about it, and he was right, Johnny was huge in Wales, he was a really popular boy, and I had a big following in London. 'You know what, Johnny, you're right, mate, we should do it; that would be a great fight.'

Of course, Johnny was a bantamweight by then, and I was only a flyweight, but I'd beaten him as an amateur and I'd beaten George and John Feeney too; George was at lightweight now, and

John at bantamweight. I'd also thought about moving up in weight, because, despite training like an absolute madman all through my career as an amateur and professional at flyweight, I was always struggling like mad to keep my weight under the flyweight limit, even though I was never out of the gym. I felt I would be stronger at the higher weight where my punches would be heavier and I'd have more stamina over the later rounds, which was something that seemed to become a problem for me as I got on in age.

I'd beaten him before as an amateur, and I couldn't see any reason why I couldn't handle him as a professional. I felt stronger as a professional than I had as an amateur, and Johnny wasn't exactly known for being a massive puncher. Me and Johnny shook hands and we said we'd have a chat with our management about it, me with Terry Lawless, and him with his dad. I don't know whether or not it would have ever happened, but we thought it was a good idea. But, after his win over John Feeney for the British title, which he'd won, he got his shot at Lupe Pintor, and I never spoke to Johnny again after that night in my dressing room.

My last memory of Johnny Owen is a very sad one. I remember, not long after Johnny died, I was at the Boxing Writers Association's 'Best Young Boxer' do, and I saw his dad in the crowd. I tell you what, that man made me cry right there in that room in front of everyone. He walked over towards me, holding his hands out with his arms way out, and he threw his arms around me and started crying. I was struck dumb, I just didn't know what to say to him, and the tears started tumbling down my face, two grown men crying in a room full of people. I guess he must have remembered that moment all those years ago, when I was just a young kid really, who he invited along with his son to his house. It broke my heart to see that bloke so upset, and all those memories came back to me. I'll never forget that moment, and I'll never forget the kindness of Johnny and his family to me that night in Cardiff after the show. It was so sad for the family, losing him, he was such a lovely kid. He was so dedicated to boxing that he never had a girlfriend; he was totally devoted to what he did. He bought his parents a house with the money that he made as a fighter. It's only right and proper that they put up a statue to Johnny in his home town in Merthyr, and that his dad and Lupe Pintor, the man who killed his son in the ring, finally made their peace with each other in memory of Johnny. I would have been proud to have got in the ring with Johnny Owen and fought him.

CHAPTER 13

First Time Round

They say that there's a first time for everything. Well, for me, 1972 was one of those years. In fact, that year saw quite a few firsts for me, and you could say that it was the first big landmark in my boxing career.

At the age of 14, I became eligible to start entering the National Association of Boys' Clubs (NABCs) competition and the Junior ABAs, and it was also the first time that I started being trained by my gaffer, Jimmy Graham. Now up until this time, I had always been trained by Tommy Adams, who was responsible for the juniors at the Arbour Youth. Up until then Jimmy had occasionally taken me to one side and shown me a few moves, because I think he could see just how hard I trained; he would take me into a little side room, and take me on the pads now and then and show me a few things, but mostly it was Tommy who was my full-time trainer. Jimmy never used to do a lot of pad work with the lads at the Arbour Youth, but he used to take me aside and show me some technical work; he singled me out if you like. When I turned 14, though, Jimmy took over my training full time, and now he could train me to be a proper fighter, and it's no accident that once I started working with Jimmy full time, I really started to hit the big time. I will never underestimate just how much I learned from working with Jimmy; he was really the man who made me the fighter I was. Jimmy taught me so much that later on, as a professional, all I had to do was make some small adjustments to adapt to being a professional fighter.

Jimmy Graham was just brilliant; he was fantastic as a trainer because he knew *what* to tell me and *when* to tell me it to get me the win in fights. He knew when to calm me down, and when to gee me up. If the boy was tall – which, let's face it, at five-foot-three, most of them were to me – he'd tell me to look at their necks; if they had a skinny neck, he told me to aim for the point of the chin so I could knock them out. If a guy was moving around a lot, he'd tell me how to step off them and then cut off the ring so I could get my body shots in. Jimmy had an answer for everything.

Jimmy was a man on his own; he'd been married, but he wasn't any more when I was training at the Arbour Youth. I was close to Jimmy and, in some ways, he was like a second dad to me really. It's funny, but I always remember him looking like an old man in a school uniform. Jimmy was a man of habit and he always had the same outfit on, never varied, dark blazer, grey tie and suit trousers.

I used to love talking to him about boxing, and the two of us would sit at the club sometimes and I'd talk to him for about an hour or so before training. I looked up to him, and he took a big interest in my career which made me feel special as a young amateur; it gave me encouragement that Jimmy took me under his wing like that. I think Jimmy liked working with me because he could see I had talent and the desire to go with it; he wanted me to do well and make the best of my talent.

He gave me so much confidence that man that I felt I could do anything when he was in my corner. Jimmy really knew the boxing game inside out, and was a great trainer. That's why I had such a great amateur career with him.

The first big thing that happened to me with Jimmy at my side was winning my first proper boxing title. Though it's pretty well known that it was the year of winning my first Junior ABA title, that wasn't the first title I won. In fact, it was the NABC title that was the first for me.

The NABC tournament was different to the ABA Championships; for an amateur boxer, then, just like now, the ABA tournament is the big one that decides who is the best in the country at the weight. It's the biggest tournament of the year for amateur boxers, and everyone wants to win it. The NABC was an open tournament, which every club could enter their boys for, so you had people entering from all over. It wasn't as old as the ABA Championships, but it was a proper national tournament where clubs could enter their boys, and in its way it was a big competition. Although it wasn't as well known as the ABA title, it was still full of right good fighters, and you could be up against much more experienced boys in the tournament.

It's funny how you remember that first title you win, and, in a way, I was just as excited about winning the NABCs as I was about any of my titles as a champion later on. It meant I was a champion, a winner, and, once you start winning titles, you just don't want to stop. That first time you get called a champion, it means the world to you as a fighter. I'm sure other sportsmen would say the same, whether they're footballers or motor-racing drivers, that first time you hear your name with the word champion, well, it's special, isn't it? It kind of sticks in your mind, and, every time you fight after that, you think you're a champion, it's a sort of mental advantage.

The finals of the NABC tournament were held at the Piccadilly Hotel in Manchester, in front of this massive crowd, and it turned out to be a really big event. All the Manchester United football team were there – Georgie Best, Denis Law, Nobby Stiles, Bobby and Jackie Charlton – all watching. I'll never forget it, I was so bloody nervous. When I was standing in the ring, I could see them all sitting at ringside, pretty much the whole team sitting there looking back at me, all the proper football legends – it was incredible. To stand in the ring knowing they were all there made the night even more special, but more nerve-wracking as well.

I was the second fight on, and it turned out that I was up against this kid called Lance Johnson who I'd fought before. I'd met him first time around in a London v Yorkshire tournament and he'd beaten me. I thought I'd won it, but the judges didn't and that was that, a loss on my record.

So, anyway, now I'd got a return, and it was a whole new ball game, a whole new competition and a chance for me to get revenge.

Johnson was a Chinese-looking kid, known for being a bit of a stylist, and he was a right flash type of fighter, with these fancy white boots on. He looked really tasty as he was warming up for the fight. The first time I fought him, he was really hard to pin down, but this time I figured I had to get right on top of him straight away, because he was really nippy on his feet and a right cagey sod. But I got really nervous and I thought, 'I want to win this really badly. He's beaten me before and this is the finals, this is my big chance.'

I went out there that first round and, I tell you, I boxed out of my skin. I fought like my bloody life depended on it. The first and second rounds I was winning it; I'd gone out more aggressive and I knew I was winning it big time. But, during the second round, he seemed to be finding his rhythm a little bit, and he was starting to make me miss. He started lying on the ropes, doing all these canny little moves and stuff, fighting with his back on the ropes all the time, right flash git he was, trying to make me miss all the time, trying to make me look silly. I was starting to worry this fight might go the same way as our first one.

But I needn't have worried, because good old Jimmy had all the answers as usual. After the second round, Jimmy said, 'If he lies on the ropes again, Charlie, as soon as he lies on them, step back, and then move to the side, and bang in a left hook to the body; that will be the key punch, you'll catch him every time with that.'

We went back out for the third round, and again he went to the ropes to try to counter me. I remembered what Jimmy told me and I did this little move. I stepped back and to my left side, and threw in a lovely short bottom left hook; it dug right in under his ribs, and he went straight on the floor. When I dropped him, and the kid went down, the referee motioned to me to go to a neutral corner. Jimmy was going, 'Oh you've got it, you've got it.' He knew that there wasn't enough fight left in him to win the bout. They would have counted him out then and there, but the bell went for the end of the round and, with the rules the way they were back then, you could be saved by the bell in any round. But I won it on points and I'd boxed my way to the title. I was a champion for the very first time!

That night, at the NABC Championship, as well as being my first title, it was also the first time I ever put someone on the deck in the ring. It was all down to Jimmy as usual; he knew that, if I made some space for that left hook to the body, I could drop the kid and really hurt him, and if it wasn't for the bell ending the round that would have been my first knockout in a competition then and there. I'd stopped others at club shows, but not in a competition.

Denis Law gave me my trophy. I had a photo with him, but sadly I never got a copy of it, which was a shame.

Being called a champion for the first time, and winning the competition and the trophy, was an unforgettable feeling and one of the strongest memories I have of boxing. It meant the world to me that I was a champion, and it was a feeling I wanted to have again and again.

CHAPTER 14

Save Me, Joe Bugner!

Because I won that first NABC title, I managed to get another first under my belt that year. It was like I was on a bit of a roll. That year I got to go to Holland on the Joe Bugner Scholarship.

At that time, Joe Bugner was the British Heavyweight Champion. The year before, he'd beaten Henry Cooper, who'd been British Champion for donkeys years, and Cooper was so unhappy about losing the fight that he retired. Bugner was a big well-known heavyweight at the time, and was fancied to go on and do well, and so Ford Motors, the people who sponsored the NABCs, saw they could get some good publicity by using his name to sponsor this scholarship. Joe organised this scholarship programme to bring on the British amateur boxers who had done well at the NABCs, and the winning finalists in all the weight divisions, in both the A and B classes, were taken over to Holland to learn about the Olympic boxing programme, and also to have a bloody good time.

There was 20 of us went, all of the winners from the NABCs. There were the lads in the class As, like me, who were 15, and those who'd won the class Bs, who were 16. After that age, you were classed a senior and no longer allowed to fight in the NABCs.

It was lucky that I was doing my class A and B at that time, because they were the only two years they ran the scholarship. I think I was the only one who got to go both years, because I won the NABC titles twice, first in the class As, and then the year after in the class Bs.

We all went down to Bedford Square in the West End, and we were picked up by this coach and taken over to Holland. There were loads of us – me, Jimmy Batten, Clinton McKenzie, Ricky Beaumont, Sylvester Mittee. We were all mates, and we had a right old laugh. Most of us had never even been abroad, and now we were off to Holland for two weeks! You can imagine what a great time we had, all of us at that age away in Holland. A bunch of East End boys in Amsterdam! Well, we'd never seen anything like it in our lives, running around Amsterdam in the red-light district.

We were warned by the people who ran the scholarship to be careful in the red-light district, and not to get up to any naughtiness. But, of course, at that age, you're not listening to anyone telling you anything, and, once we knew about the red-light district, nothing was going to stop us going down there. They also warned us not to start waving any money around if we did go down there, but because we were all young lads we took no notice, or at least I didn't, and we got ourselves in right bother one night.

Me, Jimmy Batten and Clinton McKenzie and a bunch of the other lads were all walking through the red-light district and we had all got the spending money we'd brought. All these prostitutes were in their little windows with the lights on touting for business, so we stood in front of one of the windows and there I was with my money out, waving it about in front of one of them, taking the piss and having a right old laugh.

Next thing we knew, this fucking huge black geezer appeared out of nowhere from a doorway, looking well pissed off, and he started shouting something at us in Dutch. I guess he was one of the minders for the girls. He went absolutely fucking nuts and came racing towards us. We all took off and started running, and the geezer was chasing us. I don't know what he was saying, but I know it wasn't friendly, especially as he had a look on his face like he was going to kill us! We were running for our lives down this dark alleyway. We were having it on our toes, just trying to get away from him, when, all of a sudden, up ahead of us, we saw this massive fucking bloke, this great big shape coming towards us in the other direction, and we heard him say in English, 'What's going on here then?'

We were really shitting ourselves now; we were trapped with nowhere to go, with the guy chasing us from behind, and this other massive geezer up ahead of us.

The bloke ahead of us came running towards us and said, 'What the bloody hell do you lot think you're doing?'

We could see him coming towards us, and he stopped in front of us in the streetlights, and suddenly we all let out a sigh of relief. It's only fucking Joe Bugner! 'Thank Christ!' we thought.

Joe went over to the bloke and said, 'So what's all this about then? What have they been up to?'

The guy told him, and Joe said to us, 'Right, so which one of you was acting the idiot waving their money around?'

I stuck my hand up straight away and said, 'Sorry, it was me, I was only having a laugh.'

I got a right bollocking from the ABA officials and all that, but it was a lot better than what would have happened if that massive geezer had caught me – never mind a bollocking, he would have had my guts for garters!

It was a great trip over to Amsterdam. Every day, we'd all get taken out on a minibus to the town centre and we were pretty much left to our own devices. God, we had such a laugh, it was unbelievable. All that, and we got to do Olympic-standard training like the seniors did; it was such a terrific experience. It is one of the best memories of my life.

While I was there, I got friendly with this Dutch geezer called Rinze Van De Mere. He was a boxing fanatic and he knew everyone and everything about boxing in Holland. He used to come and watch us all training during our trip over there, and one day Rinze said to me, 'Charlie, if you carry on like you are now, you're going to be very big in this sport.'

At the age of 15, it was really something to hear someone say that to you, that you're going to be very, very big in your sport. I never forgot those words, and it gave me a lot of confidence to hear that from someone who was considered a bit of a boxing expert in Holland. In fact, the whole trip gave me a massive boost as a young man just starting out on his amateur career. From there, I felt like I could go on to do some really big things in the sport.

Rinze, can you believe it, kept in touch with me right up until last year, when I last heard from him. He used to send me a little letter from time to time, or some bit of information about a boxer whose career he'd been following, and sometimes he'd come over. He's a bloke you can easily get in touch with because everyone knows him over there.

To tell you how much of a fanatic Rinze was, I heard he once camped out in Regent's Park, just to watch Carlos Palomino doing his roadwork in the morning! Can you imagine that? Now that's what you call a fan!

I think Rinze is still involved in boxing in Holland, and he writes for *Boxing News* now and again. I guess he's one of those blokes whose life, like mine, was all about boxing.

CHAPTER 15
Junior ABA Titles

The big prize for amateur boxers in England is the Amateur Boxing Association (ABA) title, which basically means that you are the top boy in the country at your weight. Except for international titles like the Europeans, Commonwealth and Olympics, that was the top prize if you were in England and an amateur, and it was the same back then as it is now.

In 1972 and 1973, I was entered by my club for the Junior ABAs. Having done the class A, then class B the next year, you're then a senior fighter and you have to enter the proper ABA tournament. I'd won the NABC title in 1972, and that same year I won my first Junior ABA title. I don't think I was really fancied to win it that year, as my opponent in the final, McDermott, was reckoned to be the top boy in the competition; he was the England Schoolboy Champion and heavily fancied to win.

I had to have two fights in one day to win my first Junior ABA title, and they were hard fights. The semi-finals were in the afternoon, and I beat this kid called Fitzgerald to get through to the final that evening, where I was fighting a kid called

McDermott from Coventry. He was the favourite at light flyweight, and the England Schoolboy Champion and the top boy in the South division; in fact, he was this, that and the other, according to everyone else!

I beat McDermott in a very close hard fight, and I was now the Junior ABA Champion. Winning the Junior ABA Championships for the first time, oh, it was fantastic! I felt like I was a World Champion after that title. I was on cloud nine. Having that first ABA title to your name feels really special, because it means you're the best in the country, that you've proven it to everyone and nobody can say otherwise, because all the best boys at your weight have been entered into the tournament.

Unfortunately, not everyone seemed to be quite so happy for me. The same night I won my Junior ABA, I went down the West End with a load of the other lads to celebrate. I was standing by the bar, ordering an orange juice, because I didn't drink at all at that age, and all of a sudden this woman appeared and she said, 'Do you think you won that fight, do you?'

I said, 'Yeah, I won it, I reckon.'

All of a sudden, bosh! She slapped me right round the face! I was well shocked, I can tell you.

A geezer came running over and he shouted at her, 'What the bloody hell do you think you're doing, you stupid woman? You can't do that, that's out of order; he boxed his bloody heart out. That's wrong, that is.'

Someone told me afterwards that it was McDermott's mum and dad having an argument right in front of me! I guess his mum hadn't taken him losing the finals too well.

When I entered the Junior ABA title for the second time, I was one of the favourites to win for the first time, and there was good reason for that. By this time in my career, I was literally knocking them all out, everyone. I was strong at the weight and, working alongside Jimmy Graham, I'd turned into a proper puncher. Now, when I got into that ring, I was just beating everyone up. I think it's fair to say that, every time I went in the ring, my opponents were scared of me landing a big shot on them. I had a reputation and, when you've got a reputation, it does half the job for you, before you've even got in the ring. You're confident because you know you can hit them and hurt them, and they're worried because they know it too. It's a real advantage to have in boxing, but it can also suddenly turn against you, which was something I learned in my second Junior ABA finals against Mohammed Younis.

Younis was the favourite with a lot of people going into these Junior ABAs, and he'd earned that reputation in the run-up to the tournament. I had a reputation too, of course, but Younis was knocking everyone out. He'd had something like 30 KOs or stoppages up until that final just in the course of the year.

I figured it would be better to get him out of the way than have to face him in the final, and, before they did the draw for the next round, I said to Jimmy, 'I want to fight this Younis. I want to fight him next.' I was getting all worked up about it.

Jimmy told me to relax. 'All right, son, calm down. You don't even know if you've got him yet. Let's wait and see, shall we?'

The time came for the draw and they started to pick the names out of the hat. I heard my name called out, and the next thing I hear them say is: 'Younis … Magri, Younis will fight Magri in the next round.'

Of course, this was the draw I wanted, but, now that I'd got him, I didn't feel so great about it!

Jimmy said to me, 'Well, that's just what we wanted, son, wasn't it? You've got him, haven't you? Happy now?'

Well, I tell you what, I was really nervous. As an amateur, I used to get really nervous before a fight. Funnily enough, years later when I was a professional, my nerves got a bit better. I think that when I was training in the Royal Oak gym, which was full of professionals who were champions, it made me feel better about it. Because I was in there training with them, I felt like one of them, like a champion, but as an amateur I used to be in pieces before a fight.

Usually before a fight, Jimmy would take me off into a little side room and give me a plan for the fight, but this time he didn't say anything to me. I went off on my own for a while and I was thinking, 'What am I going to do?'

Jimmy was a right funny bloke sometimes. I was always desperate to hear what he wanted me to do in between rounds, but sometimes he would say something that would really throw me off. Like one fight, I don't remember which one now, but I came back from the end of the first round and, as I was sitting in the corner, Jimmy went, 'So, Charlie, what do you want to know about the situation in the Far East?'

I said, 'What?'

'Don't worry, son, you're boxing beautiful; you just keep on doing what you're doing and you're going to be fine. If you need to change anything next round, I'll let you know.'

I think it was just his way of having a joke and relaxing me, but I wasn't relaxed at all before the Younis fight, because Jimmy wasn't telling me anything, except that he'd tell me nearer the time.

I went and locked myself in the toilet for a while, and just prayed I'd get through the fight. I was so nervous before this fight that I didn't even want to talk, but eventually I went over to Jimmy and said, 'What's the plan then?'

'Don't worry about it, son; when we get into the ring, I'll tell you what to do.'

'But, Jimmy, it could be too late by then.'

Remember, this kid had been knocking everyone out on his way to this fight, and I didn't know what we were going to do. I knew he was a big puncher and I was worried about how I was going to handle him, because I was used to being the puncher in fights.

Jimmy just said, 'Don't worry so much, Charlie. This kid's a big puncher, he can give it out, but can he take it as well? Don't forget, Charlie, you're a big puncher too; let's see how he likes being hit hard for a change. We'll talk about the tactics later, Charlie, but remember, those that can dish it out can't always take it in return.'

We went over to ringside to get ready for the bout; we got in the ring while they did the preliminaries. I had a little gargle and I looked over at Younis, who was jumping up and down, really pumped up. He had muscles like a grown man. I thought, 'Bloody hell!' He really was built like a proper man; he even had a little beard and he was only 16 years old. Now I was really nervous.

I was sitting in the corner, waiting for the referee to call us over to touch gloves and that, and finally, right before the fight, Jimmy came to me and gave me some advice. 'Right, Charlie, here's the plan. When you get to the centre of the ring, and he stands in front of you before the fight, I want you to look right at him, and say something to upset him.'

'Like what?'

'I don't know, Charlie, just think of something to upset him. Get him right mad, so he comes charging right out at you. When he does, I want you to throw that combination we've been working on in the gym all the time, right hand, left hook, right hand, bang, bang bang. Got it? Right hand, left hook, right hand!'

'OK, got it.'

So we got to the centre of the ring, and I was thinking about what Jimmy had told me to do. Younis stood right in front of me with his face right in mine. I stared right back and said to him, 'Have you been eating curry, mate? 'Cos you don't half fucking stink!'

Well, he was an Asian lad, and his breath did smell a bit, but I didn't mean anything by it. I didn't have anything against him because he was Asian; I just had to find a way to get under his skin, but, as soon as I said it to him, cor! He went completely mad and went charging back to his corner all steamed up!

Jimmy saw him going back to the corner all angry, and he turned to me and said, 'That's it, Charlie, that's it, you've got him! What did you say to him?'

'I'll tell you later.'

'Remember what I said, Charlie. Right hand, left hook, right hand.'

I had my back turned to the kid in my corner and, as I turned round, he was going completely berserk and looked like he was going to kill me! I tell you it was so funny – obviously not at the time, but when I thought about it afterwards.

The bell went, and Younis came flying at me like a bull. He was really mad and, as soon as he came in range, I went 'right hand, left hook, right hand', just like Jimmy said. Bang, bang, bang! I landed the straight right, banged him with the left hook, and went to throw the last right and ... Bang! He'd already gone. It was over, he'd gone. He was out!

They had to take Younis to hospital after the fight, because I'd broken his jaw. He had to have his jaw wired up afterwards apparently, because I'd done such a number on him; he'd walked right into a massive left hook.

Like I said, Jimmy knew what to tell me and when!

So that was the semi-final. Jimmy came to me and said, 'Right, you've got this other boy now in the finals. You've got Alan Murray from Hull, he's a right smart little boxer; you won't be able to do to him what you did to that Younis, he's too smart for that. So do yourself a favour. He's watched you knock out the favourite. Knocked out Younis, good and clean.

'If you see him, whisper in his ear and give him a little fright so he thinks we're going to do the same job.'

So I went out to look for the kid I was fighting. I said, 'Hello, all right, mate? How did you go?'

He said, 'I won.'

'Yeah? I never saw your fight.'

'I saw your one.' He looked a little bit scared, and his voice sounded a bit wobbly.

'Here, be careful, because I know how to punch, mate.'

A bit later on, Alan Murray's trainer came in. He said, 'I don't know what you've said but you've frightened the life out of him. He doesn't want to fight you.'

We're in the Junior ABA finals and the kid doesn't want to fight me!

I said to his trainer, 'Well, tell him I won't go too hard on him.'

The trainer went back out there and he told him. Later on, the kid came in the changing room with me, and he said, 'Thanks very much for saying that.'

I got in the ring, and Jimmy said to me, 'He's scared now, just go for him and he'll fold up.'

Not surprisingly after that, I won it. I went out, bumped him a few times and he just went; he didn't want to fight by then. Really, the kid was overawed by what he was up against after he saw what I did to Younis.

So now, I was Junior ABA Champion with two knockouts in under a minute! It was absolutely unbelievable.

It was a bit of mind games, as they say, and it worked a treat, but that was Jimmy Graham for you – he was a bloke who knew his way around boxing.

CHAPTER 16

Magri Goes International

After winning that second Junior ABA, in 1973, I was completely on top of the world, but what I didn't realise was that I was about to receive one of the biggest honours that any boxer, in fact, any sportsman, can receive. I was about to represent my country as an international amateur. For a lot of fighters, what they achieve as an amateur is the biggest thing they ever achieve. There are no guarantees in boxing that being a top amateur means you'll be a top professional. Fortunately, it worked out for me pretty well, because my style was suited to the professional game anyway, but for a lot of people their amateur career turns out to be as far as they go in terms of getting results, and success. So for any young amateur fighter, representing your country at any tournament is a very big deal.

I went down the Arbour Youth as usual one day, a few weeks after winning the Junior ABA title, I think, and I was called into the office by Jimmy Graham. 'Charlie, I've just got off the phone with Kevin Hickey, and he just told me that he wants you to represent England at an upcoming England v Germany tournament, which they're holding in Germany.'

Kevin Hickey was the Great Britain coach, and he wanted me to represent England as a junior!

Well, you could have knocked me down with a bleedin' feather, I couldn't believe it! In two years, I'd gone from winning my first title, the NABC, to the Junior ABAs, and now, after winning them both twice, I was off to Germany to represent my country! What an unbelievable couple of years they were, some of the very best years of my career, of my entire life really. They were great days that I've never forgotten.

It's hard for me to explain what it meant to me to be representing England, and especially against Germany, who were always big rivals in any sport. For me, from the day I started boxing, I always wanted to do everything as a boxer. Oh yeah, I wanted to do the lot. At first, you want to represent your local area, for me, that was to be the best in East London; then, once you've done that, you want to represent London; you do the area divisions in the amateur code, and then try to win the ABA finals to become the best in England. To represent England was the next step, it felt natural; but I never expected to get called up so soon because I hadn't even fought in the ABAs as a senior by then!

I can honestly say now, hand on heart, that, if amateur boxing then was like it is today with the lottery funding, I really don't think I would have turned pro. I don't think I would have felt I needed to, because these days you can earn a decent enough living if you're a top amateur fighter. I felt absolutely unbeatable as an amateur, but there was just no money in it at all, and everyone has to make a living, right? I wasn't ever going to make any money boxing as an amateur, but, at that stage, I still wanted to achieve things. I wanted to go on and prove myself the best in the business at my weight.

To be picked as an international was just incredible. Everything seemed to be happening so fast in my amateur career; suddenly I was going to Germany. It was unbelievable for me to be representing my country at such a young age. I was just 17 and I was going to Germany to box this kid who they were putting right up there; the way they talked about him, you would have thought he was totally unbeatable.

The England v Germany tournament was held in two towns in Germany, two days apart. The first day we travelled to a place called Hemsbach, which was a small town in the south of Germany, and we arrived on the Friday and fought that night. We had a day off on the Saturday, and on the Sunday we travelled further south to a town called Pforzheim, and had the second fight. I was part of the junior squad, because I hadn't fought at senior level yet, and I remember Pat Cowdell, Roy Hilton and Robert Davies being in the senior squad.

I was fighting a kid called Juergen Schultz, who had fought in the European Championships and was a southpaw – the dreaded southpaw, there seemed to be loads of them in my career. I remember my fights with Schultz, because he was a really tough kid, a really bloody good boxer, very hard to nail with a clean shot, and very quick. Our first fight on the Friday was really close, but I got it; I just about won it. I was over the moon. My first ever international competition and I'd come out a winner! It didn't get much better than that.

On the Sunday, we set off for the second fight, but what I didn't know was that it was going to be a really long coach ride, about 200 miles, through this long mountain road to the second town further south. I was as sick as a dog, I got carsick on the coach and I was really ill. I was supposed to be fighting another kid from Germany, but the coaching team reckoned I'd already beaten the best they had to offer on the Friday. But I felt so bad on the coach that I just didn't see how I could win the fight that night, but I had to put in an appearance anyway. I thought, 'At least I've won one, I'm going to lose one now.'

When we got to the venue, I got on the scales. They went, 'Charlie, the boy you're supposed to fight tonight, you won't be fighting him now, because the boy you beat before, Schultz, he wants a return.'

I thought, 'Oh no,' because I had such a hard fight with him the last time, and I really thought I wouldn't be able to beat him now. Again, though, this turned out to be another little lesson to me in my boxing career. I was always looking to hurt my opponents and get the job over and done with when I was fighting. I always went looking for them, to get in under their guard and land hard short shots on them. This time, because I felt so sick, and it brought my confidence down, I thought I needed to find another way to win. This time round I thought, 'I'm not going to go looking for him this time; I've already beaten him, let him come to me.'

I decided I was going to use my jab and try to box my way to the result I wanted, instead of going burrowing in there like I normally did. I didn't feel well enough to do what I would normally do, but I still wanted to win. So I thought, 'This kid's tough; I'm just going to box, go the distance, see what happens.' I'll be honest, before that fight, in my own head I thought I was going to lose. That's not the way I normally thought going into a fight whether I was a professional or an amateur. That made me fight a different fight, and he wasn't expecting it; instead of getting stuck in, I boxed him. I just started boxing, moving around and letting him come to me. I went boom, stepped over to the left, threw a left hook; he went down, bang, heavy. I hurt him really badly in the first round. I got confident and I started eyeing him, going in there looking for him again, and I went back in the old style.

I got him under pressure and the bell went then and saved him. After the break, he still hadn't recovered from the first knockdown. I went in and I went boom, boom, boom, and I beat him easier the second time than I did the first time and I was ill!

It taught me that there was more than one way of winning a fight, because I went in there really just trying to last the distance, to make it to the end without getting bashed up, and, despite feeling really pretty bad, ended up winning it in style, and really hurting the kid as well. You learned so much as an amateur, travelling the world fighting all these kids with different styles, and having to adapt, it's what made me the fighter I was as a professional. The amateur code back then was tough, people could get stuck in and really go for each other without the fight being stopped; you had to know how to be a complete fighter to do well, how to survive under pressure and come out on top. Back then, having a long amateur career meant you had a really good head start when you turned professional, because you had to be really good to survive in amateur boxing a long time; the fights were hard, and the level of competition was very high.

The kid I beat that day, Schultz, turned out to be a bloody good fighter in his own right. I boxed him at light flyweight, but he went up to bantamweight. Two years after our fight, he came over to England to box bantamweight Norman Phillips at the Royal Albert Hall and knocked him out. I was boxing another German on the same bill and I remember seeing Schultz on the night, and we had a little chat about our fights in Germany.

I remember being in the changing rooms before that tournament at the Albert Hall and the trainer said, 'Right, I've got some good news and some bad news. Charlie, you've got a nice tall boy, you've got to go forward. You go forward and you should be able to beat this kid.'

I said, 'All right then.'

Then he said, 'Norman, bad news for you. You're fighting the guy that Charlie boxed that he beat twice in three days in that tournament in Germany. The kid's got better and he's got bigger and he's got more powerful.'

Looking back on it, I'd done bloody well to beat him over there, because he did a number on Norman that night. I did well beating that kid the first time.

That was my first taste of representing my country, and I loved it. I wanted to fight for England again, and I couldn't wait to get the chance.

CHAPTER 17

Magri Senior

If what had happened before was brilliant, then what came next for me was absolutely bloody amazing. 1974 and 1975 were two of the most amazing years of my career, of my whole life really, and so they really stand out in my mind. Those two years were probably the best run of form I ever went on, amateur or professional. They were my first years as a fully fledged senior fighter. Having won the NABC and the Junior ABAs, I was now competing as a senior fighter for the first time, and things just seemed to get better and better for me.

I went unbeaten domestically for the whole of 1974; I won the ABA, then went to Europe and won a silver medal, and then I defended my ABA title. The only loss I had up until that point was the finals of the European Under-21s! There were a lot of firsts for me in those years, and I was really on an amazing run of form. I think it was those two years which really helped give me that winning mentality that I carried into my professional career, because winning is like a habit it's hard to get rid of.

I stepped up to senior level fighting for my first full ABA title, after winning the Junior ABA two years in a row. I was the favourite to win the light flyweight title going into the ABA that year. I was starting to really mature, and, even though I was only 17, I was fighting like a proper fully fledged professional. There were no slaps or taps when I was throwing punches; I threw every punch with the intention of making my mark on my opponent. The year before, Mickey Abrams had held the title, but he had retired that same year after winning the title three years in a row. He was a good champion, and it's a shame I never got to test myself out against him.

I won my first title from a guy called John Chesters. Chesters was quite a lot older than me, I was only 17 and he was 23, and on paper it should have been man against boy, but I was starting to hit very hard by this point, and being unbeaten I was on a really good run of form and was coming into that competition full of confidence and really raring to go.

I was on him like a rash from the very first round of the fight, hurting him with left and right hooks, really shaking him up. For the first two rounds, I hit Chesters with everything but the kitchen sink. I was jolting his head back with every single shot I was throwing and, without being unfair to him, he was never at the races. In the last round, I finally managed to hit him full force with a flush shot, and I caught him with a lovely sort of uppercut crossed with a hook, and his legs went from under him. They gave him a standing count, and, as soon as the referee got out of the way, I leaped in there and cracked him with a right cross. His legs went again, and the referee jumped in to stop it; he'd seen enough. I started jumping up and down on the spot, hopping around like a bloody kangaroo; I was so excited by it all. I'd achieved one of my dreams already in becoming ABA Champion.

The same year, 1974, I got the chance to represent my country again, this time at the European Junior Championships. This was a massive great tournament, with all the brilliant Eastern Europeans there; there were so many good fighters coming out of the old USSR, places like Russia, Poland, Hungary, Romania, East Germany, all proper hard, tough little blokes. People were in awe of Eastern European fighters in those days, because they had such a tough boxing programme, which produced champions again and again. In 1974 it was no different.

The tournament was being held in Kiev in what was Soviet Russia, the old Soviet Union. I was still only 17, just shy of turning 18. The tournament started on 1 June, and my birthday was the next month, July. It was a whole week in Russia and, I tell you what, that was probably the greatest time of my life. What a great experience that was for a young lad, off travelling the world, to a country that, in those days, most people didn't get to visit, with the Cold War and that. It was just after the ABA finals, which were in May, and the next thing I know, I've been picked for England and I'm off to Kiev.

Bloody hell! Kiev was cold, I can remember seeing everyone walking around in big furry hats, and they bloody well needed them. They'd given us this big form to read for all the boys out there who were fighting, about what you should and shouldn't do, sort of guidelines for us, but again I hadn't taken a blind bit of notice of it. I was there standing in front of this big statue of Lenin, and I got my little camera out and started taking pictures. The next thing I knew, there was this great big policeman marching over to me, pointing a gun at my chest, and shouting at me in Russian, because you weren't allowed to take any pictures. Of course, if I'd read the form, I would have known that, wouldn't I? But that was me, if it wasn't to do with boxing, I just wasn't interested in it.

So this big angry, shouting Russian geezer ripped the camera out of my hands, threw it on the floor and stamped right on it. I was bloody terrified! That was the end of my photographic career right there.

I was competing at the 48kg weight for the tournament, which was light flyweight. I had to beat good men to get to the finals, like

Juergen Schultz, who was a top amateur, from West Germany, and then Paul Dragu, who was a crafty Romanian counter puncher, who I had to stick to like glue to win a points decision. I beat Dragu in the semi-finals, and then I had to face Alexander Tkachenko. Tkachenko was an absolutely bloody cracking fighter; he became a European Seniors Champion the next year, and he went on to win the Russian Seniors title, which was a big deal in itself because they had so many bloody good fighters. He was a real class boxer, who spent his whole career as an amateur. Up to that point, he was easily the best fighter I'd ever faced. Russian fighters in those days were considered to be a real threat; you felt differently about fighting a Russian, because you knew how tough they had it in their training camps.

I remember at one point earlier on in the competition, I went into the wrong changing rooms, and I saw the Russian team all warming up for their fights. I tell you what, their warm-up was like our full training routines with the England squad. They were really going for it. Seeing them training made you wonder what was going to happen when you got in the ring with them, because they looked so bloody hard. In fact, I wished I hadn't seen them training after that, because it put the bloody fear of God in me.

I did well, and I got to the finals, but I was up against Tkachenko, a really tough opponent. He was only just young enough to qualify for the junior tournament; he was bigger than me and he looked like a proper grown man compared to me. The whole occasion was quite frightening really, and the atmosphere there was strange compared to what I'd been used to. The kid, if you could call him that, was tall for a flyweight, and he was really good. He was slick as you like and I found it hard to really get near him.

I remember before the finals, I was finding it all very strange, because I was only 17 years old and a bloody long way from home, and, well, Russia was a place with a very strange atmosphere.

I can remember walking around in the main hall, waiting

around before my fight. I'd had my bandages approved and the Russian officials came over to approve my hand wraps. Kevin Hickey, who was the England amateur coach at the time, had this bloody awful routine before we fought. Kevin took me off into a side room into the shower room. I stripped down, walked in and I knew what was coming, and I was dreading it, because the next thing that came was a bucketful of ice-cold water all over me in the freezing-cold dressing room! I was already nervous enough from the atmosphere in the crowd; I could hear all the Russians in the crowd whistling – they never cheered, just loads and loads of people whistling, a right eerie sound it was – and now I was standing there shivering and freezing cold. I never really got what sort of advantage that bucket of ice-cold water was meant to be giving me, but Kevin had his reasons I suppose.

So now I was ready to enter the arena, and I was really feeling it, the atmosphere in the place and being away from home, and the fact I'm facing this right tasty Russian had got me all nervous. The wait seemed to go on forever, and I was getting more and more nervous as time went on.

I don't really remember anything much of what Kevin Hickey or anyone else said to me before the bell went. Maybe it was the nerves, but what I do remember was going out in that first round to have a little tear-up with him. I thought that I did all right, I was holding my own with him, but, when I got back to the corner, I didn't have Jimmy Graham there, and you really feel the difference in not having 'your' man in the corner with you. When you fight in international competitions, you have the nationally appointed amateur coach, which in this case was Kevin. No matter how good that coach is, they aren't ever going to know you as well as your club coach, are they? So, in the corner, I had Kevin telling me to watch this and watch that and he made me more nervous, and it wasn't my style to back off from my opponent and fight cautiously. Of course, I'm not saying it was Kevin's fault, he was just telling me to do what he thought was the best thing right then and there, but I think with Jimmy in my corner things might have been different.

In the end I was dropped and stopped by Tkachenko; maybe he was too experienced for me, or maybe it was just not fighting to my own abilities, I don't know, but I got stopped in the second round. I lost to the guy who won the tournament, so it wasn't exactly a bad result for my first proper international competition.

The thing was, though, Jimmy knew me inside out and he knew how to get the best out of me. I'm not saying I would have won if I'd had Jimmy with me, but the truth was I hardly ever lost as a senior when I had Jimmy in my corner. Most of my losses as an amateur were in international competitions when he wasn't with me. It didn't feel the same fighting without him in such a strange place, so far from home. I didn't have the same confidence I might have had. Still I was proud of my performance, and I couldn't exactly be upset with a silver medal for my first proper international competition. If anyone had told me a couple of years earlier I'd win a silver medal at the European Junior Championships, I'd have told them they were mad. It had all happened so quickly, I'd only just won my first proper ABA title, and now I was a silver medallist in Europe! Top draw!

Tkachenko got the gold medal that year, then the following year, 1975, at the senior competition, he won the light flyweight gold. He went on to win the Soviet Championships and competed at the next Olympics as well as a light flyweight in 1976. There was no shame in losing to him; he was class and, let's face it, I was still only 17, so, as far as I was concerned I was doing really well getting as far as I had in my first major championships.

That competition sticks in my mind for another reason, because, when I was out in Kiev, it was also the first time I met Kirkland Laing, who was part of the England squad. As a boxer, Kirkland Laing was a different breed. His nickname later in his career was 'the gifted one' and was he ever gifted! Even as an amateur, you could see that Kirkland could do things in the ring that just came naturally to him, stuff you couldn't teach Unfortunately, he had the attitude that he was so good that he didn't even need to train or try, which was really his problem in the end. He was a law unto himself, a bloke who just did his own thing.

Kirkland was out there with us, preparing for these European Juniors and what a bloody character he was! I'd never seen anything quite like him, he was a complete and utter nutter, totally individual, didn't listen to what anyone had to say. I don't think I'd ever seen anyone quite like Kirkland, a big tall black geezer with an afro from Nottingham, who walked with his feet out to the side like Charlie Chaplin.

Kirkland was boxing an East German kid out there who was supposed to be unbeatable, but it didn't bother Kirkland, he just didn't bloody care. I was nervous as hell, but Kirkland wasn't worried about anything.

The trainer told him, 'Listen, Kirkland, you've got to watch this kid, he's been bashing everyone up; he's big and tall …'

'No problems, man! I ain't listening no more, man. I don't care, I don't wanna hear no more. I'll lick him, man!'

With that, Kirkland just walked out of the room; he'd heard all he needed to hear.

In my first fight, I was boxing this little East German kid. He was shorter than me and I thought, 'I'll do this no problem.' I hardly ever had an opponent shorter than me. Then I saw him at the weigh-in; he took off his shirt and I couldn't believe the muscles on the kid. I was shitting myself! In the end, though, I gave him a right hiding. I knocked him all around the ring. I absolutely battered him for the whole fight and beat him on points. It was like I couldn't miss him during that fight.

Kirkland came over to me at ringside, and he said, 'Yes, man! They're scared of us already, Charlie, you've battered one of them, and I'm going to batter another one.'

Cor, was he ever confident! So Kirkland came into the ring for his fight, and there was this massive East German kid, Ewe Franz, I think his name was. This kid was standing up all tall and stiff with his guard up, like most of the European fighters did in those days, and pretty much still do, and Kirkland was standing there with his hands down by his side, weaving around, ducking, stepping to the side, making the geezer miss. He had him falling around all over the place! He made this kid look like a complete novice; he was getting really frustrated.

The geezer went for Kirkland, and, as Kirkland sidestepped him, the bloke went flying right through the ropes and on to one of the judges' tables at the side and hurt his leg. When Kirkland saw the guy limping back into the ring, he shouted out, 'Yeah, man! He's hurt his leg. No way he's going to beat me!'

Kirkland walked the rest of the fight, absolutely embarrassed the kid. Kirkland should have gone on to the finals, but he was blatantly robbed in the semi-finals; he fought this geezer called Tadijar Kacar from Romania, but I thought he'd won it easily. He got a bronze medal in the end.

There was George Gilbody as well, who lost to the guy who went on to win the gold medal in the end, a Russian called Vladimir Sorokin, and he got a bronze medal as well, so three of us came home with medals.

The following year, 1975, was my second ABA title, and I beat a bloke called George Sutton in the finals that year. Sutton was a Welsh lad from a fighting family, a really proud and brave sod. His dad and his uncle were both boxers, and both of them had held the Welsh flyweight title as professionals. He was a proud man from a proud family, and I knew that, in the final, he wasn't going to give me an inch.

He was absolutely bloody huge as well. He must have been about five-foot-eight which was really tall for a flyweight, and he wasn't that skinny either. How he made flyweight is beyond me. His chin was bloody miles up in the air, and he kept trying to drop a long right hand on my chin. The first two rounds were a right tear-up; he was coming forward trying to nail me with his right, and I was dipping in with left and right hooks underneath his guard. I hit him with some really hard shots in both rounds, but he just kept on coming, and was still in the fight. He started to slow towards the end of the second round, and it looked like his strength was fading, and I tried to finish him off the next round. I trapped him in the corner and hit him with some really spiteful hooks to the body and a big one to the head, but he just wouldn't fall. At the end it was a pretty clear win, but Sutton had never been out of the fight; he'd hung in there and never stopped trying all the way.

So, by now, I was already an England international, and, after my second ABA title, I had another massive tournament coming up, which was the Senior European Championships. Now, as I was over 19, I was eligible to fight for the senior squad. With two NABCs, two Junior ABAs and now two Senior ABAs, I was expected to do well in the competition. People were getting used to me winning, and I wasn't going into competitions as an underdog, so most people expected me to get a medal from the European Championships. It was a different feeling knowing that people expected you to be out winning things, more pressure, but I loved it; I loved being a winner, and I never wanted the feeling to stop. Now I was about to go and try against the best in Europe again, this time as a senior, and only one man, Tkachenko, the European Under-21 and Russian Champion, had beaten me as a senior.

That year, the competition was being held in Katowice, Poland. I was well fancied to pick up a medal, some people in the papers even thought I might win gold, but everyone knew it would be a tough call against all those top Russian and Eastern European fighters. Our team that year was me, Clinton McKenzie, Pat Cowdell, Desmond Gwilliam and Garfield McEwan at heavyweight. There were also lads from Ireland, Scotland and Wales there. George Sutton, who I beat in the ABAs, was there representing Wales at my weight; Dave Larmour from Ireland was fighting at flyweight, and John Lawless was representing Scotland.

I remember, before the competition started, there was a bit of needle between the English camp and the boys representing Ireland, Scotland and Wales. They all used to sit at their own tables in the big dining hall away from the English team. One day, Dave Larmour started giving me a bit of stick as I went to eat my food, and he shouted over at me, 'I'm going to do you, Magri. I've got you in the second round, you wait and see, the Irish are going to get one over the English this time.'

I shouted back, 'Oh, yeah, you reckon, do you, Dave? Well, why don't you ask your mate there, he's fought me before, see what he thinks.' I was talking about George Sutton, who was sitting next to him. 'Go on, be honest, George, who's your money on, mate?'

I looked over at George, and George sort of shrugged his shoulders and said, 'Sorry, Dave, I've got to be honest, after fighting Charlie, I think my money's on him to beat you.'

For my first-round fight I was up against a guy called Paolo Castroville, who went on to become Italian Flyweight Champion, and I beat him 5–0 on the judges' cards. And then, in the next round, I had Dave Larmour from Ireland, who was a well-rated amateur. Despite his big talk before the fight, I beat him hands down; it was a unanimous decision with all five judges giving it to me.

Incidentally, Dave Larmour had won the gold in the Commonwealth Games in 1974, and I hadn't been picked for the team, because they said I was too young and inexperienced, and yet I beat him on all the judges' cards at the European Championships! I always felt I missed out a bit on that one, because I'm sure I'd have beaten him at the Commonwealth Championships if only they'd let me go and compete at the tournament.

In the semi-finals, I came up against a guy by the name of Vladislav Zasypko, who had won a bronze medal at the World Championships the previous year. He was a really experienced fighter, a top-ranked Russian amateur, and he'd won a medal at the European Junior Championships in 1972 and at the World Senior Championships in 1974. He was absolutely brilliant, but I gave him a bloody good run for his money. The judges gave it to him 3–2; I thought I'd done enough to nick it, but that's the way it goes. You don't expect any favours if you're at a competition in Poland against a well-known Russian fighter, and it was bloody close either way.

I did enough to get a bronze medal and, looking back at how well I did against fighters who were top-rated amateurs with more experience than me, I was pleased with what I'd done.

Pat Cowdell won a bronze medal after losing to Ristic, the Yugoslavian, and Desmond Gwilliam lost to the eventual winner, Simion Cutov from Romania, in one of the earlier rounds.

All in all, over the previous couple of years, I'd gone from being a promising junior to the top amateur in the country, and a medallist at European level. It was an unbelievable ride, and I was still only 19 years old. It felt like I had the world at my feet and nothing was going to stop me, but, as I was going to find out, things don't always go to plan, and sometimes when you feel unstoppable is exactly when it all comes crashing down.

CHAPTER 18

A Funny Proposition

You never know what's around the corner in life, and especially in boxing, and not long after winning that first Senior ABA title, something, or someone, very unexpected came along. I was approached to turn professional, but not by someone I would have expected; this was someone who wasn't even from the boxing world, but from a different walk of life to me completely.

I'd come back from the European Championships, and this strange bloke turned up at the Arbour Youth. I was training and Jimmy Graham came over to me and said, 'There's someone outside who wants to talk to you. Now it's up to you if you want to talk to him, but I'm just letting you know. If you want to talk to him, go talk to him. I'm just letting you know he's out there.'

So I went outside, and fuck me! There was this bloke standing beside a big pink Rolls-Royce, with a white fur coat and a big diamond earring. To be honest, I'd never seen anything quite like him in my life. I'll be honest, at that age, my first thought was: 'What's this geezer want with me?' I was only 19 years old and I'd never seen anyone quite like this mush in my life. I couldn't imagine any reason someone like that would be hanging about the Arbour Youth. As it turned out, he was interested in my career.

He said, 'Charlie, I've been following your career since you were a junior. You might not ever have seen me before, but I know all about your boxing.'

'I haven't got a clue who you are, mate, to be honest with you,' I said.

'Fair enough, Charlie, my name's Justin De Villeneuve, and I've come to make you an offer. I manage Twiggy, who you've probably heard of, and what I'd like to do for you is to manage your career. I've got it all set up.'

Of course I'd heard of Twiggy, she'd been a really famous model in the 1960s and was all over the telly when I was a kid, but this was coming right out of the blue. I wasn't quite sure what to make of this geezer with his pink Rolls-Royce, his fur coat and his earring. I didn't know, of course, that Justin De Villenueve wasn't his real name; in fact, he was called Nigel Davies who had become famous after he apparently discovered Twiggy. He was a hairdresser who'd actually done a bit of boxing himself when he was younger. Funny thing is, as I found out years later, he was an East End boy a bit like myself, though you'd never have guessed it from his accent. He was a bit of a chancer, as they say.

So he told me his idea. 'I live in America, Charlie, I come over here for work, but I live over there. I'd like to manage your career for you; I want you to turn professional. I've got you a trainer lined up over in America. I've got you a place to live, a gym for you to train at and sparring partners. I know you're only 19 years old, Charlie, but I'm offering you a big opportunity here.'

I was really taken by surprise, so I said, 'Justin, do you mind if I think about it; it's a big step.'

I didn't really talk to my family about it, or to Jimmy Graham or anyone else; I came to my own decision pretty quickly. I was too young, and I was scared by the idea of going to America. I never even rang him back; quite honestly I crapped myself at the thought of leaving the country and moving to America, and, looking back on it, and at the career I had, I think I did the right thing. Going over to a foreign country, and being away from all my family, and being in those tough American gyms full of little Mexican hard nuts, I think I would have got mullered out there. Some of the kids in the gyms over there are so tough that they're like grown men by the age of 16, and that, and being away from home, would have been too much. I think I would have been burned out, and ruined by an early age.

Also, this bloke wasn't a proper boxing geezer, not as far as I was concerned. To me he was just some bloke with money, big ideas and time on his hands, who saw an opportunity to make a name for himself by managing me. He didn't understand the sport, and he didn't have the connections to make it work. I thought to myself, 'What is he going to be able to do for me?' I think that would have ruined me had I gone out there. I'll never know how it might have turned out, but the fact is I became a World Champion, so I guess my decision wasn't too bad, was it?

When I did turn professional, I had my problems with Terry Lawless, I always felt maybe I should have got more money for the fights I had and the tickets I sold, but I'll say this for him, he knew the business, and he got me fights on TV in front of big crowds in the biggest venues in London. In those days, Terry Lawless was the man to be with if you wanted to make it in boxing in England, and I don't think this Justin De Villeneuve bloke could have got me to a world title the way that Terry did. Of course, it's hard not to wonder how things might have turned out, but I've no regrets at all about turning down that offer. I was too young and it was too early in my career for me to go traipsing around the world on my own. Boxing's a hard enough game, without being managed by people who don't know what they're doing. It's a bloody difficult business, and it's best left to the experts.

CHAPTER 19

Olympic Dream – Olympic Nightmare!

In 1976, I won my third ABA title, and by now I was pretty much regarded as the best amateur in the country, and that's not me being big-headed or anything. I'd never lost to any British fighter as a senior, and I'd defended my title for the second time, this time with a really dominating performance against Bryn Griffiths, who I beat easily. I was winning the first round with no trouble, and I dropped him with a big left hook at the end of the first round, but then right at the end of the round he gave me a little clip after the bell. I went out that next round doubly determined to finish him off. I knew the next big punch I landed would drop him, and I ducked in and out of range biding my time. He tried to have it the first 30 seconds of the round, then I nailed him with a long right cross, right on the button. He got up from that, and then another right dropped him again 10 seconds later, and the referee had seen enough.

I felt like I didn't really have any challenges left for me at domestic level as an amateur, and, without that challenge, the truth was I was beginning to get a little bored. I can remember, one time, I gave this kid called Phil Darr from Davenport a chance to fight me. At the time, he was the number two in England at flyweight, and we got him down on one of our club shows so I could have a decent opponent to fight. In the end, I knocked him out in one round. So I proved my point there. I was bashing up all my opposition so badly that it was hard to find anyone to fight who could give me a challenge.

If you're a sportsman and you believe you can be the best, you want people to test you, and the only time I was getting that was when I went into international competition. There just wasn't enough to keep me interested, and by this stage I was already starting to think about moving on from boxing. I wasn't really thinking about turning professional at this stage, because, to be honest, at the beginning I never really wanted to turn professional. I was 20 years old when I was selected to fight at the Olympics. That might sound quite young, but I knew I was ready, and I knew I was going to get the call-up. It was 1976, the year of the Montreal Olympics. I was the obvious choice at my weight as there wasn't anyone else in my weight division who could really challenge me, and big things were expected of me. All of the newspapers were talking about me like I was a big favourite to take home gold. The days of me being the underdog were long gone. I was expected to go out there and bring home a medal for the England team, and preferably a gold one.

I was working as a tailor's pattern cutter at the time. I'd started out as a cutter through my sister Rita who'd been working in the rag trade for quite a while. I was well into my boxing and I wanted a nice easy job that wouldn't tire me out too much, nothing that was really hard graft. My sister was a machinist, and I asked her what the work was like and she said it was pretty easy. She told me to go down and get a job cutting the patterns.

It wasn't brilliant pay, but like I said it was a nice easy job. You'd lay the cloth out and put the template over the top, and then you'd cut the cloth to fit the pattern. I used to do coats mainly.

Sometimes you would get a check in the cloth or a grain and you'd have to make sure they matched up in the right direction, but it wasn't anything taxing that was going to wear me out, that was the main thing, so I could save my energy for boxing training.

In fact, I carried on working part-time throughout my pro career, all the way until I won the European title, which was my 12th fight. I wasn't really earning enough money from boxing before that to live off, just bits here and there. I always thought the big money would come; there were plenty of promises, but I waited for the big money and I'm still waiting now!

You had to have a job to get by, because, if you were an amateur boxer at that time, even a top-class one, you were just that, an amateur. There was no funding to help you out. If you had to take time off work, then it was your lookout; you had to make ends meet and that was that. My club, the Arbour Youth, rallied round when I went to the Olympics and I think I got 35 quid. My brothers all chipped in, too, and in the end I got a couple of hundred quid to support me while I was over at the Olympics. I spoke to Sylvester Mittee who was my pal over at the Repton Club, and I think he told me he got something like five grand! That was enough to put down a deposit on a house in those days! There was no money around for amateurs in those days, unless you were very lucky.

I was due to be at the Olympics for five weeks, so I had to try to get the time off work. Luckily, my gaffer at the tailor's said to me, 'Don't worry, your job's there for you when you get back; just go out there and do your best.' They never paid me for my time off, but at least, when I came back, I would still have a job to go to which was something in itself.

Just before the Olympics, I got called for this England v USA tournament. There was a right good roll call of fighters there that night. There was me, Pat Cowdell, Cornelius Boza Edwards, Colin Jones, George Gilbody and Clinton McKenzie on our squad. We just beat the Yanks that night, 6–5, and I stopped my guy Rocky

Wycinski in the third round; I mean, properly knocked him spark out, really good performance it was. George Gilbody came within a whisker of beating Thomas Hearns, and Hearns was one hell of a fighter even when he was a lanky lightweight back in 1976. Christ, Hearns must have been one of the biggest lightweights ever, six-foot-one with a reach of 78 inches, as big as most heavyweights! What a nightmare he must have been to fight.

Hearns didn't make the Olympics that year; I think something went wrong for him in the Olympic trials. Funnily enough, years later, I did this big after-dinner show and Thomas Hearns was one of the main speakers. I talked to him about that tournament and reminded him about his fight with George Gilbody, and it all came back to him. I told him about beating Rocky Wycinski, and he said, 'You beat Rocky Wycinski? Man, he was a good fighter back then.'

It's funny how, as a professional fighter, you remember a lot of good kids who you fought with or against as amateurs. Some of them never made it big time as professionals but you don't forget how tough they were as amateurs, not ever.

After the win in that Olympic pre-tournament, I was really feeling good. I was going to the Olympics with another good win under my belt against an international fighter, and I was really flying.

As a result of that performance, and the run of form I was in going into the Olympics, I was one of the shit-hot favourites to win the gold medal. All over the papers, 'Magri now to win a gold medal' and all that. When I got to Montreal, what really surprised me was that there were loads of people who had made their way there from the East End and other parts of London to show their support! While I was in the Olympic village, I had loads of people come to see me, shaking my hand and wishing me luck; it was really amazing how many people were out there supporting me. I had a big following then, because people had seen me all over the television right through my amateur career. It's hard to imagine now, but, back then, amateur boxing was that big that it was live on the main channels, which is why it was such big news when I finally did turn professional.

It wasn't until I found out that it was a 10-hour journey on the plane to Canada that I realised just how bloody far it was. To be honest with you, I didn't really think about it before that, I was just so excited to be getting this massive chance.

So the whole squad got together and we spent five weeks out there training and sparring together, staying in the Olympic village. What a great feeling it was being out there, being a part of the Great Britain Olympic squad.

In the team that year were me, Pat Cowdell, my old pal Sylvester Mittee, Clinton McKenzie, Colin Jones, Robert Davies and David Odwell. Clinton was unlucky enough to have Sugar Ray Leonard in his group, who beat everyone unanimously on the way to his gold medal, and Clinton lost to him in the quarter-finals. What bad luck to have one of the greatest fighters of all time at that weight in your group! Leonard was as brilliant as an amateur as he was as a professional; he had an unbelievable record as an amateur, winning something like 140 out of 150 fights.

As it turned out, Pat Cowdell, boxing in the bantamweight competition, was the only one of us to bring home a medal. I can remember sparring with Pat as an amateur – what an awkward sod he was to fight! He was an absolutely brilliant fighter with such an unusual style; he'd stand there with his feet wide apart and he was so hard to hit cleanly. Sparring with him was an absolute nightmare, because his style was so weird, fighting out of that strange crouch. Pat was an underrated fighter. He came very close to beating Salvador Sanchez later on as a professional but lost on a split decision, and fought again for the title against Azumah Nelson, but got done in one round.

My family obviously were all proud of me; the only downer was that my sister was getting married the day after my first fight at the Olympics! All of my four brothers were there, and all the rest of the family, but not me. I wasn't going to be there at my sister's wedding, but what could I do? I know it didn't go down well at the wedding but I hope my sister understood what a big chance it was for me. I think she did, but, what with the way things turned out, it was all a bit of a dampener.

During the Montreal Olympics, there was some sort of boycott, which was all over the newspapers at the time. I think it was something to do with South Africa and apartheid and all that, but the end result was that a whole load of the African countries had pulled their fighters out. As there were loads of African boxers entered into the Olympics, this changed a lot of the draws in the first round, including mine. I'd been scheduled to box a guy from Ghana in the first round, but I got a walkover because the Ghanaian team pulled him out of the competition. Instead, I ended up in a new draw in what would have been the second round of the tournament with Ian Clyde of Canada, who I think also had a walkover. He was a southpaw, who was known to have a big right hook. Southpaws seemed to follow me wherever I went right through my bloody career!

I was doing pretty well early in the fight. I think I won the first couple of rounds, and then all of a sudden everything caved in. I guess I got a little bit careless and he caught me on the chin with a big counter right hand, and down I went, boom! I got straight up like a shot, and I can really remember the moment, because there was a big clock up there above the ring to show how long was left in the round. I was still feeling the effects of the punch, and so I looked up because I wanted to see how long I had left to survive the round, and I toppled backwards a bit. That was the worst thing I could have ever done. I'd got up too fast, my legs went all over the place, and that was it; the referee stepped in and stopped the contest, and it was over just like that. With one punch, my big Olympic dream was over. I'd gone from being a hot tip for a gold medal to going out in the first round of the competition and getting stopped. Right then, it felt like the whole world stopped moving, like time had frozen or something; it didn't even seem real to me that it could have happened. What a bloody disaster!

Now the thing was, I suppose, I had nobody but myself to blame. I'd actually been down before as an amateur, so I should have known better than to just jump up like that; you're taught to take your time and clear your head, because sometimes you might feel fine in your head, but your legs aren't steady. If you get up just a second or two too early, it can mean the difference between being stopped or managing to survive the round. If the referee sees your legs are still unsteady, they might not let you continue. I think part of what got me in that Olympic fight was that I wasn't used to being the one who was experiencing the knockdown. I'd fought in international competitions before, and, even if I'd lost, which didn't happen often, I was used to being able to hang with my opponent. In my career, I was so used to being the puncher that maybe it didn't occur to me that someone else might be the puncher too. So, when I got put down, I got up way too quick. I was hurt all right, but I was just ready to fight. I wanted to get him, I wanted to hurry up and get on with it. I should have calmed down, because you know that really you have to take your time. You should wait, listen to the count, give yourself time to clear your head, and then get up. But, when you're a naturally aggressive fighter and a big puncher and you get knocked down, phwoar! You really don't want to be beaten, so you just want to get up and fight them. It was shock, complete shock. You get up and you think, 'Ah, I've been knocked on my arse. Let's get in there and return the favour now.'

Looking back, I reckon that I could have fought on; I only had 40 seconds to go and, if I'd taken my time getting up and cleared my head, I don't reckon it was long enough for him to finish me. I thought the referee jumped in too quick. I could have grabbed hold of him and held him for about 20 seconds, as I didn't have long to the bell. I would have won on points, as I was in front. I was hurt, though, no doubt about it. He caught me good and proper, flush on the chin, bang! I went down.

My Olympic dream was over, it had all turned sour right there.

Well, at that moment, I can tell you, I felt like my whole life was over. I felt like jumping in the lake and drowning myself. I didn't want to go out, I didn't want to see anyone. I just felt so embarrassed. I didn't know what to do with myself. I thought, 'Oh, what do I do now? I don't usually get beat.' I knew I was winning the fight up until that point and then he went and hit me like that, and it was over. It took all the wind out of my sails. That was the low point of my whole amateur career – the biggest tournament in the world, and I was expected to bring home the bacon. Failing like that really hurt me.

To make things even worse, after losing my fight, I had to stay in Canada for another week. I didn't want to be there at all, to be honest with you. Me and some of the team went out and we met up with this Canadian bloke who took us all around; we even stayed at his house. It would have been brilliant normally to get shown around Montreal, which was a beautiful city, but I just wanted to go home.

He took me around with the rest of the squad, even though I wasn't in the tournament any more, and that made me feel like going home. I couldn't really enjoy myself properly, because all I could think about was that I was out of the tournament. What should have been one of the best experiences of my life had turned into a bit of a nightmare.

If I thought I felt bad when I was out there, though, it was nothing compared to how I felt when I got back home, feeling like I'd failed. I didn't really feel the effect of losing properly until I came back. When I arrived home, I could feel the disappointment in everyone, even if they didn't say anything. It's like you can see it in their faces, that they feel bad for you. I felt like I'd let everyone down by getting beaten in my first fight. I went around telling people I was going to pack it up because I felt so gutted. Everyone thought I was going to come home with a gold medal, all the papers and the boxing people, everyone had been expecting big things from me, and it didn't happen. It felt like people had lost a bit of confidence in me. I'd also not only missed my sister's wedding, but everyone was apparently on a downer on the day because news got back that I'd been stopped in my first fight, which was even worse.

It hit me so hard that I decided to have a bit of a break from boxing. I actually thought about packing it all in because I was so down about losing like that in the first round of my first fight. For a while, I really thought I was going to pack it in, but in the end I thought, 'No, I'm going to go back and try to get something out of this.'

I decided that the best way to put it behind me was to go out and prove that I was still the same old Charlie Magri that had won all those ABA titles before, by going and winning it one last time.

Everyone around me was asking me why I didn't turn pro. At the time, though, I didn't want to. I didn't want to turn professional with the last thing that everyone remembered being me getting stopped and beaten at the Olympics. I had a point to prove. I wanted to go in the ABAs for one more year and prove to everyone that I was still the same fighter who had won the Senior ABA titles for the last three years.

CHAPTER 20

Proving a Point – My Last ABA

So, like I said, after losing at the Olympics, I was so disappointed that everything had turned out so badly, and I decided that, to put it all behind me, I would enter the ABAs again. My plan was to go back, win the ABAs and then turn pro. I didn't want people remembering my amateur career from the Olympics, when I got beaten in my first fight, and I wanted to prove everyone wrong who was saying I was chinny, or that I couldn't take it as well as I could dish it out, which were the doubts that the papers and the boxing press had at the time.

In the end, my last actual ABA title fight was a bit of a disappointment. By the time I got to my last ABA finals, I'd kind of lost interest. The guy I fought in the finals was Mohammed Younis, who I'd beaten twice before, and I was just going through the motions a bit. I pretty much just walked through him, ignoring his punches, and actually walked on to a big right hand at one point, because I wasn't really keyed up for it at all. I didn't really care what he was doing in there; I just wanted to get it over with and win the ABA title one last time. I don't think that Younis even thought he could win the fight, after I'd knocked him out so badly in the Junior ABAs; he seemed to be really careful not to get hit and hurt. He wasn't putting much into most of his shots, and, even when he caught me with that good shot, he didn't follow it up.

I'd only entered the ABAs that year to show everyone else I was back to my best and that I was still the best amateur in the country. If I'd turned professional after the disappointment in the Olympics, I wouldn't have been doing it on a high, and I wanted to do things my way. Once I won that title, there was only one way for me to go really, and that was to turn professional. I didn't really have much interest in the amateur game any more. My heart wasn't really in it the same way, because I was training so hard I might as well have been a professional, but I wasn't getting anything to show for it except trophies. I was working during the day, but I was earning a pittance, and I was killing myself in the gym, training every day. Despite getting knocked out in one round, and going out of the Olympics in the first round like that, I never really had any doubts in my own mind about my ability, but I felt I'd let everyone down. I knew I just got caught with a really good shot, and that can happen to anyone. I'd made my mind up now: I was going to turn professional soon, and leave the amateur game behind.

I can remember going to talk to my gaffer Jimmy Graham, and he tried to talk me out of it. 'It's a nasty business, Charlie, it's full of crooks and conmen; they'll chew you up and spit you out. It's no life, they'll treat you like a piece of meat, Charlie, and, when it's all over, that's how you'll feel.'

Jimmy really hated the professional fight game. He didn't want me to go into it, but, at the end of the day, I had no money. It was a choice between turning professional and carrying on amateur boxing and doing the same old job as a tailor's cutter, and not making much money. So I thought, 'The only way I can earn money is my fighting. I'm a boxer, and I'm a good boxer. I can probably be champion.' So that was what I planned to do.

In fact, when Jimmy heard that he couldn't talk me out of it, he was so disappointed that he barred me from coming down the Arbour Youth any more; he didn't want me to go there and influence any of the other young kids in the gym. I was the most successful amateur that the Arbour Youth had ever had, and I guess he was worried that, if I turned professional, it might make some of the others down there think about it too. I was upset at being barred from my old club, because I'd had so many good years there, and I was so close to Jimmy, but I could understand how he felt.

I guess deep down that Jimmy was just trying to look out for me, and for the other kids, because he knew it was a hard life in the professional fight game, and he was right, it is. It's a lot more dangerous than amateur boxing, and you never know what's around the corner; there's people looking to make a quick buck out of you, and there's some really horrible sides to professional boxing, which is why you hear so many fighters say they would never want their children to go into it.

The thing is, for me, boxing was the only thing I knew that I was really good at, the only thing I really enjoyed doing or wanted to do. As much as I might say that it has its bad side, I was absolutely bloody obsessed with it; I never thought about anything else. To be honest, though, when I'd gone to professional boxing matches, the thought of it scared me; there was loads of blood and people beating the life out of each other, and it was a different world to the amateur sport. Professional boxing seemed like a slaughterhouse to me compared to the amateur game.

Like I've said, if there had been the money available for amateurs fighters at my level that there is now in amateur boxing, I don't think I would have turned professional at all. With all that lottery funding, I could have stayed amateur and made a living from it, and quite a nice one at that, being able to put all my energy into it without having to have a day job. I always thought I was good enough to turn professional, but, really, to start with, all I wanted to do was win trophies and beat other good fighters and make a name for myself.

CHAPTER 21

The Pro Game

As it turned out, before I even had the time to make the decision to turn professional, things just sort of fell into my lap. I guess it shouldn't have been that surprising. I'd had a pretty well-known amateur career and for the past six years I'd won everything domestically, and had been the best flyweight in the country as an amateur. I guess it's no different to someone like Amir Khan now. Good amateurs, especially ones who can punch, are always pretty sought after, and all the promoters sign them up.

One day, completely out of the blue, I had a phone call from Reg Gutteridge, who at that time was a well-known boxing commentator for ITV, asking to meet me for a chat. I'd known Reg a long time, as he had followed my career from the earliest days and had commentated on loads of my fights. He had been talking me up as a top prospect since my amateur career as a junior, right from when I won my first NABC title and the Junior ABAs. All of my big amateur fights had been televised, and Reg had commentated on them all. He was a boxing man through and through, really old school. He'd been around boxing all his life because his family had all been involved in the fight scene.

Reg met me at work in town, and we went out for a cup of coffee. He said, 'Do you know Terry Lawless is really interested in taking you on?'

To be honest, I had a little feeling already that Terry Lawless wanted me on his books. There were a few people wanting to take me on from what I'd heard; Terry, Johnny Clarke and Mickey Duff were all interested. What made me want to go with Terry, though, was that everyone in Terry's stable was from my little area; they were all around the East End, and I knew them all. The gym was famous for good fighters: my pal Jimmy Batten was with him, Maurice Hope, Jim Watt, who had just joined the gym at that time, John L Gardner and Ray Cattouse. I'd also heard my old amateur pal Sylvester Mittee, who I used to train and spar with, was going to him, so I thought, 'Well, he's only at Canning Town, I'm at Mile End – Canning Town ain't far, is it?'

A few days after speaking to Reg, I went up to Terry Lawless's gym, the Royal Oak, and said to him, 'I want to have a look.'

Terry said, 'Hello, Charlie, come in, come and have a look. Have you got your gear here?'

'Yes I've got it.'

'Right then, get it on then.'

And that was it really! I started training that day, and I spent the rest of my career training at that same place until the day I retired. I just got my kit on and started training, and I guess that was the start of my professional career.

You've got to understand that, when you turn professional, it's a big change. It's a different life the professional game, almost a different sport. It's a different way of fighting as well, you even spar differently. It's a harder game. The amateur side is only a few rounds, in and out. If you're good enough, you're going to win those titles. As a pro, you have to go through your apprenticeship. First, you fight over four rounds, then six, then eight, 10, 12 and, in those days, for title fights, 15 hard rounds. After nine years as an amateur, my first pro fight was set for eight three-minute rounds. I didn't even think about it at the time, I just trained myself up for that. Eight three-minute rounds! The longest I'd done before that was three rounds! You had to adapt to a whole new way of training to prepare you for longer, harder fights, and you had to have hard sparring matches to get you ready for what you were going to get in the ring for real come the night of the fight.

CHAPTER 22

A Right Royal Set-up

After my first day's training, Terry's called me to one side, and said to me, 'Charlie, what I'd like you to do tomorrow is meet me at Romford Station and we'll have a little chat.'

I said, 'Oh bloody hell, that's miles away, isn't it?'

Anyway, I got the train to Romford Station and Terry picked me up. He said, 'I'll take you home; we'll have a bit of tea and a chat.'

He took me to Park Drive where he first lived; his first house it was, he had two houses knocked into one. He said, 'Nice house, isn't it? How would you fancy one like this?'

'What?'

'You could get that; you could have one of these houses.'

At that time, me and my family were still living in the flats on the estate. It sounded like a dream come true.

We went into his house and had something to eat, and Terry said, 'Right, I've got a plan for you. You'll fight at the Albert Hall on 25 October.' (Bear in mind, this was September.)

I said, 'Oh, yeah, who against?'

'Don't worry about that, let me worry about that. Then you'll be fighting again in November, then a date at the Albert Hall. I want to get you a British title fight really quickly.'

'What do you mean by quickly?' I was only 20 years old at the time, and with no professional fights. I couldn't believe what I was hearing.

'There's two fights out there for you, and then the British title fight. I've already spoken to the British Boxing Board of Control, and I reckon that, with your previous experience as an amateur, you can challenge for the title in your third fight.'

'Oh yeah. Easy as that?'

'Leave it to me, it's all worked out. You've just got to win the first two fights.'

So that was it, I was on course to win the British title and I just loved it. How do you fancy that? I didn't even ask him about the money or anything. So now I've got my first fight at the Albert Hall – the Albert Hall for my debut! As it turned out, that fight would be against someone I'd fought before back in my amateur days.

Terry had it all mapped out in his mind; he'd spoken to the British Boxing Board of Control (BBBofC) beforehand, to tell them what he wanted to do with me. This is before I'd even signed a contract with him. He told them that, if I signed with him, he wanted to get me the title shot within three fights.

Now, if you're under a certain age, you probably won't have heard of the Royal Oak, but it was a very well-known gym back then. The Royal Oak was legendary in its day. It was famous because it was so full of great fighters that it was known as the 'gym of champions'. It wasn't a flash place, though; like most good gyms, it was rough and ready, and it was perched above a pub. There was a big room upstairs which looked a bit like the inside of an old church, and it always looked like it was on the verge of falling down, because there was scaffolding everywhere holding the place up, and there were punch bags and stuff hanging off the scaffolding. That scaffolding would come a cropper some years later, but I'll get to that later. Down the end were the showers, but they hardly ever worked, and there was only a dribble of water that came out of them.

But what a gym it was! The Royal Oak gym had one of the best stables of fighters ever in this country, in fact, probably *the* best. When I joined, Jim Watt had just arrived. The other top boys in the gym were Maurice Hope, John L Gardner, Jimmy Batten, Kirkland Laing, Jimmy Flint and Sylvester Mittee. Jim McDonnell came later on too. Now I obviously knew Jimmy Batten, because I'd grown up in the same area, and we'd played on the same football team, and Kirkland I knew from my time as an England international, when we'd been on the same team for the European Under-21s, so I felt at home straight away, because there were people I knew there. It felt great being a part of that gym with such good fighters. It made you feel like you were going to be something special, because, if you were good enough for that gym, you were good enough to win titles.

John L Gardner was British Heavyweight Champion and went on to fight the likes of Michael Dokes. Kirkland Laing was the British Welterweight Champion, and he went on to challenge for the European title; he even beat the great Roberto Duran years later! Sylvester Mittee also won the British welterweight title, and the Commonwealth title, and challenged Lloyd Honeyghan for the European title. Jimmy McDonnell went on to beat Barry McGuigan and challenged Brian Mitchell for the WBA and Azumah Nelson for the WBC super featherweight title. Jim Watt and Maurice Hope were the most successful. Jim went on to win the WBC lightweight world title, only losing it to the legendary Alexis Arguello, an all-time great. Maurice Hope was the British, European and WBC Light Middleweight Champion, and he lost his title to the great Wilfred Benitez. It really was a great gym full of champions and the atmosphere in there was absolutely bloody fantastic.

Of course, not everyone in the gym fitted in with the

atmosphere. The one character who never really adapted to Terry's regime was Kirkland Laing, who eventually parted company with the gym because Terry couldn't deal with him, and I've got to talk a bit about Kirkland here. Like I said, I'd been on the amateur circuit with him as an English international, and a few years later, when I joined Terry Lawless's gym, Kirkland hadn't changed much; he was still an amazing talent, but he was also still the same erratic and unpredictable bloke he'd always been.

When you're a fighter, you know when another fighter has got something really special. The thing about Kirkland was that he just never took it seriously. He was so talented he could have beaten anyone on his day, but it was all a big joke to him; he loved to clown around in the ring and take the piss. Kirkland lived a mad life, he was always out partying and you never knew when he'd be around. His fighting career sort of existed to support the rest of it. When he turned professional at the Royal Oak, he used to have a fight, and then he'd disappear for weeks or even months. He was the only geezer I've ever known who would be out of the ring for months, and then, when he came back, he'd be lighter than when he was in training! He'd come back and Terry Lawless would say to him, 'Where the bloody hell have you been?'

I remember him getting on the scales once after he'd gone missing. He took his shoes off and he was only 145 pounds in weight! Most fighters who fought at 147 had to sweat to make the weight, but not Kirkland, he was *under* the weight. Christ knows what he was doing to himself between fights. Kirkland was a massive bloke as well; he had arms, shoulders and a chest like a heavyweight. He must have had a hollow head and legs to get on the scales that light; he was like a freak of nature. The trouble was he couldn't put it together in the ring; he'd look like a world beater in sparring, but then he wouldn't train properly, and he'd turn up for fights he should have won and lose them.

Kirkland would have spent all his money from his last fight. He'd just shrug his shoulders and say, 'Terry, I need the money, man.'

Kirkland was so talented, but he was on another planet. He would walk 20 miles in a day. I can remember one day I was driving around and I saw him walking down the street in Barking, then later that day I saw him in Dagenham, and then I was driving around Aldgate and there was Kirkland again! He always used to have big holes in his shoes, because he would just wear them out walking all the time.

While most of us tolerated Kirk's mental behaviour, there was one geezer who really didn't get on with him, Jimmy Batten. In fact, the only really bad atmosphere in the gym was between Jimmy and Kirkland.

The thing with Kirkland was, because of his style, he ended up showing people up in sparring; it was just the way he fought, it came naturally to him. Jimmy Batten was the sort of bloke who didn't take any shit, and he didn't react well to people taking the piss out of him; he was a right hard bastard in and out of the ring. I still know Jimmy today, and he's not the sort of bloke you take the piss with. Of course, he's mellowed with age, like we all do, but, back then, well, he was a young bloke who was fit and aggressive, and he wasn't having it. It all started one day when Kirkland was sparring with Jimmy. Kirkland was clowning around, turning his back on Jimmy, ducking and spinning around and making him miss and fall about. Jimmy went berserk, and they ended up having a right punch-up; it was like a street fight rather than a sparring match.

Terry had to come and break it up, and he called a meeting with everyone in the gym.

'Right, everyone, I'm telling you right now, this has to stop. Everyone in this gym, we're all part of the same team, we're all part of the Royal Oak, and we should be helping each other, not having bloody rucks. Jimmy, Kirk, I want you two to shake hands and sort things out between the two of you.'

But Jimmy was having none of it. 'I'm telling you now, Terry, I don't like the man, it's as simple as that, and I ain't shaking hands with him.'

'I don't like you either, man,' said Kirkland.

'Why don't you just let us train at separate times?' Jimmy asked.

'Yeah,' said Kirkland, 'we just don't like each other, let us train separately.'

It was about the only thing the two geezers agreed on.

Terry shook his head, but said, 'All right then, have it your way. We'll sort it out so that the two of you can train at different times of the day, if that's what it takes.'

I can remember one day seeing Kirkland sparring with Dave Boy Green, who was down for some sparring before a fight. He was a great bloody fighter, a world-rated welterweight when he came down for a bit of sparring with Kirkland. Dave went on to mix it with the likes of Carlos Palomino and Sugar Ray Leonard, and no disrespect to Dave, but that day Kirkland gave him all sorts of problems. He was dancing about with his arms by his side. Dave couldn't get near the feller; a lot of the time, nobody could. This is a guy who was a world-class fighter! He did the same thing to Maurice Hope in sparring. Maurice was bigger than Kirk, and he was a World Champion as well at light middleweight at the time, but he turned round and said, 'I'm not sparring with this geezer, I can't fucking touch him.'

But, of course, it's no good being the king of the gym, because you don't win world titles in sparring.

I tell you something that sums Kirkland up. A few of us went up to Nottingham with Terry to give Kirkland a bit of support, when he and his brother were both fighting on a bill up there. Kirkland was in the corner with Terry, and I was sitting close to them and I could hear Terry Lawless shouting at Kirkland, 'Stop whistling, Kirk, and bloody well listen to me, will ya?'

Kirkland was whistling like a bleedin' canary, without a care in the world; he was like someone from another planet at times. He boxed this feller who he could have stopped any time he wanted, but he let it go the distance because he wanted to get a workout, so he treated the fight like a sparring session.

Later, Kirkland left the Royal Oak because he wasn't really fitting in there. He pulled off a massive upset in Detroit when he beat Duran in a non-title fight, and there was talk in the gym that his new people were lining up a fight with Thomas Hearns. Kirkland was offered a chance to go over and fight Hearns, and there was apparently a massive chunk of money on the table for the fight to happen, but he didn't even turn up for training and went on the missing list again, for a whole bloody year! He only turned up again when all the money from the Duran fight was gone. What a waste!

Kirkland was the sort who, on any given night, could have beaten anyone you put in front of him, but he was just so erratic and unpredictable he could also lose to anyone. Sadly, he's had a lot of problems since his boxing career ended, but he was one of the most naturally talented geezers I ever saw put on a pair of gloves.

Personally, I can honestly say I got on with everyone at the gym, me, Sylvester Mittee and Jimmy McDonnell were particularly close; Sylvester because we'd been in the England amateur squad together, and Jimmy because, being two of the smaller guys in the gym, we trained together a lot.

I have to say, I gelled straight away with Terry Lawless, right from my very first day in the gym. Terry had a way about him; I suppose you could say that he had the gift of the gab, and he made you feel like you were important, like you were special.

He wasn't a boxer himself, he'd never had any amateur or professional career to speak of, but he had a way about him; he could say things to you, and get inside your head. He was brilliant at the psychology of the fight game, that's why I never left him my whole career. I always felt safe with Terry when I was in the ring the same way I guess I felt safe with Jimmy Graham. Like Jimmy, Terry knew what to say, when to say it, and how to say it to get you in the right frame of mind to get you to win the fight.

When it came to tactics, he wasn't that technical about it, but then he didn't need to be. The people in his gym, me included, were all ready made. We'd all been successful amateurs, and I'd had a long amateur career, including fighting for England 28 times. What Terry did was to try to get inside your head and keep you happy, simple as that; psychology, that's what it was. That was why I always felt safe in his hands, and I always left everything to Terry and just got on with fighting.

I adapted to life at the Royal Oak really quickly, and I think part of the reason was that I was always a fit boy, for as long as I can remember, and it's all in the head. I really believe that, most of all, it's in your head. If you *think* you can do it, then you can do it. Where some people find reasons that they can't do it, other people just get on with it, knuckle down and put the work into it without any second thoughts, and that's the way my mind worked. I just loved the challenge of proving that I could overcome whatever was put in front of me. You've got to have the arsehole so that when someone says, 'Can you do this, or can you do that?', you just say yes. It's as simple as that. If you haven't got it in your head to do that, you shouldn't be in it. Everything was a challenge to me, it didn't matter what I had to face, I'd do it, I wanted to succeed. I loved training; I never missed training because I was scared that, if I missed something, I'd lose. I guess you could say that I was paranoid really, because I was always worrying myself bloody stupid over training. The physical effort I put in was nothing compared to what was going on inside my head all the time. I fought every fight about 10 times in my head before I ever got into the ring.

I was made to feel welcome by the other lads in the gym. On the first day, I wasn't there early enough, so I'd missed the run, and they said they were all going running in the morning. They used to run in Greenwich, so John L Gardner said he'd give me a lift in his car, and the next morning he came and picked me up from the Burdett Estate.

So me, John and Jimmy Batten were all running together round Greenwich, through the park, through the foot tunnel under the river and everything. I was the new kid on the block, and so that first day, when we went out running, they decided to give me a bit of a wind-up. They said to me, 'Right, we're going on a bit of a longer run, but you go that way, down that shortcut, and we'll meet you on the other side of the park.'

Of course, when I followed the route they gave me, I got completely lost! They used to do that a lot; they had me running all over the place, they were right sods! They were great times, though, and there was such a good spirit at that gym. We were all in it together, all part of a team, and we were made to look out for one another by Terry Lawless.

As a professional, my main sparring partners were bantamweight Ivor 'the engine' Jones and lightweight Ray Cattouse. Ivor wasn't with the gym, but he was brought down and paid by Terry Lawless as a sparring partner. Ivor was a Welsh lad, and we called him 'the engine' because he used to make loads of noises when he was sparring, sort of hissing like an old steam engine, and around that time there was a kids' TV show called *Ivor the Engine*. He was a jockey as well. He started out as a stable lad at Newmarket, and he learned to box while he was there, because they made all the stable lads do boxing training.

Ivor was a really good kid, very strong, and he was a really good lad to spar with because he was always in fantastic shape, and he could go for it round after round without getting tired. Years later, when I fought Eleoncio Mercedes for the world title, Ivor was his chief sparring partner before the fight. They had a line in the newspaper about it before the fight saying, 'SPY ENTERS MERCEDES CAMP AND GIVES MAGRI THE INSIDE LINE'. He told me a few things about him.

I must have had a million rounds with Ray Cattouse and Jim McDonnell, who went on to challenge Azumah Nelson. Ray was one of the most underrated fighters I ever met, he was never well known because he wasn't a big ticket-seller; he was British Champion, and challenged for the European title, and got a draw, but he never got the return match. Then he lost to George Feeney for the British title, but I know for a fact – because I went out on a run with him – that, on the morning of the fight, he was weak from trying to lose weight before the weigh-in. He was winning the fight, but in the end he ran out of gas and lost in the 14th round to George. He was just exhausted at the end, and both of the Feeneys were like animals, they just kept on coming at you.

Ray was a lightweight; he was about 10 stone, and I was only 8 stone 2, and sparring with him really gave me strength, because two stone is a lot in a boxing ring when you're a little guy. People used to say that they'd do eight miles when they ran, but I used to do three miles a day, and I felt that was enough. I used to do it at a hard pace. I always thought that, if you do too much running, you can injure yourself, especially running on the roads, so I kept the roadwork down a bit, but pushed myself harder over a shorter distance. I'd walk, then sprint, then jog, then back to walking to break it up, putting some hard sprints in there.

The thing I used to like most was the sparring, because I used to spar with a lot of bigger boys. I always wanted to prove myself in sparring, and it would piss me off if I got caught. I never thought that sparring should be really hard. You're in there to sharpen up, practise your moves and get yourself ready for a fight, not get the living daylights bashed out of you. Some fighters and trainers thought differently, and wanted to have a tear-up every single sparring session, but I preferred to keep it technical. Don't get me wrong, if someone wanted to have it with me, I'd have it with them back, but, if not, that was fine with me too.

When I sparred as an amateur, we used to go to Crystal Palace where I'd train with the England squad, and everyone there had something to prove, and people would try to knock you out in sparring. I used to have some right tear-ups, I tell you. They'd come at you, and you could see in their faces they wanted it, that they wanted to spark you out, but, if that happened to me, then I'd let them know that I wasn't there to be pushed around.

Personally, I think that, if you're the step above someone, you should take it easy. You should take your sparring according to your level of competition. I was never a bully, but, if someone brought it to me, if they started it, then I'd have a tear-up. When I'd spar with the bigger boys, I'd like to prove a point and make them think how hard I punched for a flyweight, and I like to think I usually got that point across.

I felt so happy at the Royal Oak. I liked everything about the set-up, it was like a dream come true. I was with one of the top trainers in the country, and part of the most successful gym, and I was looking forward to my new career as a professional fighter.

CHAPTER 23

42 Days

So, finally, after my first training camp, after all the talk, having signed a contract with Terry, and all the other preparations, I was about to have my first professional fight. It was 1977, and I was 20 years old. I'd won the ABAs that year and now I had turned pro and was having my first fight. What a buzz. I suppose I should have been worried about it all, about the step up to professional, but I didn't feel that. Maybe it was because I'd always trained so hard as an amateur, and had been doing so well, but I honestly never even gave it a second thought.

The fight was set for the Royal Albert Hall on 25 October 1977. I was up to fight against Neil McLaughlin, and my old pals Sylvester Mittee and Jimmy Batten were on the same bill as well. It was a great first fight to be a part of. McLaughlin was the Northern Irish Bantamweight Champion at the time, and he'd had a great amateur career. We'd nearly come across each other as amateurs, although it never happened, but I knew his style. He was a little bit older than me and was used to fighting at bantamweight. He was also much more experienced; he'd had nine fights before fighting me, winning two, drawing two and losing five. Even though his record wasn't great on paper, having that extra experience made the fight dangerous. Neil had fought at the 1972 Olympics, four years before I went. He'd boxed at bantamweight as an amateur, but he came down to flyweight as a pro to fight me, and we boxed at 8 stone 2. I just knew I'd beat him, although I thought it was going to be a hard fight. As it turned out, I overcame him quite easily really. Truth was, I just couldn't wait to get in the ring with him, and I had no second thoughts about turning professional.

Having said that, it was a really hard first round as a professional! It was fought at a really fast pace, and he was an awkward customer; he was circling the ring with a high guard, and I was trying to cut the ring off and close him down. I was sticking the jab out to make him counter and miss a few times. I caught him good with the jab a few times, but he was making it awkward for me in the first round. Then, at the end of the first round, I caught him with a three-punch combination and put him down in the corner, and the crowd went mad! It was a really good atmosphere, two little guys fighting at a really fast pace; it was an exciting fight. After the first round, I went back to the corner, and Terry Lawless gave me his instructions. 'That's the way, Charlie, lovely stuff, but I want you to do something, you're going for his head a bit too much, remember the body, Charlie. What I want you to do is get your shots in under that guard of his; he's got a high guard, so his body's wide open there. Dip yourself down from the waist and to the side and bring the hooks in up to his ribcage.'

So I went out and went for the body, boom, boom, boom! And he was gone, right out of it. It was set for eight three-minute rounds that fight, but I took him out quickly.

After that fight, Terry called me into his office again and said, 'We've got you another fight, this time it's over 10 threes at the York Hall, and it's an eliminator for the British title!'

I couldn't believe how quick all of this was happening. I'd only just turned professional and I was fighting an eliminator, but I just wanted to get on and do it, I couldn't wait for it to happen. This was less than six months after I'd won the ABA finals, and now I was going to be fighting a British title eliminator! Not just that, but I was fighting a 10-rounder in my second professional fight!

The British title eliminator was against a guy called Bryn Griffiths. Bryn was from a Welsh fighting family, and his dad had been a successful fighter in his own right. Now, as you know, I'd fought Bryn before as an amateur, and beaten him in my third ABA title at flyweight. I'd really given him a big going over in our amateur fight, stopping him in the second round when the referee jumped in to save him after he was knocked down for the second time. I'd done a number on him, and I had absolutely no worries about facing him again. He tried his heart out, I'll give him that; he was a tricky southpaw, but I had his number. I thought I'd go right at him and prove to him that I was still the same boy that had beaten him before. If you've beaten a boy once, you go in there knowing you can do it again. I beat him the same way as before; I stopped him in the same round, and I even put him down in the same corner.

Back when I was fighting, the British title was a really big deal. Every fighter worth his salt wanted to win a British title and most fighters would go for the British title before they even thought of going for a world-title shot. Today, with so many belts flying around, WBA, WBC, IBF, WBO and all the rest, a lot of the best fighters don't even bother fighting for the British title, and because of that it doesn't mean quite as much as it used to. But, even now, the British title and the Lonsdale belt that comes with it are still a big deal, and that belt is one that any fighter would be proud to have in their collection.

After the fight with Bryn Griffiths, I got a call from the British Boxing Board of Control, because the fight had been an eliminator for the British title, but they weren't sure about me

Main picture: Keeping my promise, I marched up and down Bethnal Green Road the morning after I got my WBC belt presented to me at the *This Is Your Life* studios by Eamonn Andrews.

Top: The Magri clan. *Left to right*: brothers Walter, Tony, George, Joey, Mum, Dad, sister Rita. Me and my little sister Mary in the front, all at my brother Joey's wedding to Maria.

Below left: Magri the angel, aged five.

Below right: Me and my Rolex – well, actually, my mate lent it to me for the photograph!

Silver medal for me at the 1974 European Under-21s. On the left is George Gilbody with a bronze medal, next to me is Kevin Hickey, and on the right Kirkland Laing with his bronze.

Road running past the back of the Arbour Youth Club, East London.

As a young amateur I was proud to have boxed for Arbour Youth ABC.

Top: Winning my last ABA finals, beating old foe Mohammed Younis, who I'd knocked out in one round previously in the Junior ABA.

Middle: Me with Jimmy Graham who taught me so much about being a boxer and a man.

Bottom: Returning to my old amateur club Arbour Youth, after winning the British title, and my old gaffer Jimmy Graham finally forgave me for turning professional.

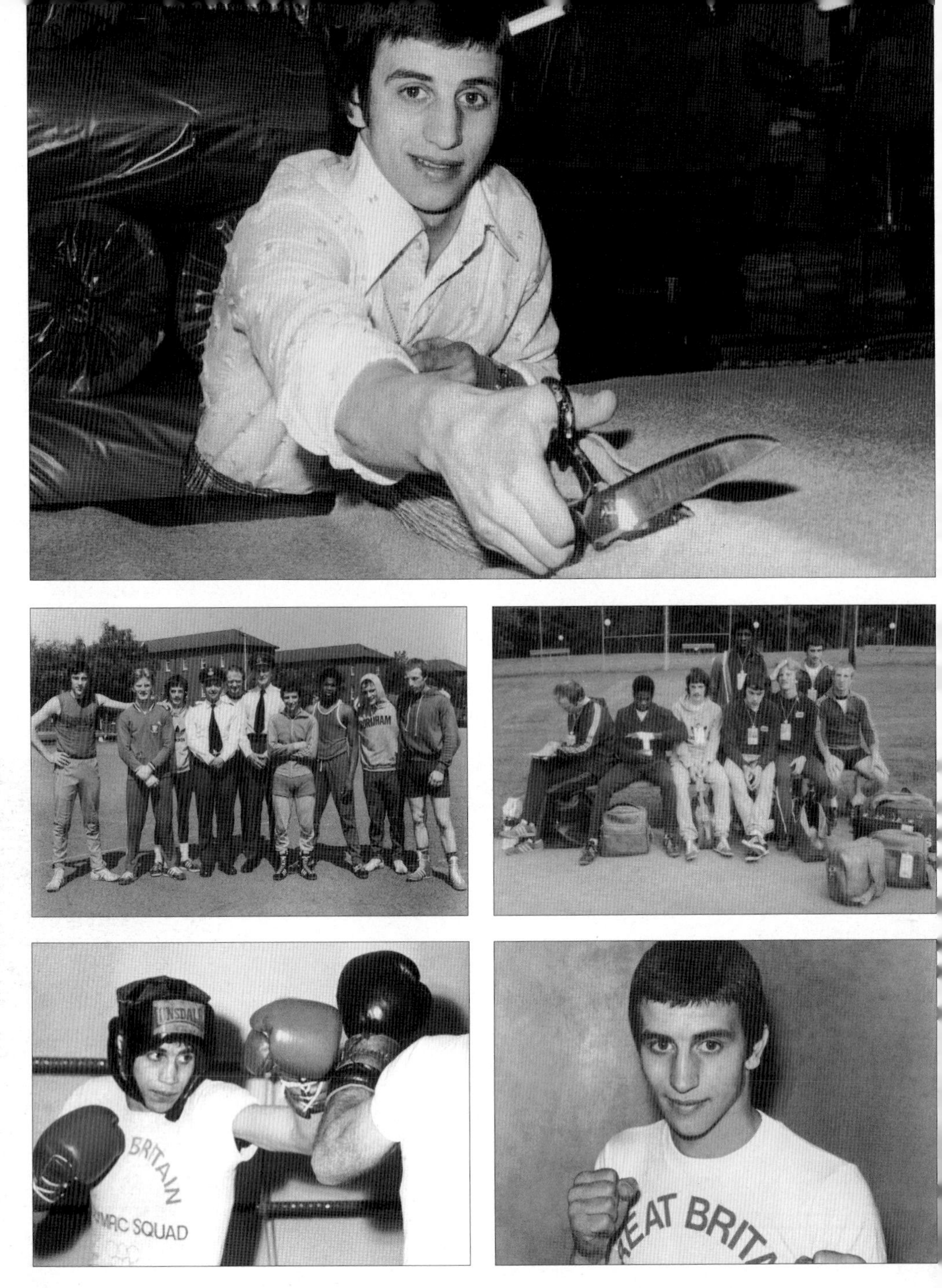

Top: Cutting the cloth at Carlinders, Great Orex Street in Whitechapel, where I worked as an apprentice just before I left for the Olympics.

Middle left and right: Great Britain Montreal 1976 Olympic boxing team. Left to right: Dave Odwell, Colin Jones, Pat Cowdell, Kevin Hickey our coach, me, Sylvester Mittee, Chris Davis, Robbie Davis. Robbie didn't go in the end and was replaced by Clinton McKenzie. I don't know what those two warders were doing there!

Bottom left and right: Been there, done that, got the T-shirt. Proud as punch to be representing my country at the Olympic Games of 1976.

Top left: Getting stuck in for the first time as a professional at the Royal Oak.

Top right: Me with Terry Lawless on the left, and Frank Black on the right, just arriving at the Royal Albert Hall before my fight with Dave Smith for the British title.

Bottom: Over and out! Knocking brave lad Dave Smith through the ropes, en route to winning the British title, just 42 days after turning professional.

I may have been one of the little guys, but I was a big ticket-seller, and topped the bill regularly fighting alongside some of the biggest names of the 1980s.

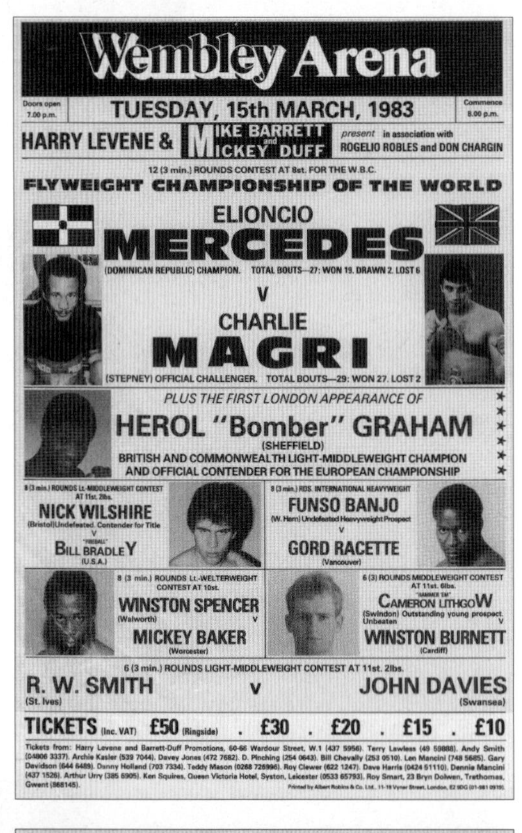

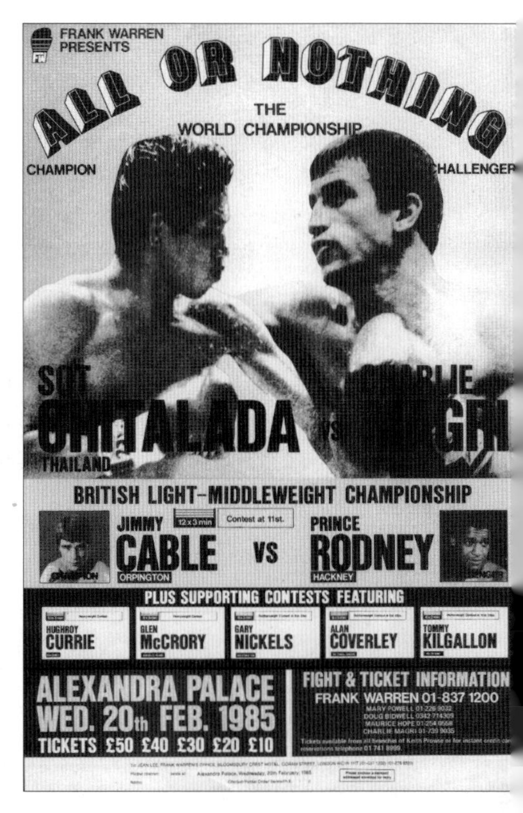

challenging for the title because I had only recently turned professional. At first, the BBBofC didn't even want to allow it. So I had to go along with Terry for a meeting with the BBBofC at their offices, which back then were still in London.

They said to me, 'We're only thinking of putting you forward for this because of your amateur career. You've got so much experience that we think that you're probably good enough to do it.'

I said, 'OK. I don't know why you called me up here then.'

'We called you up to tell you that we're thinking of accepting the fight, the British title, so quick. How do you feel about it?'

'Well, I'm fighting Dave Smith for the British title.'

'Yes, but Dave's had a lot more fights than you; he's a lot more experienced.'

I didn't care. I said, 'Well, I fought Dave Smith before, and I beat him before. I beat him in the London ABA finals. Why can't I beat him again? I mean, how is he going to feel?'

'Good comment. You're confident, aren't you?'

'I beat him before, I'll beat him again. This is why I'm fighting for the British title. I ain't fighting someone that's miles too good for me. Dave Smith I can beat.'

'Right then! The fight's accepted. You're fighting him.'

And that was that.

They had just wanted to talk to me to make sure I was all right and ready for it, to see if I was scared or what, even though I think they knew that I could beat the guy they were agreeing for the fight. Me? I just *knew* I could beat him, I knew I was better and I was good enough to do what they wanted me to do. Terry had it all mapped out. He'd done his homework, and he knew what I was all about, my amateur background. I had a terrific amateur record and, even though Dave Smith had more experience, I knew I was just too good for him. Like they say, if you're good enough, you're old enough.

There was loads of press coverage for my British-title fight; it was all over the papers and, before the fight, there was a big press conference on the BBC. The fight was a sell-out, it was a South London v East London clash, and it was big news. I knew that I'd beaten Dave Smith before in the ABAs, but he kept going on about how he was more experienced and how he'd had more fights than me.

So we were there at the press conference, and I said to him, 'I've beaten you before, Dave. How are you going to beat me? Tell me that, how are you going to beat me?

He went, 'Errrrrrr, I'll outpoint you.'

I said, 'You're not going to knock me out, though, are ya, Dave? You can't knock me out, can you?'

He didn't know what to say; I knew I'd made a point.

One day, when I was at the gym during a break in training during the run-up to the British-title fight, this reporter turned up at the gym. It was nothing unusual to have a journalist coming around, because, in the run-up to that fight, they were in and out of the gym and on the phone all the time. This geezer was someone I'd never seen come around before with the other newspaper people. He came in with this little notepad with him and told me he was a reporter from a South London newspaper, but it was a newspaper I've never heard of. He started asking me all these questions about my preparations, what sort of training I've been doing, how my weight was, what I'd been working on in the gym. Then he started telling me how he'd been with Dave Smith in the pub the other night.

Now, I knew that Dave Smith was from South London, and something about this geezer wasn't ringing true; he seemed to know a bit too much about Dave Smith, and so I said, 'I tell you what, mate, I reckon you're wasting your time. Go on, piss off! I know what your game is!'

'What's that then?' he said.

'You're asking me all these fucking questions, but I know you're something to do with Dave Smith. Tell Dave from me that I'm going to knock him out, and I tell you what, if you don't piss off right now, I'll knock you out an' all. You're not a bloody reporter. Now take your notepad and piss off.'

That was the last I saw of him. It made the newspapers though: 'Spy reporter ejected from Magri camp'.

I remember one day not long before the fight, maybe about four days, I came home from training and, as I walked through the door, who do I see on TV but Dave Smith, who's being interviewed on the six o'clock news. He was saying how he was going to do this and do that to me, giving it the big 'un.

My family were all there, and they said, 'Isn't that the man you're fighting, Charlie?'

He was going on about how I'm not ready to fight him, how he's had more fights than me, and how he's going to outpoint me. I remember thinking how he said he was going to beat me on points, and I'd already told him I was going to knock him spark out. Seeing his face on telly and hearing him mouth off made me really angry, but it made me more determined than ever to shut his mouth. I'll give him credit, he talked a great fight; it was all very convincing the way he was talking, but I knew I'd already beaten him as an amateur and I was convinced I was going to do a number on him.

During the run-up to the night of the fight, my brother Tony was there with me, keeping me company. It was great having him around and it really helped me relax. Tony was the best person in the world to have around before a big fight. I used to get really nervous before a fight; I'd get so tense it was almost unbearable, but, with Tony there, he always had a joke to crack, or he'd do something stupid which would just take my mind off the occasion a bit and let me relax my mind a bit more.

Tony was the only one who used to come to all my fights. When I was doing well as an amateur, if I had a show on, he'd make sure he took a day off work so he could get there early and be with me before the fight.

I'll never forget this one day with Tony when I boxed at the semi-finals of the ABAs. What a laugh! We were boxing at this venue called the Bellevue Manchester. Me and Dave Rodwell were boxing in the semi-finals and, before our fights came up, we decided to go for a walk together and get some fresh air. As usual, Tony had come up to Manchester with me to keep me company, and he decided he'd come along too. We had quite a while to go before we were on, so we decided we'd go along to Manchester Zoo. Tony went to the kiosk, and bought this big bag of peanuts, the kind they give you to feed to elephants, monkey nuts – which, as it turned out, was quite funny in itself.

Tony was right on form, and the three of us were laughing and joking, pissing around, cracking jokes, as we're walking around the zoo looking at all the animals. We came to the monkey house, and we were looking in through the mesh at all these monkeys. There were loads of them in this big cage. We looked up, and there was one hanging off the mesh right up in the air, and, as we looked up at it, it turned round, and flashed its arse right at us. We all started cracking up, and the monkey kept doing it, turning round making this screaming noise, then flashing its arse right at us. There was this big red raw arse, like a sodding blood orange, staring back at us!

Dave said, 'Fucking hell, Charlie, look at that monkey! What a cheeky bastard!'

Tony started laughing his head off at this monkey, then he went, 'I'm going to do that fucking monkey in a minute.'

So next thing, he grabbed a handful of nuts and chucked them right at the monkey, and one of the nuts went right up its arse crack and it let out this really loud screaming noise. The monkey literally went nuts! It went completely mental, and came jumping at us and landed right on the bars of the cage. We nearly jumped out of our skins. Fucking hell! It was so funny I could hardly breathe! It was making me crack up so much that I forgot all about my nerves.

Another time when I boxed in Spain, when it was in the bull

ring. Tony had a moustache at that time, and my opponent had a moustache as well. When we were in the dressing room before the fight, I said to him, 'Don't stand too near to me, Tone, because he's got a moustache, and you've got a moustache, and I might get confused.'

We had such a laugh. I was screwing him out and he was pissing himself laughing. Tony was the joker of the family; he was my right-hand man and he came everywhere with me.

I think everyone needs company before a big fight, or at least I did. You have to have some way of loosening up. For me, having Tony there made all the difference.

The day before the British title, I was training and checking my weight throughout the day to make sure that I was under the limit. I was always mental about making weight. The day before a fight, I'd hardly eat anything. I'd be absolutely starving, but that's what you've got to do when you're making weight. That's just how it is.

I had a light training session, but as usual I wore sweat gear for the whole day's training. I'd do 15 minutes' shadow boxing, 15 minutes' skipping, three rounds on the pads and three rounds on the punch bag. I suppose I should really have been resting the day before the bout, but I was really keyed up for it and could never stay out of the gym the day before a fight.

Throughout the day at the gym, the day before the fight, there'd be people passing in and out to come and say hello and wish you luck, and the atmosphere in the gym would be different, because everyone knew you had a fight the next day. You were treated that little bit special before the fight; the other fighters would give you that bit more space and stay out of your way when you were training. If it was a big title fight, then you'd get even more 'special' treatment. The press would turn up for some last-minute quotes before the fight, to try to get some snippets. Before the British-title fight, because it was such a big deal to fight for the title so soon after turning professional – only 42 days since my first fight! – there were absolutely loads of press down the gym taking pictures and trying to get quotes.

I remember I had a picture taken by the press photographers on the day of the fight. I was at the gym checking my weight before the official weigh-in. I had this massive sheepskin coat on and this great big wide-brimmed hat. I felt really big in the fur coat, but, I tell you, I was as skinny as you like underneath; with all the making weight I was like a rake.

Before a big fight, you would feel like a giant; you wanted to win and prove yourself, you felt like a gladiator getting ready for combat. I used to love the occasion; it was another opportunity, another hurdle to jump over, another chance to prove yourself. I loved the build-up to the fight. Before the British-title fight, I was even more excited; this was my big chance to prove myself, and, really, I was still just starting out as a professional. Back then, fighters dreamed of winning the British title; it was a really big deal. That was the route you went, British title, European title, world title. It's not like that these days; because fighters can get hold of a world-title belt so much easier, they don't even necessarily bother themselves with the British-title.

After the weight check in the afternoon, I'd eat lightly, maybe a little bit of fish, and a couple of little boiled potatoes, and that would be my last meal before the weigh-in the next day, a whole day with nothing to make sure you came down to the weight limit. Then, that night before the fight, just before I went to bed I'd eat a whole lemon before I went to sleep. That was an old trick that my old trainer Jimmy Graham taught me; he told me that, if you ate a lemon, it would help you shift water weight out of your body. Lemons are like a diuretic tablet; they flush water out of your body, and make you piss like nobody's business. You put loads of clothes on you when you went to bed, and you sweat loads, then when you woke up in the morning you just couldn't stop going, and the weight would come off with it. Just by eating a lemon, I would lose another pound-and-a-half in weight.

The morning of the fight, I'd go down the paper shops and pick up the papers for the day, then I'd go for a really long stroll, just trying to kill the hours before the fight. Time was the big killer before the fight, the day just seemed to drag on and on, and you were always trying to kill time, just dying to get in the ring and fight; the wait was torture.

CHAPTER 24

British Title – The Fight

That day, the day of my British-title fight, I swear to God, the whole of the East End of London was completely dead, everyone from round my area was going to the fight. You could've walked the streets and you would've thought there was some sort of bloody curfew going on there were so few people walking around. It was really spooky. I tell you; it was like the little bit of the world round me had come to a standstill.

You've got to remember that, up until this time, the flyweights in Britain were pretty much invisible. It was a long time since there'd been any interest in a flyweight fight in Britain, and there hadn't been a British World Flyweight Champion since Walter McGowan won the title in 1966 and nobody had really even come close since. The flyweight division hadn't had much excitement in this country for a long time, and, let's face it, it hasn't got much now. Flyweights who sell tickets are as rare as rocking-horse shit; ask any promoter, and they'll tell you the same thing. Most flyweights don't score many knockouts, and most people don't want to see two little blokes whacking each other round after round. Even though the fights are entertaining, people want to see a massive knockout; it's what helps put bums on seats. I'd been giving them tear-ups in my first few fights.

The thing is, it's the little guys who usually produce the exciting fights, but normally nobody knows who they are; it's the same these days. But this British-title fight was massive because of all the press attention that had surrounded me turning pro, and because it was a record me going for the British title, only 42 days after turning professional. This fight was all over the papers and on the news, and it was being talked about everywhere in the weeks leading up it.

The weigh-in was at the Odeon Leicester Square at one o'clock in the afternoon, and it was a massive event with a huge crowd outside. It was like a film premiere and I felt like a movie star. I've got to be honest, and I'm not being big-headed here, but I loved every single minute of it; it made me feel special, important, to see all those faces out in the crowd, all the photographers and people calling out my name: 'Over here, Charlie!' and all that sort of thing. I absolutely loved it. I wasn't a show-off or flash or anything like that, but, God, it was enjoyable.

So we did our weigh-in, and we both made weight. It was all over by two in the afternoon, and there was seven hours until the fight. I was straight off home and, as soon as I got in, there was a massive roast dinner waiting for me. I tucked into it and demolished it. Christ, did I enjoy that meal, after eating like a sparrow to make weight! After eating it, I felt as strong as an ox; I felt like nobody was going to beat me, and I had plenty of time for the food to settle.

I always made my own way down to the venue and met Terry Lawless down there. My brother Joey was a black-cab driver, so he gave me a lift down to the Albert Hall with my other brother Tony. I always got there well early, because I liked to get a feel for the place and see the crowds in the arena, who'd be there for the undercard fights. It was my little routine before my fights to get myself settled. I remember when I arrived at the venue with Tony, when we got to the gates, there were hordes of people arriving, and the place looked like it was absolutely packed. Remember, this was only my third professional fight, and it was already my second time at the Royal Albert Hall! The Albert Hall in those days held something like 8,000 capacity, but there must have been more like 10,000 packed in there, because there were people practically hanging from the rafters.

When we got down there, I could see people in the queue that I knew; everyone from the Burdett Estate where I lived had turned up for a start, and lots of faces from around my area that I recognised. It started to dawn on me just how many people had turned up to see me. I got to the dressing room, and met up with Terry, and there were a still a couple of hours to go before the fight. I wasn't on until nine when the TV coverage started. I used to feel a bit keyed up when I was waiting to fight, and I was getting pretty nervous, so I wanted to go for a walk to clear my head.

I told Terry, and he said to take someone with me, because he was worried I was going to get lost. The Albert Hall was a massive place, with loads of corridors everywhere and little side rooms. It was vast and the last thing Terry wanted right now was me going off and getting lost in the building before the fight.

So Tony came with me for a walk around the venue. We found one of the doors leading out to the arena, and I said, 'Come on, Tony, let's have a look and see who's here for the fight.'

Tony said, 'What are you worried about, Charlie? You're going to be fighting in a couple of hours, let's go back.'

But I talked him into it, and, when I opened the door, I let out a massive gasp of air. 'God!'

I couldn't believe the crowd. I could see people I knew from Mile End. There were people's faces I recognised from all over the East End, and plenty that I didn't expect to see. All the Sinclair brothers, a well-known family who I knew from around the area, were there. It surprised me, because, although I knew them, I didn't know them all that well, and they were all a bit older than me. They came up and asked me, 'So are you going to beat this Dave Smith geezer? You going to do it for the East End, Charlie?'

''Course I am,' I said.

I realised that pretty much the whole of the East End were out there in the crowd, expecting me to win, and it made me really bloody nervous knowing all these people were out there, waiting to see me fight. It also made me want to win more than ever. Dave Smith was South London and I was East London: East London pride was at stake.

So I did a little tour of the arena, and I loved it; everyone saw me and they were saying hello and waving, and I felt like a little superstar really.

When I got back to the dressing room, which was only about an hour before the fight, I just couldn't sit still. I was jumping around, cracking jokes and pacing up and down all over the place. It was making Terry Lawless nervous, so he said to Tony, 'Keep an eye on him, will you, Tony? He's getting all overexcited.'

The thing was, I felt better moving around than I did standing still. It had only just really hit me what I was about to do. It was only 42 days since I'd turned professional, and now I was fighting for the British title.

I went to the toilets, and who did I see in there? Dave Smith standing up against the urinals. I thought, 'Well, I can't turn around and walk out now.' I didn't want to look like I was backing down, so I stood next to him and had a piss, and I said, 'How you feeling then, Dave?'

'Yeah, I'm all right,' he said.

I could see he wasn't all right, though; he looked really nervous for having seen me before the fight, and right then I thought, 'I've got him.' He was absolutely shitting himself.

He said, 'Yeah, I'm all right, mate. What about you? Nervous, are you, Charlie?'

'Yeah, I am, but I'm not half as nervous as you, mate.'

'We'll see about that!'

After walking around the arena with Tony, I made my way back to my dressing room with my name on it and all that and I was sitting in there before the fight all on my own. As usual, I found my little corner of the dressing room to get comfy for a bit, get my boxing boots out, my little crucifix from my mum, a little bag with holy water and a set of rosary beads in it. I'd get the holy water out and I'd put it over my knuckles and wash my face in it; it was a little touch from my mum, meant to bring me good luck, and I'd always have it with me for every fight. It was a superstition, I suppose, that I'd done ever since my amateur days.

Right before the fight, there were two officials and my brother Tony. I could feel the attention begin to focus in on me. It's a very strange feeling; it's like the eyes of the world are all bearing down on you. You start to feel the pressure of the occasion getting to you. The thing that helped me was that, from day one as a pro fighter, I'd been in the limelight; there was such a big fuss when I turned pro, and my first two fights had been big occasions. I'd already boxed at the Albert Hall in my first fight, and so it wasn't a completely new experience. I was top of the bill in my first two fights, and I'd backed it up and won.

That night I wore my white silk dressing gown, and it was at this fight that I started off the tradition of always going to the ring last, which really you're only supposed to do as a champion. I used to make them wait for ages, give them the time to get anxious and nervous. I made my way to the top of the steps, which led down to the arena, and then the spotlight hit me and the light was shining off the silk dressing gown. Suddenly, I could hear the roar of the crowd, and I could hear, 'Charl-eee! Charl-eee! Charl-eee!'

Cor! What a feeling, what a buzz that was! I could feel a rush of energy coming from the crowd, and then it dawned on me that I was about to enter the ring and fight this bloke that I could see standing over the other side of the ring all the way over the other side of the arena. It's the strangest feeling but it's a lovely one: the butterflies are fluttering around your stomach, and you're nervous, excited, scared, all in one. It's a good man that can overcome those feelings and win a fight, because, when you see that other geezer in the ring bobbing up and down and screwing you down with his stare, well, it's a frightening feeling; you're getting in there to fight another man. You have to take control of those feelings and make it work, because your opponent isn't coming for a ride, he's coming there to bash you up.

Dave Smith was the sort of bloke who had a lot of bottle in and out of the ring; he'd have a row outside the ring if someone wanted to give him one, and he wasn't someone who was easily intimidated. I remember that, when I made my way to the ring, his expression didn't change, he just looked right back at me; despite me thinking he was nervous at the press conference, he was no bottler.

I went out there in that first round, and I went absolutely mental. I was throwing hard shots at him to the head and body with both hands, non-stop. I caught him early with a long left and dropped him, and he was all over the place. I was going to finish it right there and then; within 30 seconds I had him on the deck. It was a dream start, and I thought, 'I've got him, that's it.'

He was badly hurt from the knockdown; he looked completely finished, and I wanted to finish it. I wanted to get it over with as soon as possible, and I went in for the kill. Thing was, he wasn't ready to quit. How he survived that first round I don't know, because I was really bashing him up; he was a brave lad Dave, a very brave lad. I remember I caught him with another cracking left hook that was nearly as good as the first but he just wouldn't fall.

I tell you what, I was convinced that the referee Roland Dakin was against me in that fight. The ref was pulling me up for absolutely everything: 'Watch the head, Magri; keep your shots up, Magri.' Every time I was on him, the referee was on at me about something. It seemed like they were never going to stop the fight;

I kept putting him down, and the referee just kept letting him carry on. I think that fight ruined him, because he took so much punishment. Round after round I was giving him a terrible going over. I knocked him right out of the ring in the third round, his legs had gone and he just slid through the ropes right on to the *Sun* newspaper table. He sort of dropped to his knees after a body shot in the sixth and, when he got up, I whacked him with a little low blow. I'll be honest, *I* was getting knackered from hitting him so bloody much, and Christ knows how he felt! I'd hit him so many times and he was still there, and I figured I needed to rough him up a bit to try to take the fight out of him, so I cracked him with a little low blow to try to take his legs away. I hoped he'd bottle out, but he didn't. If you look at me at the end of the fight, I was absolutely knackered. I'd hit him with everything I had, and I don't know what I'd have done if he'd somehow survived another couple of rounds, because I didn't feel like I had much left in the tank. I knocked the guts out of him in the sixth, and eventually he fell, but he wouldn't stay down. What courage that guy had! The referee should have stopped it there, he had nothing left. He got up at eight, and he was bloody smiling when he went back to his corner! I couldn't believe it!

The first jabs I landed in the seventh wobbled him; every shot was taking his legs away, and there was nothing coming back at all. I dropped him again with a really big left uppercut and left hook and he went through the ropes again. He got up at eight, but there was no point letting him carry on.

I had a good fight that night; I really got stuck in there. He was a nice kid, a really nice feller, and I actually liked him, but we'd become big rivals as amateurs and the needle at the press conference got to me, and I took it out on him in the ring. But there was no malice there afterwards, which is normally how it is with boxers, and I still speak to Dave now; he's got a pub out in Kent, and he phones me up sometimes.

I often think about Dave, and I feel a bit sorry for him that he took so much punishment during that fight. Why the referee let it go on is beyond me, as every punch I landed was hurting him. I definitely think he let the fight go on too long and I think I knocked a lot of his career out of him that night. I honestly think he could have gone on to be British Champion but for that fight, as he left a lot of himself behind that night. He wanted to win so badly that he kept on getting up when a lot of other fighters would have called it a day, and, in my opinion, the referee let him down a bit by not stopping it earlier. It's a tough job refereeing, but you've got to protect the fighters in there above all, and make sure they don't take too much punishment. Dave won and lost a few after that, and challenged for the British title, but lost in challenges against Johnny Owen, and then John Feeney.

After the fight I did something I wanted to do as soon as I'd won the title. I went to Stepney Green to Arbour Youth to show the lads at the club the Lonsdale belt that I'd got for winning the British title. I hadn't been down there since I told Jimmy I'd turned professional, and I was still barred from going down there, but I went up and knocked at the door. Jimmy opened the door and I said, 'I've come down to show you the belt.'

I wasn't sure how he was going to react to that, but then he smiled at me and said, 'Come in, Charlie.'

I went in the club and showed them the belt. After that, we stayed in touch; we stayed close, because he was more than just my trainer when I was young, he was someone who was there looking out for me, and someone I looked up to for advice. Jimmy was a man of principle, someone I respected. I wanted to share the belt with him and the club, and it felt right to bring it to him to have a look, because without him I never would have won that British title.

CHAPTER 25

The Fame Game

As I've said, I was pretty well known as an amateur; I'd won the ABA title a total of six times, and represented my country, and I was used to having my fights shown on TV because the BBC used to show a lot of amateur boxing back then. But, after I won the British title, things went right to another level. The press were phoning me up all the time, and I was on TV, in the newspapers, everywhere. It was such a big deal because of how soon after turning professional I'd won the British title; winning it in 42 days was a record, and that made it even bigger news than it would have been otherwise.

Now I'd be a liar if I said I didn't enjoy being famous; being well known for what I did gave me a buzz, and, if you're a sportsman and you reckon you're good enough to get to the very top, it's one of the perks that comes with the territory. I loved all the attention during the weigh-ins and the pre-fight verbals; it was all fuel to me, it made me feel good, feel special, and the way I see it there's nothing wrong with that. Who in their right mind wouldn't enjoy it? I didn't feel any pressure from stuff like that. I loved it all.

I was never one of those to complain about being famous, as most of the time people were nice to me because of who I was, and I didn't get any hassle from the press people. Truth is, though, being famous can sometimes be a pain in the arse as well as a bonus. Sometimes, it seems to bring out the worst in people, whether because they're envious or they think you're giving it the big 'un, I don't know, but sometimes you get someone acting like a complete and utter muppet. Sometimes, though, it could be pretty funny as well.

Not long after I'd won the British title, Terry Lawless organised a personal appearance for me at this big amateur show, where I would get up after all the boxing was finished, and make a speech for all the people at the dinner show. It was a bloody long way away, in Whitehaven somewhere near Carlisle, right in the Lake District. My brother Walter was living in Carlisle so we met up and went along together.

After the boxing, I got in the ring with the microphone, and got myself ready to do the speech.

'Good evening, gentlemen,' I started. 'It's a real privilege to come and speak here tonight at this dinner show, because I remember what it was like boxing on these shows as an amateur, and how excited I used to be.'

You get the general idea anyway. So, I'm going through, talking about my career and fighting in the ABAs and all that stuff, and saying how much the shows mean to the kids involved, that sort of thing, trying to kind of set the scene for everyone there, and make the kids boxing on the show feel a bit special.

Suddenly, I heard this voice booming out of the crowd. 'I was a flyweight!' this voice shouted out.

I went, 'Oh yeah! That's nice, mate, who's that?'

'I reckon I could have beaten you!' shouted back this voice from the crowd, in a funny accent, so I think he was probably local.

'Oh yeah!' I said. 'Who are you then?'

I looked into the crowd and there's this little fat bloke, who must have been in his late forties. He was fat and round with a big thick set of jam-jar specs on, and he looked like Ernie the Milkman, the character from Benny Hill's song.

I had the mike in my hand, so I said, 'Oh yeah, mate, I reckon you're a bit over the weight now, ain't ya?'

The crowd all started laughing at him and he went all funny, saying, 'Oh right! There's no need for all that, is there?' The geezer looked pretty pissed.

I said to him, 'How old are you then, mate?'

'I'm 45!'

'Well, you're a bit too old for me, mate. You weren't around when I was probably.'

'Never mind all that! I'll do you right now!'

I thought to myself, 'Oh no!' and the crowd started geeing him up, so for a laugh, I said, 'Look, Ernie the Milkman's come to have a go!'

That didn't seem to bother him, though, and he came marching through the crowd towards the ring.

The crowd all started chanting, 'Ernie, Ernie, Ernie!'

He came charging into the ring, completely pissed up, and he said, 'All right, here's how it is, we'll just do slaps, and my three mates over there can be the judges.'

I pissed myself laughing at him and I said, 'Go on, get away, will ya?'

The geezer ripped off his bow tie and started undoing his jacket and he started chasing me around the ring. The crowd are all chanting, and I'm running round the ring trying to get away from him!

In the end, some people from the crowd had to get in and pull him out of the ring because he wouldn't listen. Later that night, when I got back to the hotel, the people who'd organised the evening took me into their room and showed me a video of the night and there he was, this fat geezer trying to have a row with me! God, it was funny.

So, you see, being famous can have its drawbacks, and sometimes people want to have a pop at you because of your name, but I think this guy was probably just pissed!

One of the funniest nights I can remember, though, was during the time I was doing some managing and training, when I went down to this boxing show at the Rivermead Leisure Centre in Reading with a mate of mine. I was there, because I was managing Nigel Benn's cousin, Paul Bowen, who I had on the bill. The main fight on that night was between Mark Baker, who's from a traveller family, and Dean Francis, a black fighter, and the heavy crowd that night seemed to be divided up between all the local black geezers in the area supporting Dean and all the travellers who lived on the manor backing Mark.

There was a right heavy atmosphere there, and it felt like something was going to kick off. Sure enough, as soon as it was announced that Mark Baker had lost, you should have seen this place go off! There were ashtrays and bottles flying everywhere, chairs whizzing across the room, and bodies falling all over the place, as the two sides started kicking lumps out of each other.

My mate went, 'Fucking hell, Charlie! I think we'd better get out of here before we get hurt.'

So we started going for the door, trying to get through the crowds of people who were knocking seven bells out of each other, when all of a sudden I heard, 'Charlie! Charlie, over here.'

I thought, 'God! Why's someone calling my name? I'm not getting involved with this.'

I looked around and there was this massive traveller bloke covered in tattoos and blood, who was holding this black geezer in a headlock with one arm and punching him in the face with the other. He let go of the geezer, who dropped to the ground in a heap. Then he fished in his pocket, and what did he do? He only brought out this little scrap of scrunched-up paper, which he handed to me, saying, 'You haven't got a pen, have you, Charlie? I'd love to get your autograph. I'm a big fan of yours.'

I thought, 'This is fucking mental! I'm in a bloody madhouse. The geezer's in the middle of a fight and he's asking me for my autograph.'

I tell you what, it was like something out of a film. You couldn't have made it up if you'd tried.

I signed the geezer's bit of paper, and he went, 'Cheers, Charlie!' Then, just like nothing had happened, he went back to rowing and started laying into some other geezer. Honestly, some people, eh?

But the time that I think made me laugh the most was much later on in my career, after I'd won the World European title. I was obviously pretty famous after that night, because I was European Champion, and Terry had arranged for me to do a speaking engagement at a show in Norwich. There was a boxing match, then I would do a bit of compeering and after-dinner-speaking stuff at the nightclub.

So we agreed a price and it was all set up. On the day, I got on the train to go to Norwich, and, as I was going to the toilet, I went past these two blokes sitting next to each other looking at me, and I can hear them arguing with each other and saying, 'It's him. It is him!'

'No it's not!'

'It is him, it is, I'm telling you!'

So when I came back, I sat down, thinking, 'I wonder when they're going to come over.'

One of the blokes came towards me and said, 'Look, I've had a bet with my mate sitting over there for 20 quid; he reckons he knows who you are, and I *know* I do. So, can we clear this up so I can get my money?'

I said, 'All right, mate. So why don't you tell me who you think I am first.'

'Oh, I know who you are.'

'Oh, right, so who am I then?'

'I know who you are, you're Charlie Minter.'

I burst out laughing. 'Don't be silly, mate, go away.'

He walked off all embarrassed and had to tell his mate that he was wrong and his mate started laughing at him, and giving me the thumbs-up sign.

When we pulled into the next stop, the two blokes were getting off and, as the train pulled into the station, the geezer who won the bet came over to me, smiled, nudged me and went, 'Cheers, Barry!'

So much for being famous, eh?

CHAPTER 26

On the Road to Europe

After I won the British title, Terry Lawless and Mickey Duff had it all planned out for me as usual. With their contacts with the venues and TV, they had sure-fire dates for me to fight on. I was getting a pretty big following, and they wanted to keep me on a roll. So, a few days later, Terry took me to one side and brought me into his office at the Royal Oak, and said, 'You're doing everything we've asked you to do, so we're going to get you the fights to get you the European-title shot.'

Terry and Mickey had all the right connections with the European promoters, so Terry knew he could get me a shot at the European; it was just a matter of me winning the right fights. Terry had it all mapped out, where I was going to fight, when and who. The idea was basically that I worked my way right through the European rankings, from number ten up to number one, fighting all the people I had to fight, one after the other until I was in a position to fight for the European title. That way, they could keep me busy, and keep the crowds flooding into all the venues like Wembley, the Albert Hall and all that. And, along with the crowds, money came rolling in at every fight, and that's the way promoters like it. I set out on my way to getting a shot at the European title in 1978 and, for the next 18 months, it was the busiest time of my whole professional career. Fight after fight with hardly a break in between.

The first fight was set against European ranked Nessim Zebelini. Terry had the fight lined up for 21 February 1978 at the Royal Albert Hall, the same place where I'd won the British title a couple of months earlier. Terry Lawless, Mickey Duff and Mike Barrett had deals with the Royal Albert Hall and Wembley, so they put shows on there all the time, and I was hardly ever out of the ring for more than a couple of months.

It was like I was on a rota. The way my career was mapped out, I'd fight the same venues over and over again. I'd go from the York Hall, to Wembley, to the Albert Hall, to the York Hall, to Wembley, to the Albert Hall and so on, and they had the venues every year. Terry would have 10 bookings at this place and 10 at that place, and, when you're their biggest ticket-seller, you're making them a fortune. They earn more that way, don't they?

It was all about keeping you working, keeping the shows going and the money rolling in, rather than getting you a world-title shot, and then having you only fight twice a year. At the end of the day, boxing is just a business to your management. It's a business to them because they've got Charlie Magri on the bill. Then they get someone else, Jimmy Flint or Jimmy Batten, who sells tickets. Get them three together and you've got a show. With three ticket-sellers, you can fill the hall out. It's all about the bill and making it work for them – and, of course, making money. That's the boxing business for you, bums on seats.

Frenchman Zebelini had a record of nine wins and 12 losses coming into the fight, and, although that wasn't a great record, he was much more experienced than me. He'd fought for the European title the year before against Franco Udella and got stopped in the ninth round.

Zebelini was quite an awkward fighter; he had that French style of sort of tearing around the ring, bouncing about, with his guard up high, which made it hard to get at him. Once I found my range, though, I had a pretty easy night's work, stopping him in three rounds, which was a good result considering he'd taken Udella nine. It was a good impressive win that I'd been able to take him out so quick, because he was a seasoned fighter with a lot more experience at European level, and it made a statement.

Dominique Cesari was next up; he was the French Bantamweight Champion, as well as fighting at flyweight. He came in for the fight over the weight, well over eight stone, but we took the fight anyway. I battered him in three rounds. It wasn't even a close fight.

Believe it or not, my next fight was only three weeks later. Can you imagine a fighter doing that today? Fighting two ranked European fighters back to back in three weeks. To me, it didn't matter; I liked to stay busy and, as I was never out of the gym anyway, I never felt like I needed to rest. There was no need to have long layoffs because I wasn't getting bashed up in there; I was going in there and taking them apart.

Manuel Carrasco was my next fight, set for 25 April, my fourth fight in four months, including the British-title fight! It was less than six months since I'd turned pro, and it was my seventh fight!

To be honest, I didn't know very much about him, except that he was ranked in the top 10 in Europe and that meant I could move into the top-10 rankings if I beat him. I knew he was a big tall lad, but I never watched any tapes of fighters, because I didn't really want to know about their style; I wanted them to worry more about my style. I learned my technique as an amateur; I'd fought all styles, shapes and sizes, and I'd learned to adapt in the ring. I was a pressure fighter, but I could box if I needed to, so I wasn't worried about whatever they had. I guess I was a little bit superstitious as well – I felt that if I saw them before the fight it might be bad luck.

Carrasco, though, my God, he was a tough cookie! I gave it to him for eight rounds, pounding him everywhere and anywhere, but he just wouldn't fold. He was my first distance fight as a professional and, as I would find out later, he was one geezer you just couldn't get rid of. Another fight, another notch up the rankings, another step closer to my goal, which was to win the European and then world title.

During the run-up to the Carrasco fight, I'd had breathing troubles. I'd had my nose busted before, but in that fight the damage got too bad, and I couldn't train properly, or breathe properly during the fight. It happens to a lot of boxers after they've had their nose broken, but it only gets to be a big deal if it affects your breathing seriously enough to affect your training, which mine had. So, right after the fight, I had to have an operation to remove the cartilage in my nose, because I could feel myself getting tired in training and during fights and I was having trouble eating because I couldn't breathe properly when I had my mouth full. So, after the fight I went to Harley Street and had an operation done to remove it. The operation, of course, came out of my purse, and I think it cost me about £600. It was a bit frightening having to go under, but it had to be done. Even after that I only had a week-and-a-half off of training; I just avoided sparring for a little while. The worst part about the whole operation was when they took the packing out of my nose which was there to absorb the blood after the operation and it hurt like mad. After they took the packing out and I looked at my nose, I got a bit of a shock, because my nose was completely flat. I'd had a nice long pointy nose before that, but now it was flat as a pancake where they'd taken all the cartilage out. I could have had another operation if I'd wanted to, which would have corrected it, but I guess that was my trademark really, people knew me for that. People always recognised me partly because of the nose, and it was like my mark from boxing, so I just kept it.

As I've said, back then, it was a lot harder to get a world title than it is now. You've got to remember that, in those days, there were only two belts. There was just the WBC and the WBA. The IBF wasn't even around yet, and the WBO, well, that was a long way off.

Miguel Canto was still the WBC Champion. Terry Lawless and Mickey Duff had good links with the WBC, because John Conteh had won their title, and Maurice Hope went on to win it too, so they were on good terms with their president Jose Sulaiman, and it was that title I was going to go for.

In those days, most British fighters, if they wanted a shot at the world title, had to go the traditional route: first the British title, then fight their way up the European rankings, then get the European title, and finally work their way up towards a world-title shot. You really had to fight your way to the top. Nowadays, a fighter can pick up a belt without ever really having to fight a top-class fighter, and I think it's a lot easier for a fighter to call themselves a World Champion, because there's four world-title belts, and they are always being stripped from fighters, and people fight for a vacant title. It's like a bloody merry-go-round these days.

Anyway, after beating Carrasco, I beat Sabatino De Filippo in seven rounds, then Claudio Tanda in three a month later, followed by Mariano Garcia in three just before Christmas 1978. In just over a year I'd gone from a novice professional to one of the top fighters in Europe. It was like being strapped to a rocket; everything was happening so fast that I barely had time to think.

Then Terry told me that there was another bill coming up on 23 January 1979, and I was going to be fighting to get my number-one European ranking on that bill. All I had to do was beat this guy and I would be the main contender to Udella. I'd already fought my way right through the European rankings. Only two years after my last ABA title, I was fighting for the number-one spot in Europe! I knew this was the big chance. I had to beat this geezer to get where I wanted to go to get at the European title; all I had to do was beat Filippo Belvedere.

It turned out to be a bit of an anticlimax really, because I took him out in under a round. I battered him from pillar to post, as they say, and the referee had no choice but to step in when I trapped him in a neutral corner and started teeing off on him; he was completely helpless by that point. Belvedere had gone the distance with Italian Champion Giovanni Camputaro and, though he'd lost a lot of fights, nobody had ever stopped him until now; in fact, I was the only one who ever stopped him in his whole career. I was on top of the world, and I was one fight away from one of my boyhood dreams.

I remember, after the fight, me and Belvedere were sitting on the ring apron like fighters do, and Harry Carpenter came over to us. Harry said to me, 'Right, Charlie, I'm going to speak to Belvedere through an interpreter now, and then I'll talk to you.'

Harry spoke to the interpreter who relayed the questions to Belvedere.

Then Harry pointed the microphone at me, and said, 'Belvedere's said that he didn't realise just how fast you were. He said you threw so many punches he thought he was fighting four people.'

I was laughing my head off at that. I'd really gone to town in that fight; I'd thrown punches from every angle you could imagine.

Now that I had my number-one ranking, my management thought it would be good to face off against something a bit different, so they brought in an American import. His name was Mike Stuart, a flashy black American fighter who had Hedgemon Lewis in his corner. Hedgemon was a bloody good fighter in his day, he'd gone the distance once with Jose Napoles, and then lost a return in nine rounds; he'd drawn with Carlos Palomino; and his last fight was a losing effort against John H Stracey. Hedgemon had been trained by the legendary Eddie Futch, one of the greatest boxing trainers of all time, and the man who trained Joe Frazier. So, he was a geezer who knew a thing or two about fighting.

In the build-up to the fight, Terry had told me that I had to let this kid know early on that I could hurt him, because he was a stylist who was slippery. Mike Stuart was quite highly thought of in the States, and a lot of people thought the fight could be a bit of a difficult one for me. He was the first American I'd faced in my career, and people always tend to think the Yanks are a bit special, but I didn't show him any respect. I was on him from the off, and, although it took me a while to figure out his slippery style, after the first round, I knew there was nowhere for him to hide, and he knew it too.

In the second round, I caught him with a nice right hook which hurt him badly. In the third, I hurt him again at the end of the round; he was out on his feet, and he grabbed hold of me for dear life.

Terry Lawless was going mad in the corner. 'Push him off, Charlie, come on! Push him off, get some room, shove him off!'

He was worried that the guy would get time to recover, and wanted me to finish him off. So I shoved him with my shoulders and his legs went and he fell right through the ropes, boom! He was out of the ring, and on to a table at ringside; he landed on the TV monitors, and then bounced off and on to the floor. The referee, Harry Gibbs, just started counting – which he shouldn't have done really, because he'd not been punched out of the ring – and counted him out before he made it back into the ring.

Stuart's corner went mental. Hedgemon Lewis went mad at the referee, rightly so as it happens, because it wasn't a knockout. I'd hurt him badly, but he shouldn't have been counted out as I'd shoved him out of the ring, not knocked him out of it, but the referee wasn't having any of it. Well, what was I supposed to do? Argue with the referee to give him another bloody chance? Not likely.

So that was that, Stuart was done for. I had my number-one ranking, and now all I needed was for my management to come to terms with Udella's promoters and make the fight.

CHAPTER 27

The Guv'nor of Europe

So, finally after fighting my way right up the European rankings, I got word that I was going to get a title shot, against European Champion Franco Udella. He was coming to London, and I'd fight him in front of my home supporters in their thousands at Wembley Empire Pool! What a day it was when I heard that!

Now, here's the funny thing. Many years before, when I was still at Arbour Youth, I think I was about 15 at the time, one day, I was doing my skipping in front of the television. There was an old black and white TV set there and, on a Saturday, they always showed *Grandstand* with Dickie Davis. So I was skipping away, and there was the European flyweight title being shown on television. It was only Franco Udella defending his title! It was against a Spaniard, I think. He was bashing the guy up, and I was still skipping, but I was watching the fight and analysing Udella and the way he fought. The more I watched it, the more I could see flaws in the way he fought, because, although he was big, strong and aggressive, he was stiff. I stopped what I was doing and

I turned around to the lads in the gym and said, 'He's stiff. He's strong and tough, but he's all stiff.

'I'm telling you, I could beat that geezer there.'

Well, all the boys in the gym just laughed. 'Go away, mate,' they said, 'you can't beat him. He's a grown man and he's the European Champion, he'd slaughter you.'

Funny to think that now, years later, I was about to box him at Wembley, when he was 32 and I was only 22, but I'd never forgotten that moment. I'd never forgotten that moment when I said I could beat him. I'd only just won the Junior ABAs but I knew I could beat him. So I guess that was the first moment where I thought I could turn professional and do well.

We went out to San Remo in Italy to make the fight against Franco Udella. A whole bunch of us went out there, because my stablemate Maurice Hope was challenging for the WBC light middleweight belt against Italian Rocky Mattioli. The plan was for Terry to speak to Udella's promoters while we were out there. The fight was a mandatory title shot, as I'd boxed my way through the other top-10 fighters in the European rankings. Terry had won the purse bids and had brought the title to Wembley, and I couldn't have asked for more than a shot at the European title in my own backyard!

There was a whole load of us went over to watch Maurice win his world title, and, in the hotel we were staying at, they had a stage set up with drums, a microphone, a guitar and all that, where the hotel band would perform. The British boxing press got us all dressed up like we were in a band, and took a photo of us. It was really funny. There was Maurice Hope, Cornelius Boza Edwards, John L Gardner, Jim Watt and me all dressed up like we were the Beatles or something.

For me, winning the European title wasn't just about the title itself, as, if I won the European title, I would then be ranked by the WBC and WBA as well, and I wouldn't be far from a title shot. Well, so I thought at the time, but things didn't quite turn out quite like that.

At the time the fight with Udella was signed, Miguel Canto was the WBC Champion, and I badly wanted to get a shot at him. Canto was a real legend. He was a tiny little bloke, only five-foot-one, but he was a great fighter; his nickname was 'El Maestro', because he was such a clever little fighter. He'd been fighting since the age of 21, and he'd been champion since 1975. Harry Gibbs Sr, the famous British referee, had refereed Canto's title defence against Shoji Oguma in Japan, and Canto had just about nicked it, but he was run bloody close. I ran into Harry at a show one night and he sat down next to me and told me, 'Charlie, I spoke to Terry Lawless. I saw Canto fight recently, and I told Terry that he should make the fight for you as soon as possible. I'm telling you, Charlie, you could take him right now.'

As it turned out, a couple of weeks after the fight with Udella was announced, someone else got there first, and Canto lost his title in Korea. Harry was right, he was there for the taking, and I was right in my prime. As it happened, I'd have to wait four more long years to get my shot at a title. Now maybe I wouldn't have beaten Canto at that time, but I felt I was young and strong enough to rebound from a loss and come back again, and get the experience of being in there with a champion. Anyway, I think I'd have given Canto a run for his money at that time, as he was getting on a bit and had been champion for almost four years; from what I heard, the old legs weren't what they used to be and, as a mover, he was vulnerable. I was younger and fresher, and he wasn't the kind of puncher I would have had to be scared of.

Anyway, now I knew I had the title shot, and I knew it was against Franco Udella. I was 22, a young fighter on the way up, and he was 32, the old champion. He'd been European Champion for donkeys years, and he'd never lost a European title fight. He'd won the WBC light flyweight title, in 1975, but was stripped of his title for some reason. Then he won the European flyweight title, and vacated the belt to fight for the WBC light flyweight title in 1976. After losing, he'd won the European flyweight title again in 1977, and now he had defended his title four times. He was a good champion, but I was confident that I could beat him.

The fight was lined up for 1 May 1979 and the plan was that I would win the European title, and then box later the same month at the Albert Hall on one of the many shows Terry and Mickey Duff had booked throughout the year. Terry and Mickey had shows going on at the Albert Hall, Wembley Conference Centre and the Wembley Empire Pool venues all year around, and, if I came through the fight in good enough shape, I'd appear on the next bill.

I had a long training camp, 14 weeks, for the Udella fight. Not that I was ever really out of the gym, but, instead of just ticking over in training, I had a long hard training camp to prepare myself for what was, after all, a big fight. This was going to be a 12-rounder, and Udella was known for being a right tough little sod. He'd been stopped before, but only in world-title fights; nobody had ever beaten him in a European-title fight, and we were prepared for a full 12-rounder. I knew he was a tough man and I would have to be in top shape. I did six 15-round sparring sessions in the weeks leading up to it to prepare for a long fight. It was the longest time I had ever had between fights since I started my professional career. Normally, I fought once every two months, once a month, or even more often. In 1978, I'd fought twice in April alone. But I was being given a really long training camp to prepare myself completely for this fight; nothing was being left to chance.

Despite training so hard, I had a real fright the evening before the official weigh-in. I got on the scales, and I got a right shock! I was six pounds over the weight! That was really unusual for me, because I would normally be bang on or even a couple of pounds under the weight the day before the weigh-in.

So I had to get the sweat suit on and I skipped for half-an-hour, followed by five rounds of shadow boxing and 15 minutes on the bike, and, fortunately, the weight came off. It was mainly

Top: Me at the Royal Oak, skipping, with the big figure of Frank Bruno in the front. Jimmy McDonnell chats to Terry Lawless in the background as Mark Kaylor works out in the ring.

Left: The famous Royal Oak lightweight Ray Cattouse on my left, heavyweight Neville Mead on the bike. In the background is friend of the gym and all-round character 'Jimmy the Biscuit'.

Top: Terry Lawless towels me down during a break in one of my hard training sessions at the Royal Oak.

Middle: Miles away, dreaming of one day being World Champion.

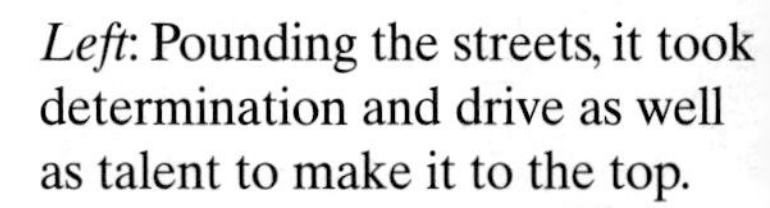

Left: Pounding the streets, it took determination and drive as well as talent to make it to the top.

Top: 'The gym of champions.' *Back row, left to right*: John L Gardner, British Heavyweight Champion, soon to be European Champion, Jimmy Batten, British Light Heavyweight Champion, light heavyweight Johnny Waldron, Maurice Hope with his British, European and WBC light middleweight belts, and British and European Champ Jim Watt, who added the world title just over a month later. *Front row*: Me with my Lonsdale belt with Terry Lawless and Jimmy Flint.

Middle: Me and Frank Bruno, in Cagliari, Italy, before my European-title defence. Frank came over to keep me company during my training. I'm doing my Stan Laurel impression.

Bottom: Me and Frank were the little and large of the gym who became good friends and here we are both working hard as usual. Like me, Frank never wanted to miss a day's training.

The early bird: I was
always the first in,
because I was the
lightest weight, and
also because
I hardly ever
slept anyway.

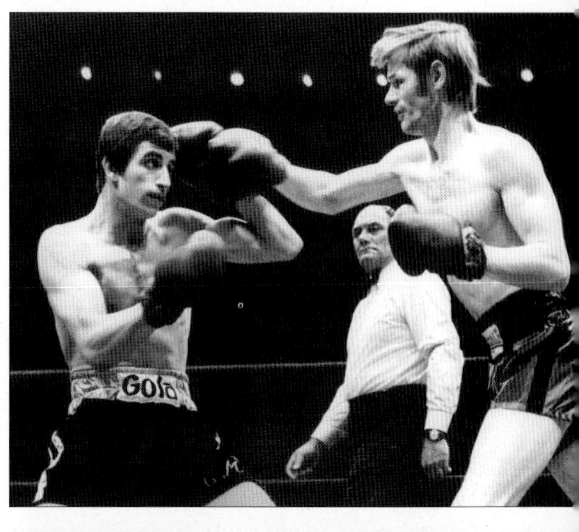

Top: 1977, blocking a shot from Neil McLaughlin, my first professional opponent. I won in two rounds.

Bottom: And the winner! Terry and Frank Black hold me up to show me off to the crowd at the Royal Albert Hall after beating McLaughlin.

Those bloody Mexicans! Juan Diaz who stopped me in six rounds in 1981, ending my unbeaten run, and setting back my dreams of becoming World Champion.

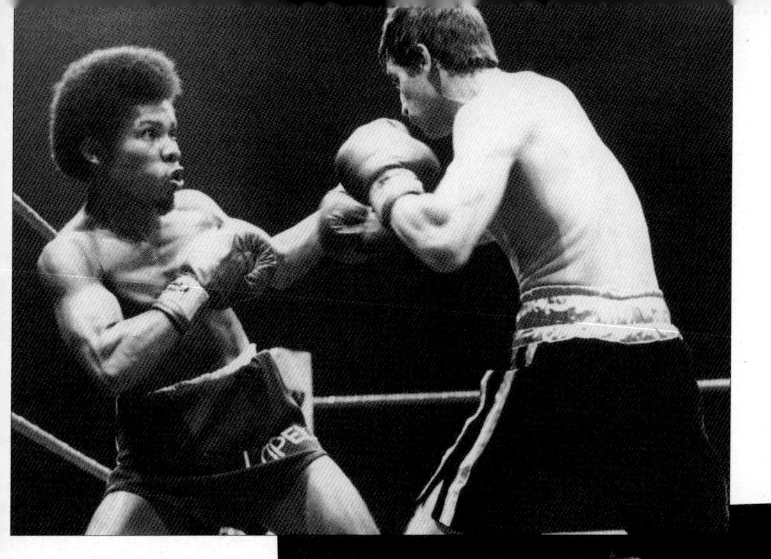

1980, having a proper tear-up with former World Flyweight Champion Alfonso Lopez, who I beat over 10 rounds. It was the best win of my career up until that point.

Top and middle: 1980, the hardest 'warm-up' fight you could ever wish for, against the great Santos Laciar, who went on to become one of the best flyweights of his era. He dropped me like a sack of spuds in the first round, but I recovered and went on to win.

Bottom: 1980, Aniceto Vargas, former light flyweight challenger, he went in three rounds.

just liquids that I'd had which had pushed me over the weight. When you've really killed yourself to make weight, and you're starving yourself and dehydrated, your body holds on to any liquid you take in.

If I'm honest, I'd been a bit naughty a couple of nights before the weigh-in. I used to stay at Terry Lawless's house before a fight, so I was there two days before the weigh-in, and Terry was going out with his wife; he left me there alone with a load of videos and stuff, and said to just chill out before the fight. I did something really odd for me and had a glass or two of wine. It was totally unlike me, as I hardly ever drank really, and I ate this big bunch of grapes that I'd seen lying around. It was stupid really, I was sitting there like bloody Caesar, with a glass of wine and a bunch of grapes, scoffing away. I paid the price for it the next day, I can tell you.

I didn't watch any videos of Udella before the fight; in fact, I never watched videos of anyone. My old amateur trainer Jimmy Graham had always told me, 'If you're good enough, you'll know what to do when you see them in the ring.' I figured that was right; if you learned your trade properly, there shouldn't be anything in the ring which could surprise you. I'd been a top-class amateur for six years, I'd faced all kinds of styles in the ring and, at that time, I felt there was nothing there that I couldn't beat with my skills and my desire to win. I didn't see how Udella could do anything to beat me; I was younger, fitter, stronger and better. I think all the good fighters didn't ever need to study people; they could make their adjustments in the ring. If you're the best, you can adapt to whatever happens; it's no good going in there with a plan, and then finding that you don't know what to do when the plan doesn't work.

Terry Lawless was an excellent corner man. He didn't talk tactics before the fight, but he'd give you some good information of what to expect from the fighter. Jimmy Graham used to tell me that, if you have a southpaw, the best way to deal with them is to get them on the ropes. When they aren't able to get their right foot forward, they're no longer a southpaw, and you've neutralised their advantage of having everything reversed. Take that away from them, and suddenly they've lost their biggest weapon. That's what we worked on for this fight, driving Udella back where he couldn't make use of the southpaw stance. This was something that had worked for me over and over again in my career, driving the southpaw to the ropes so that his feet were both level with the back ropes, and then letting my punches go downstairs and up, and simply overwhelming them with my workrate and fire power.

Before the European-title fight, the atmosphere in the gym was electric. I felt so secure being surrounded by all these fighters that I knew like brothers. Jim Watt was already a European Champion and Maurice Hope had just won his WBC world title from Rocky Mattioli in San Remo. I felt so good going into that fight once the weigh-in was over; I went back home and tucked into a nice big meal and looked forward to getting in the ring with this man.

When I got down to the arena that night, the atmosphere was amazing. Dave Boy Green and Alan Minter were also on the bill, and there was a massive crowd there for the fight. That night, I didn't really feel any nerves for once. I felt so sure I was going to win, I was completely focused and I was just in the zone the whole time until that bell went.

The bout with Udella was fought at a right pace from the off. Udella liked to come in and fight on the inside, and so did I. I could box clever, but I always wanted to get in there and make my mark on my opponents early on, and let them know I was there to hurt them. Rather than back away from Udella, which people probably expected, because he was a really good inside fighter, I let him get close and got right up in his face from the word go. I wanted him to know I was going to hurt him if he got close and I wanted to make sure he had no room to use that southpaw left hand. I really tore into him in the first three or four rounds; I hit him with massive shots to his ribcage over and over again and I think I knocked most of the fight out of him in those first four rounds. I came out banging away to his body and really giving it to him, I never stopped punching, and I didn't let him get set to get his own shots off. As tough as he was, he was feeling the punches, and he wasn't firing that much back in reply.

When he didn't go down in those four rounds, I pretty much knew that it was going to be a distance fight. He was such a tough little man. Udella came to fight, but I could tell that he was determined not to get stopped, and he'd settled for losing the fight after about four rounds. He had a little go in the fifth and sixth rounds, and came back into it a bit, but I was hitting him with massive body shots in every single round, and I took control back from the seventh on, pummelling him for the rest of the fight.

I knew I'd won, but when I heard the scorecards I got a right shock, as it was a split decision, and one of the judges, Frank Marti from Switzerland, had scored it by one round to Udella! 'What the fuck is that about?' I thought.

In a way, I was glad to go the distance again. It was the first time in my career that I'd ever gone 12 rounds, and it felt good to know that I could do a distance fight, because most of my wins were stoppages, and I'd only done one 10-rounder before that. I went out really hard and I never really let up in the whole fight; I fought at a really hard pace all the way through. I learned more in that fight and in the Carrasco fight than in all the other fights put together up to then. When you know you've got someone in front of you who isn't going to fold, you have to knuckle down and get on with controlling the fight and winning it. If I'd knocked him out in a couple of rounds, I'd have probably gone on thinking I could just bowl everyone over, but in fighting Udella I learned that the higher you went in the rankings, the harder they were to put away.

To this day, I don't know how that Swiss judge had Udella winning the fight! At the end of the last round, even Udella raised my arm to say that I'd won, and his manager Umberto Branchini said that he was mystified by the card that had Udella winning and that he thought I'd won it fair and square. Branchini said that they thought I would go on to make a terrific European Champion, and, well, when you hear your opponent's manager say that, you know you've won the fight hands down.

Mickey Duff put it even better about the Swiss judge's scoring when he said, 'I've seen people get bird for less!'

CHAPTER 28

The Long and Winding Road

After winning the European title, I thought that the road to the world title would soon come along, but I had another thing coming. After beating Franco Udella, I thought that, within a year, maybe two at the most, I'd be fighting for and winning a world title, but it didn't quite work out that way for me. Getting that title shot would turn out to be like the bloody Holy Grail, and I would be chasing it for a long time to come. I learned the hard way that getting there would be much harder than I thought. You might have thought that, having won that title, I would have had a layoff, but, no, I was back in action within a month.

The first sign of how hard it was going to be from then on came in the same month I won the European title from Udella, when I had a fight against a geezer by the name of Freddie Gonzalez. Terry, Mickey Duff and his partners had dates to fill, so I was back in the gym again, training for what was meant to be nothing more than a keep-busy fight. Gonzalez was a Mexican fighter, one of many I'd end up facing in my career, and, like all of them, he carried a bit of a sting in his tail. What started out as a routine fight ended up with me being plastered all over the papers.

Although I won the fight in the third round, I got decked in the first round, when I walked into two massive left hooks from Gonzalez. I think what got me was the style. Gonzalez didn't really box like anyone I'd faced before; he had that Mexican style where he liked to throw hooks whether he was in close or at range. I had my hands out in front of me, rather than tucked up round my ears, and in the first round he caught me with a couple of big wild punches. I wasn't really badly hurt, but it definitely gave me a bit of a shake-up. After that, I figured out his style, but he was still standing and trading with me, even though I was much stronger than him. I made him miss in the second round, and started really raking in those body shots, and then, in the third, I hit him with one of the best punches I ever landed. After I cracked him to the ribs with a one-two, I nailed him with a massive uppercut, which completely did for him.

Even though I ended up winning the fight, it was the first time people had really seen me hurt, and I think that's when the papers had got the idea that I was a bit chinny. The rumour had started after I'd been knocked down by Ian Clyde in Montreal, which was stupid, as up until then that was only the second time I'd been stopped as an amateur, and both those times were at international competitions. One was against a top Russian, Alexander Tkachenko, and the other, well, that was just me walking on to a shot really. It can happen to anyone, but now doubts began to surface again. Still, I'd won the fight, and now I was on the long road to getting rated in the top 10, and getting a shot at the world title.

There was one other reason that night stood out in my memory, though, a much nicer reason. That was the one and only night in my career that I shared top billing with Muhammad Ali! It's true. Ali was doing a tour of Europe at that time; he was more or less retired, as he'd announced his retirement after he won the title back from Leon Spinks the year before, but Mickey Duff arranged this European tour for him, with Ali boxing exhibition bouts and making appearances. He boxed some exhibition bouts with John L Gardner and a couple of other people, nothing serious, just a bit of fun. I can remember walking up and out of the arena, just as Ali and his entourage were coming down the steps, and Ali stopped, looked at me and tapped me on the shoulder. 'Hey, boy! How'd you get on in there?'

'Knocked him out,' I said.

'Good work, son,' said Ali, and then just winked and walked past.

If ever I was starstruck in my life, it was right then and there. Although it was just an exhibition bout, and Ali was well past his best by then, he was still a legend, and passing him on the stairs on his way down to the auditorium at the Royal Albert Hall that night was something else! Ali was a living legend, and for him to ask me how I was doing after a fight was just out of this world!

After a four-month layoff, that same year I had two stoppage wins over Raul Pacheco and Candelario Iglesias, in six and three rounds, and, then before the end of the year, I had my first European title defence at the Royal Albert Hall. If you're the champ, then, of course, you've got to defend your belts. I'd been European Champion for seven months, and it got to the time to defend my title. I'd had two pretty easy fights on the way there, which was just as well, because my first defence turned out to be a bloody hard night's work.

When I heard who I was going to be fighting, I thought, 'Oh no, not you again.' I had to fight Manuel Carrasco, who had been the first fighter who'd taken me the distance early in my career in an eight-rounder, and this time it was going to be a 12-rounder with the title on the line.

Carrasco was a big tall southpaw, the worst kind of fighter for me through my career. He used to tear around the ring and he just threw punch after punch after punch, and kept on moving. He wasn't much of a puncher, there wasn't much put on each punch really, but he was a sod to nail because he was always flying around the ring throwing out these shots at you. Carrasco was like a bad smell; you just couldn't get rid of him. Since fighting me the first time, he'd fought for the European title against Franco Udella, the guy I'd won it off, and gone the distance with him. You know what? That geezer took everything I could dish out to him for 20 rounds over two fights, and he never really came close to going down. He was one of the toughest geezers I've ever seen in a boxing ring.

The fight went just like I expected it to go, with me chasing Carrasco all over the ring for the entire fight, and him soaking it all up. He was a big tall feller, for a flyweight anyway, and he had a great big afro, something I seemed to run into a lot of in my career! I think I fought about five geezers who had afros – Mike Stuart, Manuel Carrasco, Aniceto Vargas, Alfonso Lopez and Santos Laciar all had big barnets.

In the first fight, I'd headhunted him a bit, so, in the second fight, I went for the body a bit more, and I'm telling you I landed a lot of hard body shots on him. I hurt him in every round, but he was a tough proud man, and he soaked it all up, even though he must have lost every round. I learned an awful lot fighting that guy because you had to fight hard to win against him; there was no way he was going to lie down for anyone. I was used to blowing people away in a few rounds, but, against Carrasco, you knew you were in for a long hard fight, and it forced you to pace yourself.

By the time I faced my next opponent, Aniceto Vargas, I was finally the number-one challenger to Chan Hee Park, from South Korea, who had won the flyweight title from Miguel Canto, the long-reigning WBC Champion, and I had to keep winning to maintain that status. It is a weight on your mind, because all the time you're number-one challenger you know that, if you lose, bang goes your number-one status. It's why some fighters stop fighting so often once they realise they are the number-one contender, hoping that they get their mandatory shot at the title. I never had that luxury, as I never had enough coin coming in for my fights to do that, and Terry and Mickey Duff had their regular shows to put on, and wanted me headlining.

Vargas was a good, tough fighter. He'd started his career at light flyweight and he'd fought the champion at the time, losing it in 14 rounds, to a bloke called Yoko Gushiken. I was the favourite to beat this kid, because his record at flyweight wasn't so good, but a quick stoppage was what I needed to keep on impressing.

Early on, I was hurting him with body shots, and in the second round he pulled this funny face after I whacked him with a couple of rib-ticklers to the left and right sides. It didn't take long before he was under pressure, and in the third round I caught him with a massive right uppercut which hit him right on the button, followed by a lovely left hook which dropped him, sending him through the ropes and out of the ring, right on to the ringside seat of Harry Carpenter, landing right on the TV monitors! He got up and tried to get back into the ring, but he didn't make it before the count of 10, and he was counted out. Vargas's best shot of the night was a little kick he gave me during a clinch. He was a martial artist in his spare time, so I guess he figured he needed whatever chance he could get. I can remember Harry Gibbs the referee giving him a little warning and laughing to himself about it.

After that, I defended my European title again, on 28 June 1980, at the Empire Pool in Wembley, against a geezer called Giovanni Camputaro, who I stopped in three rounds, which was probably the best display I ever put on. I don't think he laid a glove on me that bloke in the entire three rounds. I felt like I could have stood there all night and I don't think he could have hit me with a handful of rice. I stopped him easily and it was a really impressive night's work. Camputaro was a decent operator as well, he had a 19-3-2 record coming in to that fight, and he'd been on a good run, only losing once in his last 15 fights. Beating him so easily gave me a hell of a lot of confidence in my abilities. I was beginning to feel unstoppable, because all of the wins were coming pretty quickly and easily, give or take a little difficult patch here or there, and, considering that I had been a professional less than three years, it was all going great.

Now, for some reason, which I still don't understand to this day, despite being number one in the rankings before I fought and beat Aniceto Vargas in three rounds – and three really one-sided rounds at that – and having beaten Camputaro as well in the best performance of my career, for no good bloody reason, I went down to number two in the rankings, by the time of my next opponent Alfonso Lopez! I would still like someone to explain it to me. Now the Mexican Antonio Avelar had the number-one spot, a name that would crop up more than once in my career, though I never actually fought him. I don't know what the problem was, but I guess my management couldn't convince the sanctioning body to rank me number one; because of that I had to keep on fighting warm-up fights, and fights to try to get an eliminator. I was ready for a world-title shot right then, but I just couldn't keep that number-one ranking.

Alfonso Lopez wasn't exactly what you'd call an easy test. The guy was a former champion at flyweight, and on paper he was the best fighter I'd ever faced. He was a little bit past his best at 27, and he'd had a few losses in the run-up to the fight, but he'd mixed with top-class fighters in his career. He'd beaten Shoji Oguma before who was the current World Champion, defending his title against him in 1976, and he'd also beaten a young Hiario Zapata who went on to be a World Champion later. He'd mixed it with Guty Espadas, and Freddy Castillo, top-class, world-class fighters. He was definitely a step up, and not an easy night's work. A former champion knows what it is to be on top. There was also added pressure on me, as, because I had such a high ranking with the WBC, I was also a big scalp to anyone I fought; they knew now that, if they could beat me, they had a good chance of getting into the top 10 in the rankings, and maybe get a shot at the WBC title as a voluntary defence, and a nice payday.

It turned out to be a really rough night's work as well. I started off pretty well, and was giving him a lot of bother early on, but, as the fight wore on, he just seemed to get stronger and stronger. After the fourth round, he came on strong, which was strange, as he had a reputation as being someone whose stamina was a bit suspect, and I kind of got myself into a rut. The middle rounds turned into a bit of a nightmare, as he seemed to get encouraged, and I had bad bleeding from my nose and mouth. By the eighth round, the fight was getting closer, and over the last two rounds of the fight I had to box really smart to make the decision safe. I had to pick my shots and make sure I didn't stay in one place too long so he couldn't land any big right hands. I came away winning a close decision, but it hadn't been easy. I ended up having a really long hard fight, which hadn't really improved my chances of getting that title shot, and the press started questioning if I was really ready to face the champion at the time, the Japanese WBC Champion Shoji Oguma.

Luckily, a few weeks later, I had a much easier night's work, another one-round blow out, this time against Enrique Castro at the Royal Albert Hall again. I'd now had eight fights since winning the European title, including two title defences, but I was still waiting to get my shot at a world title, and, despite being on a winning streak, I couldn't seem to keep hold of the number-one ranking with the WBC. I was getting frustrated with it all. It felt like the opportunity was passing me by, and I badly wanted to get my shot before it was too late and I went off the boil. I was so close to being the top contender for the WBC title; I just needed to get my hands on the number one, Antonio Avelar.

CHAPTER 29

Laciar – The Warm-up

Then I got some good news. Terry told me that he'd got me a fight with Antonio Avelar, and that, if I beat him, I would most likely be ranked number one with the WBC. As I was the number two in the rankings and he was a number one, it was pretty much an eliminator for the title. It didn't quite work out, though, because this time, a couple of weeks before I was due to fight him, the fight fell through because he was injured, and suddenly Mickey Duff and Terry had a show on their hands where the headline act hadn't got an opponent – not a good situation. I was headlining the show, and also on the bill were Tony Sibson, who was fighting for the European title, Lloyd Honeyghan, who was making his debut that night, a young Mark Kaylor and Jimmy Flint. The venue was still booked, of course, and, as I was headlining the bill, a new opponent had to be found so that the show could go ahead.

Terry got on the blower with his contacts, and him, Mickey Duff and Mike Barrett came up with this bloke called Santos Bonino Laciar, a name I will never forget. I think Mickey Duff had got hold of a fax with this geezer's details. He was a young Argentinean fighter, who'd had a few losses, and they said he didn't look that dangerous on paper. Now, if you follow boxing closely, you'll know that the Argentineans have a reputation for producing tough-nut, wild-punching fighters as well as some bloody great World Champions. From Luis Firpo back in the 1920s, who gave Jack Dempsey absolute nightmares, to Carlos Monzon, one of the best Middleweight Champions there ever was, and the likes of Victor Galindez. Even now, they are still churning out really tough men like Jorge Castro and Jorge Barrios, and loads more throughout the years. The Argentineans are wild, rugged, unpredictable tough little men and you take them lightly at your peril.

Part of the problem – and most matchmakers will tell you this – is that most of these guys have untold fights; some of them are on record, but quite a lot aren't, and it's not easy, even in this day and age, to know exactly how many fights they've had, because most of their fights happen in their home country, and often nobody knows much about them. Laciar was no different. When his record came through, it didn't look anything special, but, without seeing him in action, nobody had much idea what he would be like, because almost all of his fights had been at home.

So Terry called me up and he told me, 'We've found an opponent for you, Charlie. Laciar his name is, and he's an Argentinean. He's not had many fights and he can't punch his way out of a paper bag, so it should be a nice little warm-up fight for you.'

Well, I don't know where this information came from, because, as it turned out, if you look at his record now, this geezer had been fighting since 1976, and had well over 40 fights, almost all of them in Argentina against pretty much unknown opponents. It was even harder to get hold of fighters' records then and, if you look up this guy's record, you can see he wasn't some inexperienced kid. He'd had more bloody fights than I had! Laciar, like a lot of South American fighters, had turned pro early at 17.

The problem was that I'd gone from preparing to fight a really tough and good Mexican fighter to training for what I believed was an inexperienced 20-year-old who'd never fought anyone and a bit of a walk in the park; little did I know what I had in store for me. In my mind, it had changed everything about this fight. Although I'd trained like an absolute nutter in the gym, in my head I wasn't prepared properly for what was about to come.

The first sign of trouble came at the weigh-in. The way that Terry had talked about him, I was expecting an inexperienced kid, who was barely even a grown man. When I saw Laciar take off his top and step on the scales, I couldn't believe the physique on the geezer! He was short and stocky, but incredibly muscular, with shoulders, back and chest that looked like a sawn-off middleweight. He was only little, but he was built like a bull. I thought, 'Fucking hell, look at him!' I tried to screw him down, sort of give him the evil eye, but he just looked right back at me, he had no fear at all! Absolutely none at all! That took me by surprise, and I had to figure he either didn't know my reputation or he just didn't care; he just stood there staring back at me like he wanted to kill me. Suddenly, this fight wasn't looking like the 'nice little warm-up' that Terry had described.

I was still confident, though. I'd trained hard and at that time in my career I didn't think that anyone could beat me. I liked fighting tough, good opponents; it didn't faze me at all to take on a hard nut, because I felt I could beat them, and, if I can beat them, then that means I'm a good fighter, doesn't it?

As soon as I heard the first bell, I went forward to meet him and take the fight to him, but, the next thing I know, just a few seconds into the fight, I ducked under a couple of shots and, as I came back up, he caught me with a chopping right hook, which I only saw coming as it landed. This was all of five seconds into a 10-round fight! It caught me slightly off balance, and dropped me right on my arse. I wasn't badly hurt, my head was clear, but, bloody hell, had he given me a big shock! I was trying to get up almost immediately. Laciar came steaming in when I was on the floor, and tried to have some afters before the referee got in there to pull him off. I was up and feeling OK and moving around the ring trying to stay out of harm's way, when he caught me with another good right hook, which shook me up. He saw that I was hurt and went all out to finish me off. He was banging away to the body and keeping on me, not giving me any chance to get some breathing space. Another right hook cracked me and now I was hurt and had no choice but to try to stand and fight back to discourage him. That round, I was really hanging on for dear life until the last minute of the round, and even then I wasn't right. It was the worst round of boxing I'd ever had as a professional fighter, and the first time I'd been decked like that and properly hurt.

'So this geezer can't punch his way out of a paper bag!' I thought. I was so shocked, I just couldn't believe I was on the floor, and, if you watch a video of the fight, you can see the look on my face as he hits me, complete and utter bloody shock!

Second round, I came out jabbing and managed to start boxing him. I took control of the centre of the ring, and stopped him getting me with that big right hook by sticking him with the jab and keeping him moving so he couldn't get set. I knew I couldn't let this geezer have any free swings at me, so I kept spearing him with that jab, which is what you do to stop a puncher getting their leverage in there – jab, move and jab again when they try to track you for a big shot. Laciar was good, when he saw I wasn't going anywhere soon, he started using his boxing skills; he wasn't just some crude brawler, he knew what he was doing in there. He was crafty, and he kept slipping the jab and weaving underneath my short hooks, and then he'd sling in a body shot under the elbow; he was hard to nail with a clean shot, but I managed to be the aggressor and land more shots.

I pretty much managed to control the next three rounds, but it was hard technical boxing. I had to be on my guard the whole time, and not leave him any openings, he was such a clever little fighter. By the fifth round, I'd cut him under his left eyebrow, and marked him up with my jab, and I just about got on top in the sixth, but he was never really out of any of the rounds. It all went a bit quiet in the seventh but then in the eighth he came back again, and so I had to turn it on. I really bashed him up in the eighth round. I was hitting him with some massive shots; I got him with some really good uppercuts, and he looked like he was on the way out at one point, but he could really take a punch this geezer. In the ninth, though, he seemed to just come back to life again. I don't know where he got the energy from, because at the end of the eighth he looked really gone. He came storming out like it was the first round and he had me under pressure big time for the whole of the ninth round. In the tenth, we were fighting at the sort of pace that most flyweight fights were fought in the first round, and the crowd were going mental! What a bloody hard fight it was, toe-to-toe action almost for the whole fight! It was a fantastic fight, and the crowd were on their feet at the end. It was back and forward action, with me getting the nod from the referee.

When the decision was announced and they raised my hand, I went over to Laciar, and I picked him up and held him up to the crowd. The entire audience was on its feet and they cheered both of us for a cracking fight. It was the hardest fight I'd ever had in my career, and this guy was just supposed to be a warm-up while I waited for a title shot! He was only ranked 15 by the WBC, but he gave me the hardest fight of my career so far by a long way.

Laciar turned out to be a fantastic fighter in his own right. Two fights later, he got a title shot at the WBA Champion, and he went over to South Africa to fight Peter Mathebula in Soweto. Laciar knocked him out in seven rounds in the other guy's backyard! He went on to lose and regain the title, defending it 10 times, and then went on to win the super flyweight title, before losing it against Sugar Baby Rojas. He challenged for it again in 1990 against Gilberto Roman for the last time in his career. Laciar ended up with 101 fights in his career; he won 79 of them, and he was never stopped in a 14-year career. Some warm-up this guy was, he was one of the great Flyweight Champions of the era!

On paper, I suppose you could say that was the best fight of my career, considering what the guy went on to achieve, and I put in a fantastic performance in that fight. I learned a lot from fighting someone like that too, just like I learned a lot from fighting Udella who took me the distance in a long gruelling fight. I proved I could come back from a shock against a really tough opponent, and handle it. It was a big test and a great learning fight. Thinking about it now, I was probably right at my peak then and there. I reckon, if I'd got a title shot right then, I could have done it. Physically, I was at my best; I was young and strong, and I was still in love with the game, still hungry and full of fire. I just wish now that I'd got my title shot the very next fight.

What was really hard to take was that, after all the trouble I had with Laciar, and missing out on my chance at the number-one contender Antonio Avelar, Avelar came back after injury, got his shot at Shoji Oguma a few months later and knocked him out, winning the WBC title. Laciar had got his WBA title shot and won it. I missed out on a chance of either one.

As it was, my next two fights were a defence of my European title against Spaniard Rodriguez Cal, and then another Mexican opponent. My European-title defence was an easy win; he wasn't even really at the races in that fight. I had him running for cover, decking him three times with the same shot to the ribs, and forcing the referee to end it. This guy had a good record too; he hadn't lost before he met me, and had one draw on his record and 17 wins. He also had a terrific amateur record, having won a bronze medal and two silver medals at the European amateurs. The fact that this guy couldn't stand up to my punches at all made me think I'd be in the number-one spot soon enough.

To add to my case for being ranked in the WBC rankings, I flattened Mexican Jose Herrera a couple of months later in one round in a non-title fight. The same night, the headline fight was our own Jim Watt, who lost his title in a really hard gruelling fight against Alexis Arguello, one of the all-time greats. Jim gave a great account of himself that night, but Arguello beat him in what was quite a close one, and Jim pushed him right to the end of the fight. It was Jim's last fight, and he went out against one of the greatest fighters of all time. Arguello had won proper titles at featherweight, super featherweight and lightweight; he'd beaten the likes of Ray Mancini, Royal Kobyashi, Bobby Chacon, Bazooka Limon, Cornelius Boza Edwards, and he'd won his title from my old hero as an amateur, Ruben Olivares, another all-time great fighter.

For me, I was just marking time until I could get myself a shot at the title, but that number-one ranking was proving hard to come by. I was about to find out that, while you were marking time, that was just when things could get really difficult.

CHAPTER 30

That Losing Feeling – The Diaz Fight

Like I said, after my fight with Laciar, I had a couple of easy fights. The idea was to keep me fighting and keep me up in the rankings until they could get me a title shot. With Laciar having gone on to be a champion, you would think that would be easy, but it wasn't. Laciar got his shot, won his title, but that was the WBA, and I guess my promoters and management weren't as well connected with the WBA, because there was no chance of a title shot in the offing. I fought Laciar, Cal and Herrera all within six months, because I'd been the number-one contender or thereabouts for ages now; all I had to do was keep winning, and I'd surely get my title shot sooner or later. The only thing I had to do was make sure I didn't lose. Famous last words!

That's the thing, if you're a fighter, you constantly have to live with the chance that if you keep fighting you're going to lose. Very few fighters in history have retired unbeaten if they've fought at the top level; when you're fighting other top boys, it's hard to win them all. The more fights you have, the more chance you have of losing, and the better the competition, the bigger the risk.

As I've said, it wasn't so easy to get information on fighters then; we didn't have stuff like boxrec.com to check out our opponents' records and find out their wins and losses. Often you went into a fight, not knowing much about them, just like my surprise with Laciar. My next fight was staged for October 1981 at the Royal Albert Hall, and my opponent was a guy by the name of Juan Diaz. He didn't have much of a record to speak of; he was 20–17 with one draw, but he was known to be a big puncher and, early in both their careers, he had beaten a guy by the name of Eleoncio Mercedes who would go on to be World Champion, and would figure in my own future. The Diaz fight was meant to be just another tune-up; he shouldn't have been much of a threat, as I'd beaten better men before, but in a boxing ring that means nothing. When there are two men hitting each other, anything can happen; you get clipped with a shot, and you go down, bang!

Now I know they say that fighters always have an excuse for losing, but the truth is that I'd had big problems with making weight all through my career, and, in the Diaz fight, it finally caught up with me. I always trained like a demon for every single fight; I was never out of the bloody gym and, in fact, I used to do secret training which I never even told my management about, going running at stupid times in the morning because I couldn't sleep, or shadow boxing at home in the middle of the night. I was always terrified of being unfit, of leaving anything to chance, and the truth is I think I drained myself with all the worry, all the constant training, and never having a break away from the gym. So my weight-making problems didn't come from me not being active enough between fights or out of the gym, as I was never out of the bloody gym. I think the simple fact was that I was killing myself to make flyweight.

My big worry in fights was that, with the effort in making weight, and the amount of training I had to do to keep under the weight limit, I would feel myself tiring in the second half of fights. That was my one big weakness as a fighter, that I had a tendency to slow down in the second half of a fight because, looking back on it, the way I made weight was really all wrong. The process of training like a madman day in, day out, for weeks on end and eating virtually nothing in the run-up to a fight to lose that last bit of weight has a big effect on you, especially if you're a flyweight, when you're so small anyway that your body can't tolerate drying out as much as the bigger lads. A few pounds, say three or four, is not a big deal to someone who weighs in at 160 pounds, but, when you're weighing in under 112, those extra three or four can mean the difference between coming in healthy or feeling absolutely terrible, especially as in those days you had same-day weigh-ins. You only had a few hours between the weigh-in and the fight, so, if you were badly drained from making weight, or had to go and do some last-minute training to make the weight, that was your lookout. These days, fighters have more than 24 hours between the weigh-in and the fight, plenty of time to take fluids on board, rest and recover from the hardship of making weight. Me? I spent so much time worrying about making weight that I was a nervous wreck. That's why I always wanted to finish a fight early and make sure that I couldn't tire.

In those days, fighters took terrible liberties with their bodies, and there wasn't the same level of advice and expertise around then that there is now. I wonder what it was like for fighters in even earlier eras; it must have been terrible the things they put themselves through, although, as they fought more often, they probably didn't have that much time to put the weight back on.

I honestly knew before that fight something was going to go wrong. In training for that fight, I went absolutely mental. I wanted to show that I could make the limit easily. In fact, I almost got myself in under the light flyweight limit. I got myself all the way down to 7 stone 11. I only weighed in at 109 pounds for that fight which is three pounds inside the limit! Now that might not sound like a big deal, but I was always struggling so hard to get under the flyweight limit anyway, and, at that sort of weight, three pounds' extra weight is a big deal, let me tell you. Had I lost another pound, I would have been inside the light flyweight limit! I was absolutely shattered at the weigh-in.

Diaz, though, I think weighed in on the day at 8 stone 3, 115 pounds, a whole six pounds heavier. As it wasn't a title fight, it didn't really make a big difference if he was overweight, as long as we agreed to it. When I got off the scales, my brother Joey gave me a big bottle of orange juice mixed with water, but I made a massive mistake and downed the whole bloody bottle in one go, because I was so thirsty and dehydrated I was as weak as a kitten. That was the worst thing I could have done. When you're dehydrated, you're suppose to take water in gradually, as it can make your stomach cramp up badly, because your tissues are all dried out inside, and then it can make you vomit and feel ill. The shock to your stomach of whacking loads of water down you makes it go funny. But I was so thirsty that I just swallowed the whole bottle in one go. I was so sick after that that I couldn't eat a thing when I got home. Normally after the weigh-in, I'd go straight home and tuck into a massive roast dinner, but, after that, I wasn't fit for anything. I didn't eat a thing that night, and I thought, 'What the hell am I going to do now? I've got to fight tonight.'

On top of that, because I was getting frustrated waiting around for my title shot, I don't think I had my mind right. You've got to treat every single fight as a life or death battle; if you don't you can come unstuck, and that's what happened to me that night. The first round, I had a bit of a shock, when he decked me with a jab. I was more off-balance than anything, but I'd been on the floor again in the first few seconds. I gathered myself and I started boxing well, popping him with my own jabs and cracking him hooks to the head and body. Apart from the flash knockdown, I was doing all right.

After that, things were going well. I was really tearing into him, but, because I was feeling drained, the shots maybe weren't having the same effect. I couldn't seem to hurt him as I expected to. I was really on top to begin with, and I was giving him a bit of a going over. I went out there like I did every other fight to take him apart, and, if I'd been able to get him early on, I would probably have been all right. I can remember looking over at the end of the fourth round, and I could see his corner literally shoving him off his stool. I swear his corner was having to push him back out for the fifth round, and he really didn't fancy it at all. I was leading well on all the cards, but then, well, the wheels just fell off.

The trouble was, after that, what with coming in well under the weight, and not being able to eat, the arse just fell out of it. I was so knackered that, when he caught me with a good shot, my legs just went from under me and I went down. I got up again and he hit me with another shot, and I just went down and stayed down that time. I'd taken bigger shots off of bigger punchers than Diaz before, and come on strong, but that night I just didn't have any strength to resist his shots. In the sixth round, I walked into one of these big wild swings he'd been trying to connect with all the way through, but I'd kept slipping and blocking them, and then he suddenly connected with this big wide hook, and down I went.

I can remember Terry screaming from the corner for me to get up, and I made it to my feet at six, but there was too long left to go in the round. I can remember feeling like I had no strength left in my body. He tore straight into me, and I went down again, and this time there was just nothing left. There was hardly any time left in the round, but it made no difference, I was completely shattered. I just couldn't get up. I'd lost the fight, my reputation and, worst of all, my ranking with the WBC.

I felt devastated, I'd never lost before as a professional, let alone been stopped, and it was a big, big shock to me. To be honest, after the loss, I seriously considered packing it all in. I was a man who hated losing, and especially the circumstances around that fight. I felt like I came down far too much in weight and knew I didn't go into the fight in my best condition. I'd pretty much been fighting at light flyweight for that fight, and I was really drained. I just couldn't recover like I was able to before when I got hurt. I went down and got counted out, and now I didn't know whether I wanted to fight any more.

It might sound stupid, or like I was being silly about it, but you have to understand that winning was everything to me. I just couldn't imagine the idea of going in that ring and losing, especially at that time in my career when I was unbeaten. For the next couple of weeks after the fight, I moped around, thinking of jacking it all in, because I just couldn't believe I'd lost. And not just that, I'd lost at the worst time possible, and to a man I knew I could have beaten under different circumstances. It felt like I had no chance of getting a title shot now. I'd beaten a guy who went on to be a World Champion, Santos Laciar, missed my shot at the number-one contender Antonio Avelar, and now I'd lost to a guy who wasn't even well ranked; everything had gone badly wrong. My dreams of a world-title shot looked further away than ever. I was just devastated.

All through my career, I had always thought the press were a bit funny with me. After losing at the Olympics to Ian Clyde, I was always tagged with being chinny, because I'd been stopped so suddenly. Then I got dropped by Gonzalez, and again in the first round by Laciar, and they were having a field day with me now. It really bothered me, hearing what they had to say about me, and I think it affected my confidence a lot. What happened against Diaz next gave them even more fuel for their fire.

When I lost to Diaz, the flak got even worse, because I had not only been dropped, but also stopped inside of six rounds. I think it gave me a bit of a chip on my shoulder where the press was concerned, and I didn't really want to talk to them. I used to get upset every time I read something negative in the press.

After losing to Diaz, I was really down, and, I'll say this for Terry Lawless, he stuck by me at that point, and he carried on until he could get me the opportunity. Every time I lost, it hurt so badly I wanted to quit. I never wanted to duck anybody; I thought I could beat them all, no matter how tough they were. I'd rather lose than duck someone, but I always thought I was going to win every fight.

CHAPTER 31

Bouncing Back – Cipriano Arreola

Everyone can deal with winning, that's easy; we all love winning, don't we? If you want to get to the top, whatever your line of work, chances are you've got to get ready to deal with things not going your way. They say that a champion knows how to deal with loss, and, though I'd lost, I still felt deep down that I was good enough to be World Champion. I still thought I could do it; I *knew* I could do it. The newspapers had slaughtered me after that loss. Everyone was saying how I could dish it out but I couldn't take it, how I would never be World Champion. It hurt me to read those things, it really did hurt me, but it made me want to succeed more than ever. After a big loss like that, especially if you get stopped, the idea is that your management get you a nice easy fight to work your way back in. After the loss to Diaz, I had five months out of the ring which was a lifetime for me.

You need a confidence boost to get you back into things. So Terry got me a fight against a nice easy opponent, or so he said. Now I'd already heard this sort of thing, first about Laciar, and then Diaz who I ended up losing to, and I wasn't about to make the same mistake again. There's no such thing as an easy night's work in boxing; you just never know what's going to happen once you get in that ring. I wasn't going to start thinking this was easy; I trained like a demon for this and got myself ready for a hard night's work, mentally preparing myself for the worst that could happen.

Now at this point, I've got to mention something, because it's a moment in my life that I will always remember, something that has always made me laugh when I think about it. And, right then, with my situation, I needed something to laugh at, so it stuck in my mind.

While I was doing my stuff down at the Royal Oak, during my training camp for this fight, we had a new fighter join the gym. He was a young heavyweight who had just turned professional after winning the heavyweight ABA Championship. You might have heard of him, his name was Frank Bruno. That's right, big Frank. Frank had turned professional under Terry Lawless, although he didn't finish his career with Terry. Anyway, of course, we didn't know how famous old Frank was going to become, but at the time he was still regarded as a brilliant prospect, because of the way he'd dominated the amateurs, absolutely smashing all of his opponents to bits in the ABAs and winning the heavyweight ABA title when he was only 18, which was a record.

Frank had signed with Terry Lawless's stable, and was soon to have his professional debut, fighting against Lupe Guerra on a bill at the Royal Albert Hall.

I can clearly remember the first time Frank came down to train with us, and seeing this huge hulking bloke. I was amazed at how shy and nervous he was. When he first started out, well, you've never seen anyone so timid in your life. He was so shy, he'd just clam up in company; he wasn't really a very outgoing sort of bloke. Frank was so big and powerful, but so young and immature; if he'd had a head on his shoulders, there's nothing he couldn't have done, with a bit more confidence. But, and this is the big but about Frank Bruno, he couldn't half punch. That was his big leveller.

That first day, he came down with his kit, and Terry Lawless said to him, 'Why don't you just have a bit of a workout on the heavy bag?'

Now, as I mentioned earlier, the Royal Oak gym had all its equipment set on scaffolding poles, which were all over the inside of the gym to hold it up, and the punch bag hung off one of the scaffolds. So Frank got ready, and he walked over to the heavy bag and stood in front of it. With his first shot, he's gone BOOM! There was this almighty crash, and all of us jumped out of our skins. We looked round, and there was an embarrassed-looking Frank Bruno, surrounded by all the scaffolding which had fallen down – he'd managed to bring the whole lot crashing down with one punch! Now that's what you call a punch! Imagine being hit in the head with something like that! We were lucky the whole place didn't fall down on top of our heads. When Frank realised what he'd done, he was like a big kid; he went, 'Sorry, man, I only punched it.'

Only punched it, he said! If that had hit someone, it would have gone right through their head. Terry Lawless came out of his office and said, 'What the fucking hell are we going to do now? Put the scaffolding back up.'

I couldn't stop laughing. We all had to stop training for the rest of the day. Frank used to crack me up, what a funny geezer he was.

I remember one day later on in Frank's career, in 1983, when Frank was meant to be sparring, preparing for his fight with Jumbo Cummings, the guy who almost knocked Frank spark out in their fight. Anyway, Cummings was this fucking huge great muscular black American fighter, a big lump like Frank. So they brought in another huge black American guy as a sparring partner. We were all looking forward to seeing the sparring sessions, because Frank was a bloke who couldn't help but bash his sparring partners up because every punch he hit them with was so bloody hard. Even his jab was like a battering ram, and it used to put people over.

I finished my workout for the day, and I went into the changing rooms to have a shower. I looked around and I couldn't believe my eyes: there's the biggest geezer I'd ever seen in there, he looked about seven foot tall with great big long arms like a gorilla. I thought, 'Fucking hell!'

I came out of the changing rooms and said to Frank, 'Bloody hell, mate, you wanna see the size of the geezer you're sparring.'

Frank looked absolutely terrified! 'What, man, what do you mean?'

'He's about seven-foot-five, with arms down to his ankles! He's a fucking giant, Frank!'

'What?!'

Frank went to look, and he opened the door and gasped in fear; he absolutely shit himself and looked like he was on the verge of doing a runner.

I'd finished my workout but I thought, 'I'm not going home, I'm going to watch this.'

So they set them up in the ring, and Terry told them to start sparring. The massive geezer got in the ring and he came out with a bit of style about him, really tall and quite slim, but bloody massive with it. He started coming out on his toes, all nimble like, throwing the jab and moving around, and Frank came out all stiff and tight, with those stiff legs, shuffling forward. The guy tried to move around and went for a jab, and Frank threw his own jab … BOOM! The guy hit the deck. Frank knocked him spark out, cold! They took the geezer out and he went home.

The next day, I said to Terry, 'What's happened to that great big geezer? Is he coming back?'

'No,' he said, 'he's gone home.'

We never saw the geezer again; he flew back home the same day. He flew in, one jab, BANG! Next plane back home. They always had trouble finding sparring partners for Frank, because he kept knocking them over all the time.

Frank could have been so much better. I remember I couldn't believe how well he boxed against Lennox Lewis. That was one fight he really wanted to win. There was a lot of needle in that fight between Frank and Lennox, on account of some of the comments Lennox made about Frank before the fight, which were a bit out of order, calling him an Uncle Tom and all that, and Frank fought out of his skin that night. It was more than just a boxing match to Frank, it was about proving himself, and proving he wasn't what Lewis had said he was. He was actually winning the fight on all the cards before he got stopped. Lennox even admitted himself that he had a much harder night than he expected, and that, if he hadn't found the big punch to turn the fight around, he would probably have lost. He came so close to winning the world title that night, because Lennox was the WBC Champion, but it would be another three years before Frank finally won that belt from Oliver McCall, who beat Lennox for the title.

Anyway, back to my fight with Cipriano Arreola, which had been lined up as a sort of comeback after my loss. Arreola was a young Mexican bloke, who was from a fighting family; I think there were six brothers, and all of them were fighters. In fact, John Feeney, who I'd fought as an amateur, was fighting one of them, Adriana Arreola, on the same bill.

So, it was meant to be a nice easy comeback fight, but he was another Mexican, and I always found in my career that, against Mexicans, especially in those lower weights, there's no such thing as an easy fight. Even your average Mexican club fighter is tough as nails, and loves a tear-up. I'd had a real disaster against Diaz, and this was my chance to get myself back into the mix for the title. If you looked at it on paper, then the Arreola fight did look like a nice easy fight. He'd not really had much of a career to talk about, though, looking back on it now, he'd beaten Jose Torres, who beat me later in my career.

Of course, the trouble is that fights happen in the ring, not on paper, and it turned out to be probably the hardest win of my career, even harder than when I won the world title. He was one of those tough Mexicans that people know nothing about, but who come to fight, and, being from a fighting family, he was a proud man and he wasn't coming to lie down.

The signs were there before the fight even started. While I was sitting in the dressing room with a towel over my head getting ready, John Feeney had had his fight with Adriana Arreola; someone came in and said, 'Christ! Feeney's just got done over; he's been over twice and he's been beaten on points.'

I'd already been told that Adriana wasn't as tasty as his brother Cipriano, so I should have known right then that I was going to be in for a rough night, because John Feeney was a tough man who'd been 15 rounds with Johnny Owen for the British title.

This was one of the biggest fights of my life, because I knew that, if I lost here, my chances of a world-title shot for the WBC belt were pretty much dead in the water. One loss was bad, but two losses back to back and I'd have to wait ages and win loads of fights to get a crack at the title. Sometimes a loss can get you nearer a world title, because people are less afraid to face you, but two on the trot? Well, that's another story, isn't it?

Coming into the fight, I was ranked number three by the WBC, and I had to win this fight if I was ever going to get my shot at a title. I'd already lost one big chance when I lost the Diaz fight.

As soon as the bell went against Arreola, I was right on him. In the first round I was a bit careful, but I still made sure I landed some hard shots on him and took control of the ring. I wanted to make sure he knew I was there to hurt him. In the second round, I really let him have it. I dug in hard shots under his elbows and the ribs, trying to take his legs away. I hit him with some punches that really hurt him all the way through the round. If I'd thought it was going to soften him up, though, I had another thing coming. This kid just seemed to soak up the punches; I never even saw him flinch once, and I hit him with some of my biggest punches. These Mexican fighters were always the same; it's like they were made out of rubber, you'd whack away at them, and it just seemed to make no difference at all. At my weight, I could really punch with the best of them, and other fighters would have gone down from the shots I hit him with, but he just carried on like nothing had happened.

Arreola came right back into it in the third, and he started landing some big hooks of his own. I was getting marked up as well, and a big swelling came up under my right eye. It certainly wasn't an easy fight, and by the fourth it was turning into a rough old clash; our heads were knocking into each other, and the two of us were banging in big shots standing right in close. I had to start using my head a bit, and get some distance and bang in some shots to the body. That was it from there on in, it was give and take with both of us having our moments, and Arreola wasn't going anywhere. Christ! What a tough little man that bloke was; he just seemed to soak up all the big body shots I was landing. Although it was give and take, I thought I was just edging the rounds, and felt like I was winning the fight, even though it was a really tough night's work.

Then, in the ninth round, things went badly wrong. Right at the end of the round, he threw a wide left hook which took me completely by surprise and caught me bang on the chin, and I went down by the ropes near my own corner. The fight was hard enough, but now I had a knockdown against me. Luckily, it came right on the bell, and I had time to recover; the corner were working away like mad trying to get me right for the start of the next round.

It was only a 10-rounder, and I knew I had only one more round to go. I figured I was ahead in the fight, but it was going to be a hard round; I knew that Arreola was going to come looking for me in that last round, so I had to fight back hard to keep him off me. I dug right in, and took the fight to him, bashing away to his ribs and keeping the punches going. There was no way I was going to get stopped. I had to fight every last second of the round and at the end I walked straight over to the referee with my arms out, and he raised them up above my head. I'd done it, but only just!

Even though I'd won it fair and square, that fight with Cipriano Arreola was such a tough old fight; it was the worst I ever got hurt in a fight, including the times I had been knocked down or stopped. Although I'd won it in 10 rounds, I was well and truly bashed up. My face was all banged up and my head felt like it was the size of a football; it was really throbbing inside after the fight, and I had the worst headache I'd ever had in my life.

After the decision was announced, I got out of the ring and went to the changing rooms upstairs. I told my brother Tony that I was going to have a shower, and I got in to soak under the hot water to try to take the pain away. When I got to the dressing room after the fight, I really started to feel bad. I was badly bruised, with a massive black swelling under my right eye, a right big lump. My head felt like it was 10 times bigger than it should be. I was peeing in the shower, and I looked down and I saw this thin red line of blood come pissing out of me. I completely freaked out and I shouted out for my brother: 'Tony, Tony, come here!'

Tony came running over and said, 'What's the matter, Charlie?'

'I'm fucking pissing blood, Tony! I'm pissing blood!'

Tony went completely mental, saying, 'Where the bloody hell is Terry?'

He found Terry and shouted at him, 'How much fucking money did you give him for that? Look at him, he's in a right state. He's pissing blood everywhere!'

I was really scared, and I felt terrible. When I came home after a fight, my wife usually cooked me a big roast dinner waiting for me to come back. Her parents drove me back to the house from the arena, and after I walked through the door I just collapsed on to the sofa. I honestly felt like I was dying.

She asked me how I did and told me my dinner was ready, but I just felt so terrible. I felt like my head was going to explode it was so swollen and I just went upstairs to lie down and

1982, my first of two fights against Jose Torres, another Mexican, and another loss this time. Another setback as Torres handed me the second loss of my career, stopping me in nine rounds. I beat him in our return match.

Looking the worse for wear despite winning the fight, in the toughest battle of my career against Cipriano Arreola. Later that night I felt like I was dying, it was very frightening.

Top: Alan Minter (*left*) and John Conteh (*right*) provide the guard of honour for me and Franco Udella at a photo shoot before I successfully challenged for his European title in 1979.

Left: I've got Franco Cherchi on the ropes and covering up here. I beat Cherchi twice in 1984 and 1985, both for the European title.

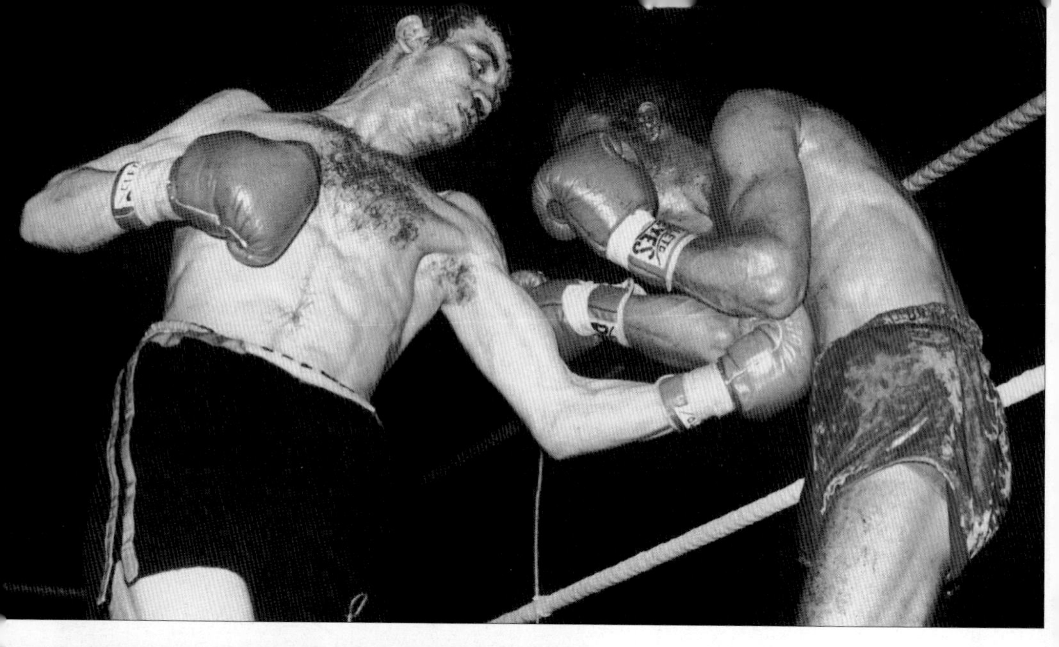

Above: Digging into the body against Mercedes in what was a blood and guts war. Both of us were cut and marked up, but in the end I came out on top to achieve my life's dream, but it wasn't an easy win. Mercedes was a tough, tough man.

Left: Some afters at the bell. Me and Mercedes went at each other hammer and tongs while it lasted, before I finally stopped him on a cut in seven rounds to become the World Champion.

Below: 1983, if looks could kill! World Champion Eleoncio Mercedes shoots one at the cameraman before our fight.

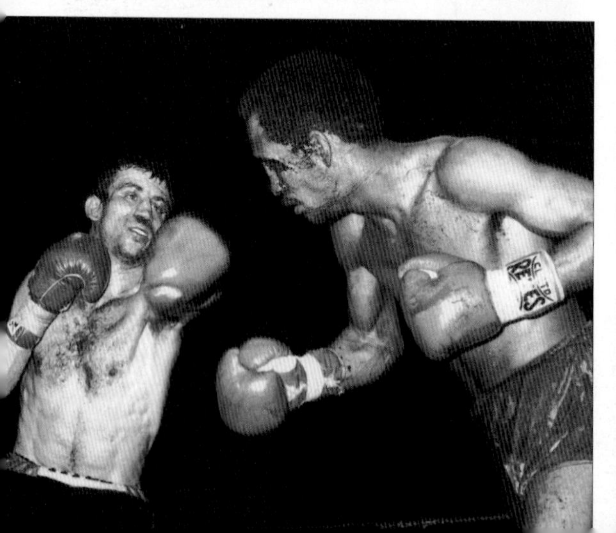

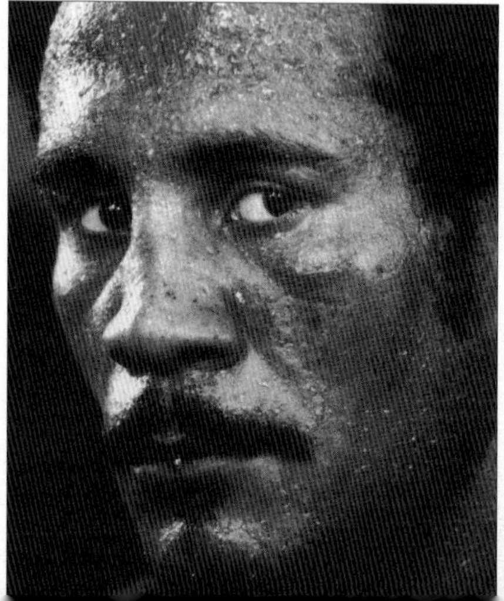

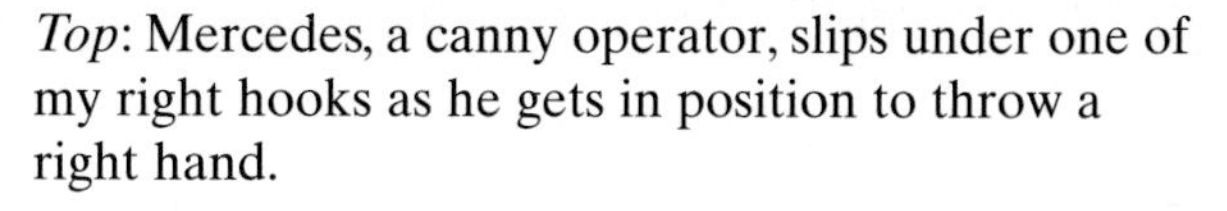

Top: Mercedes, a canny operator, slips under one of my right hooks as he gets in position to throw a right hand.

Middle: 'And new World Champion!' *Left to right*: Jimmy Tibbs, Frank Black and Terry Lawless celebrate yet another World Champion at the Royal Oak gym.

Bottom: One of many flush hard shots I caught Mercedes with during our world-title fight; that man took so much punishment but just wouldn't fold.

Main picture: I'd lost, but I knew I'd given it my best. Chitalada sportingly carried me around the ring to the crowd in appreciation of the fight I'd given him. He went on to be a great champion.

Top inset: Taking one from Sot Chitalada, who was just too good for me when I challenged him near the end of my career, in 1985 for his WBC flyweight world title.

Bottom inset: Giving Chitalada one in return; for the first three rounds I was really giving him some.

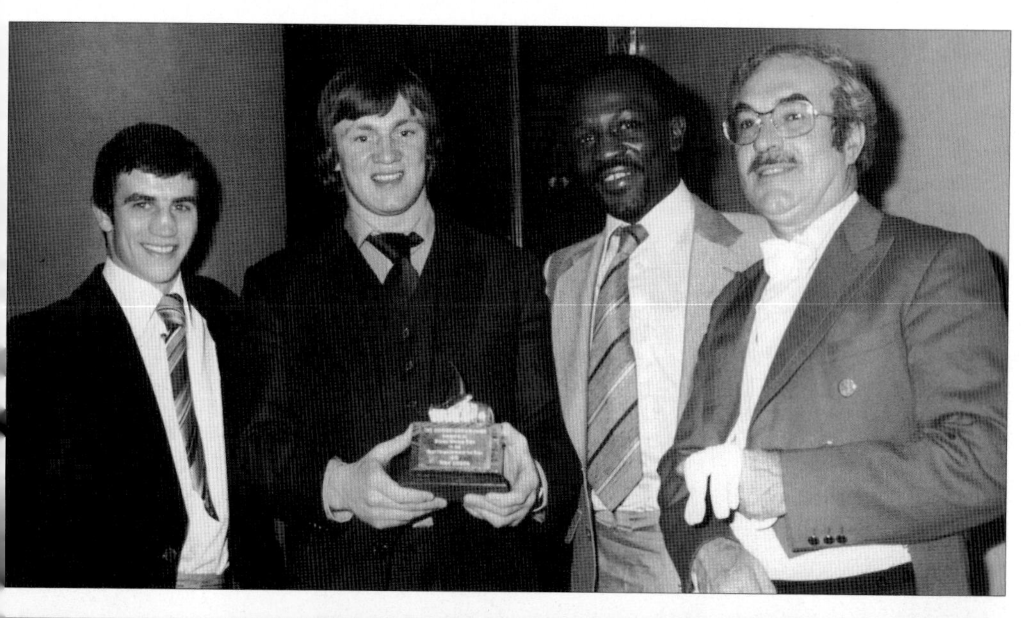

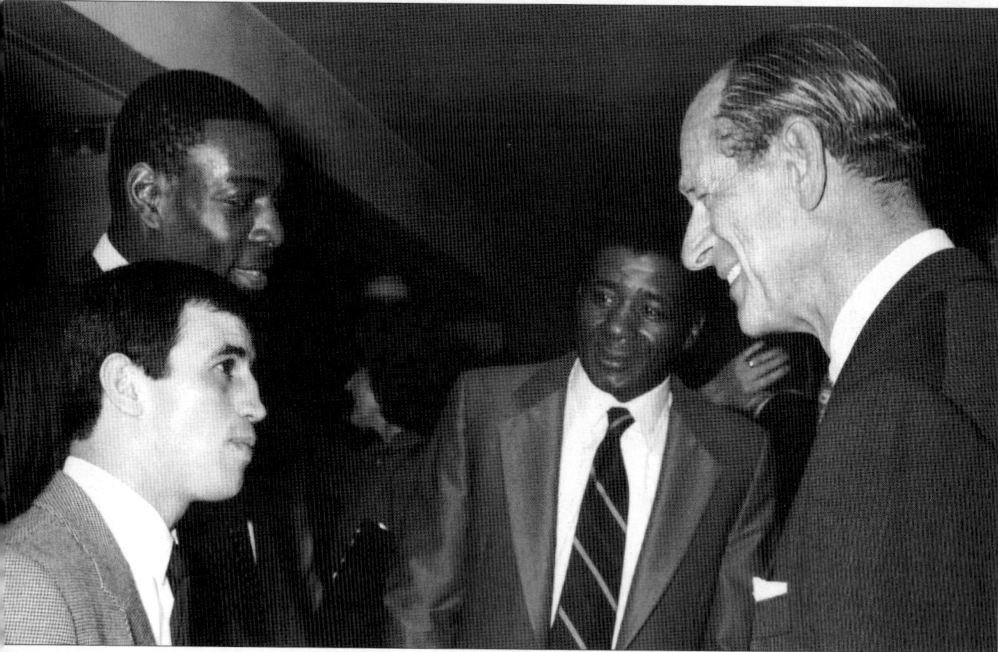

Top: The Young Boxer of the Year Awards. *Left to right*: Me, Tony Sibson, who received the award, gym mate Maurice Hope, and good pal Reg Gutteridge.

Middle: Me and Frank meet Prince Philip, and a former heavyweight king, Floyd Patterson.

Bottom right: Me with Walter McGowan, the last man to win a world title from the British Isles at flyweight, showing off the WBC belt.

You could have knocked me down with a feather! Eamonn Andrews gets me with a sucker punch as he hands me the big red book.

collapsed on the bed. I really felt like I might have some brain damage, and I was falling in and out of consciousness. I can remember waking up in the night a few times, feeling like I couldn't breathe, and then not being able to keep my eyes open and drifting back into unconsciousness.

Looking back on it, I should probably have gone to the hospital that night; I could have slipped into a coma while I slept and that could have been the end of me.

As it turned out, of course, I was fine. When I went to the hospital the next day, they examined me and told me I'd fractured my nose, and that there was something wrong with my eye as well. When I asked him what the blood in my piss was, the doctor told me with a straight face that it was 'nervous energy'! I don't know what medical school this bloke went to, but I've never heard of anyone getting nervous and pissing blood.

I said, 'Are you fucking joking, mate? I was pissing blood for about an hour!' I felt like I'd lost about two gallons of blood.

I'm sure they would've been a bit more careful about checking me over after the fight now. I briefly thought about packing it in after that, because it scared me so much, but, at the end of the day, I was a fighter, that's what I did, and I had to make a living. The thought of doing anything else just never occurred to me; it would be like asking a leopard to wear stripes for a change, it just wasn't going to happen. Believe it or not, I was back in training a week later.

Out of all the fights I've had, that was the fight that made me realise just how dangerous boxing was. I never really worried about getting hurt in the ring before that. You get scared, of course, that's natural, but I never thought anything really bad would happen to me. I felt like I could handle whatever came at me. Even when I got stopped by Diaz, I didn't feel like I was in any real trouble; I was just too weak to continue. But that night when I lay in bed, I felt like I was dying, and I wondered why I was doing this.

But, to get to the top of your game in boxing, you've got to be prepared for pain, danger and the threat hanging over you all the time of getting badly hurt, or worse. All I'd really known since the age of 10 was boxing; it wasn't just my life, it was who I was, Charlie Magri, the boxer, the fighter. That's why I came back, why I carried on, even though I'd thought I was going to die, and even though I'd never been so scared for myself in my whole life. I suppose it's hard for people to understand that, but that's the difference between fighters and everyone else: fighters see the risk, and they look it back in the eye and say, 'I don't give a shit.' You can call that bravery, or you can call it stupid, but, if you want to be a fighter, a good one, that's what you have to do.

CHAPTER 32

Disaster Strikes Again

Even after beating Arreola, the newspapers weren't off my case. Although I'd won, it had been a really hard fight, and I'd been down again in the ninth round. I was getting the reputation of being chinny big time, and the fact it had happened late in the fight meant people thought I couldn't fight for 12 rounds any more. They went on about the fact that he'd fought at light flyweight before as well. I was getting absolutely slaughtered. You'd have thought I'd lost the bloody fight the way they were carrying on in the press!

It's true, though, that, by that point in my career, I was really starting to struggle in the later rounds of fights. The constant training and all the marking-time fights I'd had, plus the fact I was starting to get on a bit at almost 26, meant that I was fading in the second half of fights. Although 26 might not sound old, for a flyweight, it's pretty much getting near the end of your career. There are not many flyweights who are at the top of their game after that age. Looking back on it, that might have been the time to move up in weight, but I'd fought my whole career at flyweight, and that was where I wanted to win the title. Moving up would have meant I'd have been back on that merry-go-round all over again. I'd been waiting so long for this title shot, ever since I won the European title really, and I couldn't really afford to change things, or so I thought at the time.

My next fight was Ron Cisneros, and I was on the same bill as my old amateur pal Sylvester Mittee, who was fighting an eliminator for the British light welterweight title. It was another easy win, with me stopping him in three rounds, and I was looking good for getting back in the rankings. Cisneros had a good record coming into the fight. He'd only lost one fight at that point in his career, and that was to a guy who went on to win the bantamweight title, Richie Sandoval. Because Cisneros was highly rated at the time, I hoped a nice quick win would get me back in the top five, as I'd dropped down to eighth in the rankings after losing to Diaz. If I could just keep on winning, then I thought it was surely just a matter of time until I got my number-one ranking back and got a shot at the title.

Then, on 23 November 1982, disaster struck all over again. I've nobody but myself to blame I suppose, as I don't think I got myself properly prepared mentally for the fight, and I paid the price. My opponent was Jose Torres, nothing special according to his record, and nothing more than a marking-time fight until I could get a title shot. Torres wasn't highly ranked at the time, so it wasn't really getting me anywhere, and I guess I wasn't that motivated.

On the night, I was getting hit by shots I should have avoided, allowing him to land big sweeping right and left hands on me. There was nothing wrong with me physically, but mentally I'd taken my eye off the ball, and came in treating it like just another fight, which is a big mistake in boxing. Torres also had a really awkward style. He was tall and lanky, with long arms and he would grab hold of me every time I got close, pinning my arms and then coming in with his head, or hitting me with a sneaky low blow when the referee wasn't looking. I found his style a nightmare to deal with, to be honest. I guess he was just one of those people that fighters have in their careers, someone whose style makes it really difficult to fight your fight; a bogeyman, I guess you'd call him.

But I was doing all right in the fight to begin with, and I think I was winning it when it was stopped. I even hurt Torres pretty bad in the fifth round, but he was so hard for me to pin down; he was always darting round the ring and I think I got a bit frustrated. In the ninth he caught me cold right at the beginning of the round, and that was the beginning of the end. I went down hard, and tried to grab hold of him and survive the round, but he wasn't having it. He knocked me down twice more, and the referee waved it over before I could get up from the third knockdown. What a bloody disaster that was. The papers and the boxing magazines all wrote me off completely after that. They said I had no chance of getting a title shot. I was written off as a no-hoper by all of the press, as someone who had absolutely no chance of winning a world title. My whole world felt like it had come to an end.

As usual, after a big loss, I really thought about quitting. I was devastated that I'd lost again, and it was such a bad time in my career that I just couldn't see how I was ever going to get where I wanted to go. At times like that, you feel disgusted with yourself and you just want to call it a day, but I knew I couldn't go out like that. I had four months off after that fight while I thought about what I was going to do with myself. The things that had been written about me in the newspapers had really knocked my confidence badly. It's hard enough losing, but, if you take all that the papers say to heart, it makes it even worse for you. I don't think the people who write for the press think about that, and I guess it's not their job to worry about it, but, when you're in the public eye, it's hard to deal with people writing things like that about you. If you're lucky, you're the sort of person who takes no notice and gets on with it, but I wasn't that sort of person. I used to sit and worry all the time about what they said about me.

I would say it was the low point of my whole career. I'd been stopped twice in less than six months, losing my unbeaten record and my number-one ranking. Luckily, Terry had arranged for me to have a European title defence. I might have lost to Torres, but I still had my European title, so, instead of sitting around moping about what might have been, I had a European title fight in the pipeline.

I was defending my title against someone I'd already beaten, Rodriguez Cal of Spain, but this time it was in his home town of Aviles, which was a little place in the middle of nowhere. Apparently, the town itself had paid the purse for the fight; I believe the mayor had organised it, and I think they thought they were making a good investment for their geezer. But I was really pissed off by this time, especially as I had to travel to my opponent's own backyard. I'd already beaten him in two rounds, and I wasn't exactly over the moon about fighting him again. I didn't expect any favours going over there, not that it made much difference under the circumstances. It was over in Spain right in Basque country, and I had the right hump when I was over there, because there were no proper training facilities, I didn't even have anywhere to check my weight, and I felt like I'd been stitched up.

The conditions for that fight were terrible. You should have seen my dressing rooms; they were literally covered in shit, bullshit in fact, because the venue was an old cattle market! All there was in the dressing room was a little table and a chair for me to put my gear on, and big clumps of shit everywhere. It was absolutely bloody disgusting. The only good thing was, with all that shit around, you were bound to have some good luck eventually if you kept walking around. I trod in that much shit I must have been the luckiest man in the world when I left that place.

At the press conference that they'd organised, Cal started going on and on about me getting knocked down by Laciar and Arreola, then stopped by Diaz, and how he was going to do the same thing to me, I got the right hump, I thought, 'Who's this geezer trying to give it the big 'un?' I told his interpreters to tell him, 'You tell him from me, Charlie Magri says he's going to knock him spark out!'

He didn't say much after that, and I knew when I got him in that ring I was going to shut his mouth good and proper.

On the night of the fight, he kept me waiting in the ring for ages before the fight, even though I was supposed to be the last one in there, being the European Champion, which was a big mistake on his part. If he wanted to wind me up, he did a good job of it, but it only made me even more determined by the time the bell went to do a right job on him. I tore into him that first round, and I knew it was just a matter of time, because I could see his arse had gone and he didn't fancy the job any more at all. I did him again in the second round, same as the first fight.

That was another fight where I didn't see how I ended up getting a small purse. The purse bids had been won by the town where Cal was from, who'd put the money up so they could give their guy a shot at the European title. What I couldn't work out was that there was a crowd of 14,000 in that arena, and yet I only got seven grand. I'd love to know what they were paying to get in. It was a mandatory fight, so I should have got 60 per cent of the purse for that fight if it went to purse bids. Unless they were letting people in for free, I just don't understand how I ended up getting so little, especially as the fight was televised on ITV. I don't understand how they let that happen, because the fight would have been worth a lot more than seven grand if it had been at home, and for a European-title defence in front of a massive audience, and televised live in Spain and England, it just didn't add up to me.

One thing I remember from being out there was this bloke who was there with us, who used to come out to my fights, called Jimmy the Biscuit, because he worked for McVitie's Biscuits. Jimmy's dead now, God rest his soul. He used to have a good job with McVitie's, and he used to come along for the ride just for laughs, or he'd hang out at the Royal Oak when we were all training.

I remember once when he came to watch Maurice Hope defend his European title in Germany, and he brought this gumshield along with him. When he got to the arena, he stood right up there at the front with the press and all the trainers, and he showed the gumshield, and said, 'I'm Maurice Hope's trainer.'

There was a press conference after Maurice Hope had defended his title. Reg Gutteridge came over to Jimmy and was having a crack at him for sneaking into another fight, because Jimmy was notorious for it.

Jimmy said to him, 'Well, at least I paid my fucking air fare myself, Reg, eh?'

We were all in hysterics. He was such a character Jimmy. I'm sure he could have afforded to pay if he wanted to; I think he did it for a laugh more than anything else, just to see if he could sneak in or not. He used to come to all the fights that the boys from our gym had; he'd be there at training sessions, press conferences, the lot, he was just fanatical. You know, I don't think I ever knew his full name; he was always just Jimmy the Biscuit to everyone who knew him.

Anyway, I'd got Cal out of the way, and given him a proper going over; I took out all of the spite and anger I felt. Everything was getting to me now, all the comments in the papers, the years and years of waiting and all the setbacks; I was getting more and more frustrated with it all, and it was getting to me big time.

One day, some time after the fight with Cal, I went over to Terry at the gym one day and I said, 'Terry, I want to fight Torres again.'

Terry wasn't too keen on the idea at first. 'He's got a bad style for you, Charlie. I don't think we should fight him again; we'll find you someone else to fight.'

'I know I can beat him, Terry. I know he's a right awkward sod to fight, but I know I wasn't right for that last fight. I want to get in there and prove it, Terry. Get me Torres again, I've got to beat him to prove everyone wrong. They're all saying I'm finished, but I'm telling you I'm not finished. I can beat this geezer, I know I can, and I should have beat him last time if my head was right.'

In the end, after a lot of pressure, Terry agreed to the rematch and the fight was set for Wembley in November.

This really was my last chance of ever getting a look in at a world title. I knew if I lost this fight that it was all over, that I'd never get a world ranking again. Everything depended on this fight.

Again, it was a really hard fight. For one thing, his style was so bloody awkward I found it hard to nail him with a clean shot because he was always moving, and never stayed around long enough for me to follow up. I also went into the fight knowing he'd already stopped me, and, no matter what anyone says, that affects you in the build-up to a fight. If someone's stopped you, you know there's a chance they could do it again. It's not often a fighter is stopped by someone and comes back to win a rematch; it's just one of the facts about the boxing game. Someone's kind of got one over you if they've stopped you. I knew inside that I was the better fighter, but better doesn't mean anything in a boxing ring; you're a punch away from losing at any time, no matter how good you are.

The first four rounds I was absolutely all over him. I was hitting him pretty much at will, and he took a real pounding in those rounds. I hit him with a huge uppercut in the fourth round that had him all over the place. He came back at me in the fifth round, catching me with a couple of one-twos and jumping right on top of me, but I wasn't going to let it slip away this time. I used my boxing skills and kept him at a standstill for most of the rest of the fight. Right at the end, in the last round, he caught me with some good shots, catching me as I came in, but I weathered it and hung on till the end. I thought in the end that, despite a couple of rough patches, I'd won the fight a bit easier than the scoreline, which gave me five rounds to his four, with one even. It was a tough fight again, though, and, just like last time, I struggled with his style. In that rematch I took punches from him that had put me on the deck in the last bout, but I was more up for it, more focused, because I knew this was my very last chance at world honours. I knew I needed a win here to get back in the top 10. It was a close fight, and I nicked it by just half a point in the end, but I'd got rid of my bogeyman and now, finally, when I least expected it, I got what I'd been looking for.

The WBC had promised Terry they would put me back in the top 10 if I won the fight, and if I was top 10 I could get a shot at Eleoncio Mercedes, if his camp agreed to the fight. I had to wait and hope that they could make an offer to the new champion. After I won the fight against Torres, Terry Lawless got on the blower along with Mickey Duff, and they tried to make arrangements. I had no choice but to hold my breath and wait to see whether they could do it or not.

I'd come through a right bloody awful time over that 18 months or so of my career, and it was out of my hands now; all I could do was wait, just as I'd been doing ever since I'd won that European title from Udella, for the chance to finally get my shot.

CHAPTER 33

The World is Mine!

So finally, in 1983, something I'd been waiting for my whole career finally happened: terms were agreed with Eleoncio Mercedes, the WBC Champion from the Dominican Republic, for me to fight him. The fight was set for 15 March 1983, back at the Wembley venue I'd fought at so many times before. Terry Lawless, Mickey Duff and his people made an offer that Mercedes couldn't refuse to come and defend his title here. I think they offered him £80,000 to come over and defend his title in London. That was a really good purse in those days, and I'll bet it went a bloody long way if you lived in the Dominican Republic as well! Anyway, it was more than I ever got for any of my fights by a long road. The WBC had agreed to put me in the top 10 of their rankings after beating Torres, which meant I was a contender, and Mercedes and the WBC agreed to the fight.

Finally, I'd fought my way to contention; it had been a long hard battle to get there and, in fact, I didn't get my shot until I'd lost a couple of times. I'd been number-one challenger or thereabouts for years, and something always happened to keep me from that title shot. It got to the point where I thought I'd never get my title shot, but Mercedes was willing to come over and put his title on the line for a nice payday like that. Maybe Mercedes figured I'd be an easy touch because I'd been stopped a couple of times. When I was number-one or number two-contender, nobody wanted to fight me, but, when I was only just in the top 10, Mercedes agreed.

I'd won the European title in my 12th fight, and I'd held it for four long years, defended it for four years, and beaten just about everyone there was to beat from Europe, and I was finally getting my chance at the WBC belt. The wait had done my head in; I'd been desperate to get a title shot for years. I felt good enough years before when I won that European title to fight for it right away. As a flyweight, your best years are when you're young, fresh and quick. In my early twenties, I felt unstoppable; now I was nearly 26, and a lot of flyweights are already past it by then. As you get older, you lose that little step in your footwork, that extra bit of stamina in the later rounds, that little bit of speed and sharpness in your punches. It might not be by much, but enough over the course of a fight to change the outcome.

When I'd first won the European title, I'd been waiting for a shot at Miguel Canto, who had been the Flyweight Champion for donkeys, but he got beaten by Chan Hee Park before I got a chance, and then losses to first Diaz and Torres had held back my career. Since Canto, nobody had really held the WBC title for that long, and Mercedes had won the title after getting a surprise title shot at Freddy Castillo, who had been a Light Flyweight Champion back in 1978. Not many people thought he had much chance against Castillo, but he went over to Los Angeles and nicked it on a split decision.

Anyway, Lawless and Mickey Duff had made sure I got home advantage by offering Mercedes a very tasty purse. Home advantage means a lot to a fighter, though I'd had to go over to the lions' den before in European fights, and it wasn't nice I can tell you. In a way, I suppose it was worth getting a much smaller purse,

I got around 20 grand for the fight, but, compared to the chance of being a champion, that didn't mean anything to me. This was my whole life's ambition; boxing wasn't just a part of my life, it *was* my life. It was pretty much all I ever thought about, and the thought of winning a world title was a complete obsession, always there in the back of my mind.

Although I had home advantage, Mercedes seemed as cool as you like during all the preliminaries for the fight; he didn't show any nerves during his interviews, and I remember he was shown on TV lying down listening to music on his headphones reading letters from home and larking about with the cameramen. He'd just won the title himself, and I'm sure he had no intention of leaving his belt behind him when he went back home to the Dominican Republic. He looked very confident in the run-up to the fight.

The papers and most of the boxing writers seemed to think he was right to be confident; hardly any of them gave me any chance at all. I guess because of what had happened in other big fights where I'd lost, against Diaz and Torres, where I'd been stopped after starting well, the boxing magazines and the newspapers had come to the conclusion I was chinny and that, if I couldn't win early, I couldn't win at all. But I knew that night that, whether I knocked him out, or whether I had to go the distance, I was going to be the geezer who walked away with that nice WBC belt. All of the frustrations, all of the setbacks over the years, all the disappointment I felt at being shut out of a world-title shot for so long only made me burn even hotter and want it even more.

You might wonder why we'd always gunned for the WBC title, rather than trying to get a shot at the WBA title, and there were good reasons for that. A lot of people outside the boxing world don't really understand that, if you want to get your fighter into a world-title shot, you've got to be on terms with people who run the sanctioning body; it's all about having a relationship with them. That's the way it was then, and it's the way it still is now.

People still phone up the sanctioning body and put a call in making a case for their fighter to be in the ratings, and try to get their man rated highly enough to get a title shot. Terry had a good relationship with the WBC and WBC president Jose Sulaiman, and so that's why it was the WBC that we were looking at during my career.

Part of the reason was that, at that time, the WBC were a pretty new outfit really; it had only been going about 20 years, and they were up against the older big boys in boxing, the WBA, and wanted to make a name for themselves. Before that, there had only really been one boxing organisation running things, the WBA, the first of the big three bodies that run boxing now: the WBA, WBC and the IBF. The BBBofC was one of the first commissions to sign up and allow its boxers to box for the new WBC title.

Mickey Duff and Terry Lawless were on good terms with quite a lot of the Italian and French promoters, and they all used to talk to each other on the phone, and these little groups used to speak to Jose Sulaiman. At the end of the day, the promoters are putting money in the pockets of the sanctioning bodies like the WBA, WBC and IBF every time they put one of their fighters in a title fight. The sanctioning bodies want the money, but you've got to be on speaking terms with them to get your fighters rated by them, so it's a nice arrangement for everyone concerned. Back in those days, if there was a British boxer fighting for the European title, the BBBofC would get 8 per cent, so the money was going around loads of people when there were big fights; boxing is a business at the end of the day.

So finally, I was there, waiting for my big chance at the World Champion. I was never going to have a better chance than I had right then to win a world title. I had the champion over here on my home turf at the Empire Pool in Wembley, surrounded by all my loyal fans. This was my time and I wasn't going to let it slip away from me. After all of the disappointments and setbacks, I felt absolutely, supremely confident.

The fight was set for 15 March 1983, and as usual I trained like a demon for the fight. There was nothing special about the training for this fight, because, whether it was a normal 10-rounder or a world-title fight, I was always completely obsessional about my training. I lived, ate, breathed and slept boxing, or in my case, *didn't* sleep boxing, as I could never sleep. As usual, the night before the fight, I was awake almost the whole night, tossing and turning, going over the fight constantly in my mind, imagining what he might do, and what I would do to counter it. I lived that fight over and over in my mind long before I stepped in the ring the next day.

I'd heard everything the papers had to say, but I didn't care; as the fight had grown closer and closer, I increasingly felt that there was something about me the night of this fight. I felt different, I swear I could have walked through brick walls. I just wanted the title so badly I wasn't going to be beaten. I think I was the sort of fighter who rose to the occasion, and sometimes I needed that extra edge that being the underdog gave you, and I was the underdog with just about everyone going into this fight, except for myself, and my camp.

On the night of the fight, Freddie Starr was in my dressing room! He'd come down to wish me luck before the fight; he liked me and was a bit of a fan of mine, because he followed boxing. Terry brought him into the dressing room because I was a bit nervous before the fight, and Terry thought he might bring me down to earth a bit and calm me down. Freddie certainly took my mind off the fight, because he was cracking jokes and all that, and he really made me feel relaxed. What a mad sod he was, though!

In the last hour before the fight, there was a knock on the door, and Freddie said, 'Leave it to me, I'll get it.'

Before anyone had a chance to stop him, he went over to answer the door and there was a voice behind the door: 'WBC referee.' He'd come to give us the instructions in the dressing room before the fight.

Freddie opened the door and went, 'Really? Fuck off!'

He slammed the door right in the referee's face! What a nutter he was, you never knew what he was going to do next.

Terry said, 'You can't do that!' He had to go over and apologise to the official and let him in so he could give us the rulings.

With Freddie being in the dressing room that night, well, I didn't feel any nerves because he was making me piss myself laughing the whole time he was there. Freddie was a big boxing fan who used to have a boxing ring at his house, and once even sparred with Muhammad Ali, believe it or not, in his own ring!

Despite what all the newspapers were saying coming into the fight, that I wasn't going to win, that my chance had come too late, I knew that night that it was my time. Come time for the fight, I felt hard as nails and I was ready to go out there and really give it to him. I didn't believe it was possible for me to fail that night; it was as simple as that.

This was my moment. During my ring walk, I don't think I've ever been so focused or determined in my life. I entered the ring with nothing else on my mind except winning that title. I wanted to prove everyone who'd written me off wrong. I'd put up with all the criticism for years, now it was my turn to grab the bull by the horns. I don't remember much about the announcements, the crowd, the lights or anything, my mind was just turned inside, willing me on, driving me towards that goal that I'd been chasing for so long: this was it, my moment.

The next thing I really remember is that bell going for that first round, and, I tell you what, as soon as that bell went, the two of us just laid straight into each other. Mercedes was a tall lanky fighter, at least compared to me, and he was a good mover. That first round he made bloody good use of the ring, and he was popping out the jab and right hand right from the offing.

What a fight it turned out to be, one of the most ferocious I was ever involved in! We went for it hammer and tongs, and the pace we were fighting at was unbelievable. He was a pretty cool customer, because I managed to crack him with really good shots along the ropes at one point in the first round, and I kept him there for quite a while, giving him a good going over with both hands, but he never lost his calm and didn't panic. He got himself off the ropes, and I turned him again and battered him to the opposite side of the ring, landing some really nasty body shots. Right at the end of the round, though, he stood right in front of me trading shots, and landed a big right hand, something most fighters couldn't get away with, as if to say, 'I'm not moving, mate.' But, at the end of that first round, although he'd cracked me with a few good left hooks, I'd done enough to control him and keep the fight going my way.

I knew early on it was going to be a very hard fight. He hadn't come to lose his title that night, he'd only just won it, and he was enjoying being champion; he came to win without a doubt. He was such a tough man, and I hit him with some of my hardest hooks in the early rounds. Even though I knew it was going to be hard, I felt I just couldn't be beaten. I would have walked through fire to get to him.

Mercedes must have fancied it the second round, because he came out swinging for me. He was leading with the right hook and following it with the left, and, when I tried to counter, he skipped back to the ropes where he ducked under three or four shots. After that, the round turned into a right tear-up. The two of us tested each other out; it was an open battle, with both of us winging in big hooks. He landed some really good hard shots, but I wasn't going to give him an inch. I had to walk through a lot of his shots to land my own, but I knew if I stayed on him he would crack first. By the end of the round, I had a bad graze under my right eye. Terry was shouting instructions at me, telling me to get under his guard and get underneath his shots.

The third was a bit quieter. Mercedes was boxing a bit off his back foot, throwing out long jabs and straight rights in combinations to keep me off him, and I didn't really get through to him too much until the last 30 seconds, when I landed a couple of really hard hooks to the pit of his stomach, and started tearing into him, trying to soften him up. The round ended with me laying into him, but nobody had got on top either way.

In the fourth, I really started going to the body. I was dipping down from the waist, rolling under his shots nice and easy just like Terry had told me to do at the end of the second. I was in a crouch, and he had less of a target to whack away at. I really threw all my weight behind the hooks to the ribs and the stomach, and he was missing me now with his jabs and straight rights. By the end of the round, he'd gone into a crouch himself, to try to protect his body, but he wasn't done at all; he started firing back to the body and landing hard right crosses and right hooks, but I couldn't feel the shots, I could just feel myself closing in on him and his title. He could have hit me with a baseball bat and I don't think I'd have gone down that night. When you want it badly enough, and you're mentally prepared, it's like you can't be hurt; it's a state of mind as much as anything else, when you're really primed it's hard for someone to hurt you with a punch.

In the fifth, I came out to hurt him, to finish him off. I threw hook after hook deep into his ribs, ducking down low and to the side to really get the power in there, I must have hit him 20 full-blown body shots in the first minute alone. For the first time in the fight. Mercedes started to look shaky. I could see him stiffening up from the shots, and his legs would go slightly after he took one. There wasn't much coming back either and, when he tried to trade with me, I just gave him even more, and started slinging in some big left hooks to the head too. I had him under the cosh now; he was flying from one side of the ring to the other, trying to get away from me, but I wasn't having it, this belt was mine! How he stayed on his feet I don't know, he must have had guts like a horse! He even found it in him somehow to have a little go in the last 30 seconds, but I felt I'd broken him by the bell. I gave him the evils at the end of the round, just to let him know there was more to come.

Christ, though, was that geezer proud, proud and tough! The next round, I almost ran across the ring to get to him, and I pinned him on the ropes, throwing in double right hooks to the body and letting him have a nice left hook upstairs. He was bobbing and weaving, trying to get out of the way, but, even though I had him there what seemed like a good 30 seconds, when he got back to the centre of the ring, he was banging out the jab, bang, bang, bang! If I was going to get the belt, I had to rip it away from him; there was no quit in this geezer at all. If anything, he was having his best round for a while. He started to land his jab and he was throwing long punches, which were catching me on the way in, but, right near the end of the round, I hit him with a left right downstairs, and I could see his face kind of screw up. He was in pain big time. When you see a fighter grimace like that, it's normally the beginning of the end, and you know that, if you keep on banging away, they'll go soon enough. I was never shy about going for the finish, and I jumped all over him, I pushed him to the ropes and ripped into his body. At the end of the round, he had a big cut over his left eye as well, which was from our heads coming together, but he was hurt to the body as well, you could see it in his face.

When he came out for the next round, it was written all over his face that he was distressed by it all. I went for the body, and I went for the eye, and I just kept on him until the referee looked at the cut and decided to stop it. Now I'm sure that Mercedes's people weren't happy about the cut, but it was an accidental clash of heads, and these things happen in boxing. I don't believe that he could have lasted much longer anyway with the body shots I was piling into him. He would have gone one way or another that night. Those are the breaks in boxing, and at the end of the day the decision was out of my hands.

There were points in the fight where it might have seemed I was tired, but I just didn't feel it. Mercedes hit me with some really big right hands during the fight, right hands that in other fights might have hurt me, but I just didn't feel a thing. I think you've got to believe you're going to win on a night like that, and I just believed that I couldn't be beaten. Sometimes it's just your night.

When the fight was stopped, and the ring announcer said those words: 'and *new* World Flyweight Champion …' that was when I realised that I'd finally made it after all the years of frustration, all the bad things that had been said about me in the press, all the disappointments and the wanting to give up. I'd climbed my own mountain, and right then all the anger and the frustration just seemed to melt away. As I stood there in that ring with thousands and thousands of screaming fans, and then Terry Lawless lifted me up out of the ring, I felt like the king of the world. Harry Carpenter called me 'Champagne Charlie' and, right then, that was how I felt.

CHAPTER 34

This Is My Life!

When you achieve your life's dream, I tell you what, it's the strangest feeling. Lots of people have dreams, but not that many of them get their hands on what they dream about, they're just dreams. When you actually get there, it doesn't feel real, because you've suddenly achieved what you've been working for all your life. When you reach the end of the journey, you don't know what to do next, and you're sort of in a daze.

The week after I won the world title, I was on cloud nine. I was walking around in a daydream. It's an unbelievable feeling being a World Champion, because, as a fighter, that's the thing you dream about your whole career, and, suddenly, you've done it, and you're the champion. Everyone wants to talk to you and shake your hand, the newspapers are in touch with you all the time, and suddenly everyone knows your name.

Now, because of this, I guess I wasn't really on the ball, and I can remember during the week after the fight my wife kept on popping out all the time, saying she had to do this and that. What I didn't know was that she was off meeting up with Terry Lawless, making arrangements for what turned out to be the biggest surprise of my life. A week after I'd won the world title, she said to me, 'We're going to the York Hall, Charlie. Jim McDonnell's having his first fight, and they've invited us along.'

Now the thing was, my missus hated boxing, she never wanted to come along to any of my fights, and she certainly normally wouldn't have wanted to go to someone else's. But Jimmy was one of my best mates in boxing, and I'd planned on going along anyway, whether I'd won or lost the world-title shot.

I was very close to Jimmy, we always sparred together at the Royal Oak, and I'd tried to help him along in getting himself down to featherweight for his debut as professional. I sparred countless rounds with Jimmy, and there was no way that I wouldn't have gone to his first fight. He'd been there with everyone else to watch me win the world title and, as a pal and stablemate, I owed it to be there for him at his debut.

So we arranged to go to the fight and then on to this restaurant called The Venus, on Bethnal Green Road, that we always used to go to, for a nice meal afterwards. I was due to make an appearance in the ring before Jimmy's fight, just to sort of set the stage. So I was standing there in the ring, and all of sudden I saw this big bloke in a dressing gown with the hood over his face come running into the ring with the spotlight on him. As I looked round, his hood came down, and there was bloody Eamonn Andrews, saying, 'Charlie Magri, this is your life!'

'You're fucking joking, aren't you?' I said.

He wasn't though.

I said, 'I'm meant to be going for a meal now. What's going on? Where am I going?'

'We're going to take you away now, Charlie, to the television studios,' said Eamonn.

What a lovely bloke that Eamonn Andrews was, a lovely feller. He sat in the back of the car with me on the way there, and said,

'What a great little fighter you are, Charlie, it's an honour to be presenting you with this.'

'It's a great pleasure to be in this car with you, Eamonn.'

Of course, Eamonn was a boxing commentator earlier in his career, and what a lot of people might not know was that he was a good amateur boxer himself in his younger days; he was the Middleweight Champion of Ireland as an amateur.

So we went to the hospitality room back at the ITV studios, and there was a big room full of food and booze, loads of champagne, loads of grub, everything you could want, and Eamonn said, 'Help yourself, Charlie, it's all for you.'

So I had a couple of glasses of champagne to take my nerves away.

There was everyone there that night, it was unbelievable. All the England amateur squad that I'd fought with, all of Terry Lawless's stable, all the Royal Oak boys. My old pal actor Ray Winstone was there, who's been a good friend of mine from the age of 12. At that time, though, Ray was just a young actor trying to make a name for himself. Freddie Starr did a live link-up to the studio; he did this funny little boxing sketch with him falling all around the place, which cracked me up.

Even Miss Sutton, my headteacher from Stebbon School, was there, and Miss Baker, the deputy head. It's amazing how when you're on *This Is Your Life* nobody's got a bad word to say about you, isn't it? If you'd listened to my teachers, you'd have thought I was the best, most well-behaved pupil who ever walked through the gates to the school; I guess everyone wants to make it look good for you in front of the cameras, but, I can tell you, they didn't feel that way when I was actually at the school! It was: 'Magri, you're trouble, you are!' 'Magri this, Magri that!' I wasn't exactly their favourite pupil, but they certainly turned it on for the cameras.

Terry Lawless turned up with his entire bloody clan in tow – aunties, uncles, brothers-in-law, Uncle Tom Cobbly and all! You name it, they were there. My old pal Reg Gutteridge was there as well and Harry Carpenter. Dave Boy Green came, and even Walter McGowan, the last person from the British Isles to win the flyweight title.

Of course, my whole family was there as well, and I remember how proud my dad looked up there, and my mum laughing when she was telling them how many candles she burned every time I fought. Oh! It was such a great day, seeing all these old faces. It was a terrific feeling, everyone turning out to say their bit and pay tribute, well, that's something money can't buy, that was something really extra special in my life.

After the show, we all had a big party in the green room, and my old pal Ray Winstone came over to me and said, 'Magri, how d'ya like being famous then?'

I said, 'It's fucking great, ain't it, mate? It'll be your turn one of these days.'

Of course, I didn't know just how famous Ray was going to become in his own right. Me and Ray had known each other for years from the boxing circuit, because he used to fight for the Repton Club at welterweight, and he was pretty good too, winning the Schoolboy Championships twice. Most people don't know that Ray was a pretty tasty fighter in his own right, so remember that the next time you see him playing a hard nut.

The whole evening was one of the happiest memories of my life. I'd just won the world title, and to be whisked off to a studio to have my whole life gone over like that was lovely.

At the end of the show, just before they finished, they had a terrific surprise for me as well. Eamonn Andrews had heard from Terry Lawless that I'd been going mental asking where the WBC belt was, because they hadn't given it to me yet. When he'd heard this, he got on to the president of the WBC, Jose Sulaiman in Mexico, who contacted a BBBofC official, who happened to be there in Reno for Colin Jones's challenge of Milton McCrory for the vacant WBC welterweight title which was just a few days after my fight. Colin showed up on a live video link as well on the show.

Anyway, they got the belt, and then presented it to me on the show. Right at the end, they called my daughter Emma out, who was only about two at the time, and she came toddling over to me. What a day that was, standing there with my big red book, my WBC belt and my daughter in my arms. It doesn't get much better than that.

As soon as I got that belt, I kept a promise I'd made to the press when they asked me what I'd do when the belt finally arrived, and I walked up and down Bethnal Green Road. I can remember walking up and down with my title belt on, posing for the cameras and feeling like bloody Superman! I'd waited my whole sodding career for this moment. I'd been waiting and waiting and waiting for that title shot, and it had felt like it would never come, but, in the end, I got there – and whatever anyone had to say about me, all the knockers and the newspaper men – I was WBC World Champion!

After the world-title win, I was invited up to Manchester for a personal appearance. We were taken in a limousine to this big hotel, and me and my wife went up to the room, and we were just lying down relaxing. I was on the bed dozing and she was reading a book and I was thinking, 'Cor, ain't this nice.'

Then the phone rang, and the receptionist said, 'Mr Magri, we've got someone down here for you in reception who wants to talk to you.'

I picked up the phone and a voice at the other end said, 'You dirty little bastard, what are you doing upstairs? Can't you wait until you get home to give her one, you dirty sod?'

'Who the bloody hell's this?'

'Come down to reception and find out!'

So I went down there, and there was Freddie Starr with Lennie Bennett the comedian. He said, 'Come on, Charlie, we're going to dinner.'

So me, Freddie and Lennie all went to dinner and, while we were there, Freddie decided to lay on a bit of entertainment for everyone, which I won't go in to! He was a right carry-on was Freddie, some of the things he got up to were unbelievable that night.

Those weeks after winning the world title were absolutely mental. It's such a strange feeling when you've actually won the world title; you've just got where you always wanted to be, and you can't believe you've actually done it. It's one thing believing you can do something, or thinking you might do it, but actually doing it, well, your life just turns into one big daydream.

CHAPTER 35

Losing the Title – Frank Cedeno

I could have handled that feeling of being champion forever. I loved it, but, as it turned out, I didn't get to enjoy that special feeling for very long, as things didn't go the way I had planned them at all.

I didn't really have a massive celebration after winning the world title. Big parties weren't really my style, to be honest, so we all went for dinner, and then back to our house for a party; even so, I didn't get to sleep until about five in the morning. I had six months off after winning the title. I wanted to enjoy being champion for a while, and it was just about the longest break I had in my entire career. Six months out of boxing for me was like a lifetime. I had a child now, as my first, Emma had been born 18 months before my world-title shot, and I was just being a family man for a while I suppose.

My next fight was just meant to be a routine title defence, a sort of coming-home fight in front of my fans. It was set for 27 September 1983 against a bloke called Frank Cedeno. Cedeno should have been a totally routine defence, and I'd beaten plenty of better fighters than Cedeno before. He had a decent enough record, but he had always fought in the Philippines and had never really fought anyone class. It should have all been lovely, nice easy defence, and get ready for another title defence. It was the biggest purse of my career as well, I got £60,000 all in. As defending champion, I was earning proper money for a change. It was way more than I'd ever earned before.

I had quite a long training camp for the fight, because I'd been out of the ring a long while, enjoying being a father and the feeling of being World Champion. During the training camp for the Cedeno fight, I started to get a slight pain inside my right ear. It wasn't that bad at first, but, as time went on, it started to bother me more and more. By a couple of weeks before the fight, I was in absolute agony. It was like someone was sticking a knitting needle right through my ear and into my head. It was so bad I couldn't even bear sparring.

Now, I'd been a bit off-colour before fights, usually from making weight and feeling a bit weak, but this was something else completely. I'd gone down the gym the day before the fight to weigh myself, and I was feeling so bad that I was really struggling to get down to the weight at all. I said to Terry, 'I don't want to fight, Terry. I feel terrible. I feel like I want to stick a needle down my ear and cut it out.'

Terry knew we couldn't turn the fight down, even though I was the champion, and he got on to a doctor in Harley Street to come and have a look at me. The doctor examined me and said that I had a 'blind boil' in my ear. He said that ideally I shouldn't be fighting to let the boil heal, but he managed to get rid of the boil, and gave me some tablets to kill off the infection. They were absolutely huge, and looked like something you'd give to a horse! Unfortunately, they were quite strong and made me feel a bit groggy and I had to go out and fight after taking them. How can you walk into a ring for a world-title fight when you feel like that?

After the weigh-in on the day, coming into the fight my legs didn't feel right and I had no energy. When I fought for the title against Mercedes, I was bouncing around all over the place, but this fight I had nothing at all. I was so tired during the fight, that I had to go toe to toe with him and try to take him out early, but my punches weren't as strong as usual, and by the fourth round I felt completely exhausted. The first really big punch he hit me with, a left hook, in the sixth, I just went over. I got up, but I was completely gone. The next round he just piled in and finished me off. The result was that I was beaten in what should have been a nice easy homecoming fight. I lost to a guy I normally could have beaten hands down, and lost my title after getting stopped. That was it, my reign as champion was over, because I'd gone into the fight in piss-poor condition, in no state to fight.

After the fight, I went to the hospital to have the boil seen to, and the doctor couldn't believe I'd been boxing the night before. He said, 'What? You were taking those tablets for 48 hours before the fight? You shouldn't have been fighting after taking them!'

Losing my world title felt like losing my life really. I think, if I had been well enough, I would have beaten him. He was a tough bloke, and a southpaw, but I just wasn't in the right condition to be fighting that night. It made losing the title even worse to think that I'd had to fight this guy with one arm tied behind my back. I was so pissed off about it all that I felt like packing it all in, because I didn't feel I'd been given a fair chance to win. I couldn't afford to pack it in, though, because I wasn't earning enough. That's the way it is as a fighter. I'd lost my title, and, at 27, I wasn't going to get too many more chances. I felt totally gutted that it had all slipped away from me so quickly. I was pissed off with my management for allowing me to take a fight when I wasn't at my best. I got a nice payday for it, but that wasn't the point. I got the biggest purse of my career for the fight, but I could have made much more than that if I'd waited until I was better. I'm sure I'd have beaten Cedeno if I'd been in proper shape for the fight, but instead I was suddenly an ex-champion, getting near the end of his career.

CHAPTER 36

European Champ Again

I had another long break out of the ring after losing my title. I was so pissed off with what had happened I didn't even want to fight. I was really depressed at losing my title. By this stage of my career, I really wasn't fighting that often anyway; I'd only fought twice in 1983, and not at all in 1984 so far.

But, eventually I got my desire to fight back, and Terry and Mickey Duff used their contacts with the current champ Franco Cherchi's promoters to get me another crack at the European title. Even though I'd been the champion before, when you challenge for the world title, you have to give up the European-title belt. By this point most people figured I was washed up, and not many people gave me much chance of winning the European title again, and that was like a red rag to a bull to me.

The deal was that I was going to have to go over to Cagliari in Italy to fight Franco Cherchi for his European title on home turf, which in boxing and especially in Italy is a very big ask. You ask any fighter and they'll tell you, that fighting in Italy, you don't get any favours from the referee, judges or anyone; it's usually a bloody nightmare and, like they say, you've got to knock them out just to win the decision. As it turned out, I needn't have worried, as early in the first round he got a really bad cut on his left eye, and the doctor was called in and stopped the fight. Cherchi's people weren't happy about it, and the crowd were going mental, but it wasn't my fault. Cherchi kept flying in with his head, and he went back on to the ropes and came flying off them straight into me. You can see on the video how he comes bouncing off the ropes like a wrestler. It could just as easily have been me that got cut the way he came flying into me, but it was him, and, if it had been me, there's no way I'd have got the rematch, I can tell you that.

The Italians in the crowd went absolutely mental! There was a right scene, there was shit flying everywhere, bottles and tin cans flying into the ring, and I thought we were going to get strung up; honestly, it was a really nasty scene in there.

It was just one of those things, but the Italian crowd were angry that their man had lost his European title on a cut in the first round. We were dodging bottles, and all sorts when we got back to the corner, and, when I got there, Terry told me to go back into the ring and apologise.

I said, 'Apologise for what? For beating him? No chance!'

After the fight, Reg Gutteridge got in the ring to interview me. He said, 'Did you realise what happened there?'

I said, 'Of course, the referee stopped the fight because he got cut, I beat him. What do you expect me to do, say I lost?'

Reg laughed, then he said, 'Would you fight him again?'

'I'll fight him any time he likes.'

There was a rematch clause in the contract anyway, and so it was arranged that I would go back and fight him on his home turf again to defend the title. I don't know why they did that, I could have fought him at home.

There was no way on God's earth I was going to apologise to him, or his people. Shit happens in boxing, and that's that. If it had been the other way around, I can't see him or his management apologising to me, so why should I bother?

The Italians had expected Cherchi to beat me, so they'd laid on a big banquet for after the fight, and there was this massive spread of food and drink, so I went to the party and had a right old time of it. I wasn't in a good mood about the whole thing, and I have to admit I was pleased that I was there enjoying a party which had been laid on for someone who was expected to beat me.

While I was at this party, some bloke came over to me and said, 'You happy?'

I said, 'Of course I'm happy, I've won. What else would I be?'

But then this bloke told me something that really pissed me off. Now, I don't know if this is true or not, and I really hope it wasn't, but the guy I was talking to told me he was quite friendly with one of the people in Cherchi's camp, and that he'd been told that Terry Lawless and Mickey Duff had arranged for options on Cherchi's next three fights and were in line for a percentage of his purses, as he'd been in line to fight for the world title against Laciar if he beat me. I was livid! I think he told me because, with a surname like Magri, he must have thought I was Italian. It felt to me like they were expecting me to lose! Well, I bloody well didn't. But, once I heard that, whether it's true or not, my attitude towards them changed. I felt like they wanted rid of me and I was going to prove a point in that rematch.

CHAPTER 37

Last-chance Saloon – Chitalada

Not long after that my contract with Terry Lawless expired. I wasn't sure whether I should stay with him after what I'd heard in Italy. I didn't say anything to him, but inside I was wondering whether it was time I looked elsewhere, something I'd never thought before. I don't know if Terry could tell I was pissed off, but one day he came over to me in the gym, and told me he wanted a word.

'Charlie, I've got some good news,' he said. 'I've got another shot at the world title lined up. We've spoken to Laciar's people, he's still the WBA Champ, and we've arranged for you to get a crack at him in Monte Carlo. I've got £40,000 for the fight, and £5,000 in training expenses, so you can train over there for a month. We're just waiting on tying the deal up with the WBA who have to approve the fight.'

I was gob smacked – £40,000 was double what I got for fighting Mercedes, and I'd never had training expenses like that before. 'Really?' I went, and thought to myself, 'What's brought this on then?'

Terry said, 'Thing is, Charlie, though, I can't represent you at the moment, because you're out of contract at the moment. I need you to sign a new contract, otherwise I can't make the deal on your behalf, and, if we don't act quick, someone else is going to get that shot.'

Now, it was very strange, but, once I signed that contract, suddenly the fight didn't seem so easy to make. Every time I asked Terry about it, he'd say, 'It's the WBA, Charlie, they're playing hard to get, it's really difficult.'

Months went by and no word, and then, in the end, Terry told me he couldn't make the fight. I don't know what was going on, but, to me, it felt like he'd just told me what I'd wanted to hear to get me to sign again, maybe because he could see I wasn't too happy with the way things were going since losing my title. All I know is that, after signing that contract, the fight with Laciar never happened. Terry had got me to re-sign with him, but he didn't seem to have much in offing, Now, my career didn't seem to be going anywhere, even though I was European Champion again.

The one thing I really wanted was one last shot at a world title. Who wouldn't? That's what every fighter dreams about, and, when you know you're getting near the end of your career, you want the chance to make some decent money before you retire. If you get yourself a title shot, you can get a decent payday and, if you win, the chance for a bigger one defending it, especially if you travel with your title. But, whenever I asked Terry what was happening, he didn't seem to have much for me, except for the rematch with Cherchi, which wasn't exactly what I was looking for; I wanted one last crack at a world title. I'd got the European title already, and I'd won it before, so it didn't mean much to me at that stage of my career.

Months went by and there was no word of when I'd fight again. In 1983, I'd been World Champion, now it didn't look like I was going anywhere. Boxing is really cruel like that, one minute you're hot property, and then you're old news. Once you're not big news any more, your management don't really want anything to do with you, as they're looking to find new talent they can take to the bank.

To be honest with you, I felt like my own management had lost interest in me. I'd won the world title, and lost it, and now, as I was getting on a bit, the opportunities just weren't coming along. Everyone, especially the boxing press, had been talking about how I should retire for years, but I kept surprising them. They'd been telling me to retire since the loss to Torres, and then I beat Torres. Then I won the title and lost it, and they told me I should retire. Then I won the European title again, and they had to swallow it again. I hated what they said about me in the newspapers, it really hurt me a lot. I wish I hadn't listened to it, I wish I could have just brushed it off, but the truth was I couldn't; it really got to me badly.

The way I saw it, the rematch with Cherchi wasn't doing anything for me really, it was old ground, and I was told it wasn't going to be a massive payday, plus they wanted me to travel to him to defend my title. I was nearly 30 years old, and, at that age as a flyweight, you haven't got a lot of time left.

Now, around this time, I'd heard some rumours that Frank Warren, a newcomer on the boxing scene at that time, wanted to promote me and that he was going to try to get Sot Chitalada over here to fight me.

Terry Lawless pulled me up one day and said, 'There's a lot of rumours going around, Charlie, that Frank Warren wants you to fight for him, that he wants to promote you to fight for the title.'

I said, 'Yeah, I've heard, Terry.'

'Well, let me tell you now, there's no way we're going near him.'

'Oh yeah? Well, you might not want to go near him, but I want to talk to the man. There's a fight for the title out there for me and I want it.'

'Well, you're on your own, son.'

The thing was, back then, Frank Warren wasn't as big as he is now. Frank had started out having to do unlicensed shows, because the BBBofC wouldn't give him a licence to promote, and he had to fight hard to get in on the act. He'd had a hard time getting TV dates, and the BBBofC hadn't exactly made things easy for him. They finally gave him a licence, probably because they got sick of being pestered, plus Frank was getting big crowds for his shows, with or without the 'official' title of the BBBofC. Now he was looking to make his mark and become a big noise in the boxing world. He wanted to manage the big-name fighters of the day, and I was a big name, so he wanted to get a chance to promote me on one of his shows.

Terry didn't like it because there was a new kid on the block who he saw as competition. He had a nice arrangement between himself, Mickey Duff and Mike Barrett, and they had all the TV dates back then, and all the main venues tied up, so they didn't like it one bit that someone was threatening to upset their applecart. Terry didn't want me working with Frank Warren because it meant he was getting a chance to promote me and make a name for himself, but, at the end of the day, it was my career and my last chance to get a crack at a world title.

Terry was still my manager, but Frank Warren was going to put me on a big bill at the Alexandra Palace in February, and I was going to get my shot at the title. Once I signed to fight on Frank Warren's promotion, my relationship with Terry soured and he pretty much disowned me. He was taking his manager's cut, but that was about it.

To cut a long story short, I arranged a meet with Frank Warren and I said I'd meet him down at Magri's Sports, the sports shop I'd invested in. I told Terry that I wanted him to be there, because he was still my manager of record and I wanted him to represent me. Even if he was against it, he was still taking a cut of my purse, so it was his job to represent me.

So, I was there with my wife in the shop. Ernie Fossey and Frank Warren were standing in one corner, and me and my wife were sitting on the chairs we had at the back for trying the shoes on.

Terry was sitting there as well, but with his back turned to us all with the right hump.

Frank Warren looked over at him and he said, 'Look at that, Charlie. Can you believe it, a man of Terry's age sitting there like a big spoiled child? How can he be managing you?'

Terry got all upset and said, 'Don't you try and belittle me.'

I turned to him and said, 'Now you hang on a minute, Terry, this isn't about you, it's about me; it's about me getting a shot at the title, and it's not about you at all. Do yourself a favour, mate, if you're not going to help me, then go away.'

Terry said, 'Right, well, that's it then, you discuss it with him, I don't want to know.'

So Frank said, 'I can get Sot Chitalada over here for you, Charlie, definite. I've got the venue booked and everything, and we can do the fight in February next year. I want you to box for the world title on my promotion. He doesn't want you to, Charlie, but I want you to, and, if you want it, it's there for you.'

I looked round and I saw Terry just sitting there staring at the wall, and I couldn't believe he would behave like that. He wasn't even negotiating on my behalf.

So I said, 'Right, Frank, I'll go for it, thanks for the opportunity.'

Frank said, 'Thanks for listening to me, Charlie, and I promise you I'll do you the best deal I can.'

Initially, he only offered me £20,000 for the fight. I said, 'No way, mate, am I fighting that geezer for £20,000. I'm not doing it, find someone else.' I knew he needed me for his bill; I was the headliner, and it was a world-title fight.

He said, 'Tell me then, mate, what do you want?'

'Well I want more than that!'

In the end we negotiated a deal, and I agreed to the fight for £40,000. We shook hands, and Frank said, 'All in £40,000,' meaning it was a deal where I wouldn't get TV money, and I agreed.

Looking back on it, I probably could have got more money, but I didn't want to take liberties. I was given an all-in deal, Warren told me that he was going to have the TV rights, and I suppose I could have asked for a slice, but I didn't want to take the piss; maybe I should have been pushier, I'm not sure. Anyway, it was a lot more than I'd got as a challenger to face Mercedes, so I've no complaints about it.

Despite what some people might say about Frank Warren, he was the only guy I fought for who I actually felt gave me a fair whack. He asked me what I wanted and I told him, and he gave it to me, and £40,000 was a good payday to get the champion in your own backyard, and a lot more than my own manager had paid me to fight Mercedes. I only fought for Frank Warren once but I got well paid for it; in fact, it was the second biggest payday I ever had in my career and it was as a challenger. The only bigger payday I got was when I defended my title against Cedeno.

So, this was it, my last chance at the world title. It was set for 20 February at Alexandra Palace, or Ally Pally as it's known. It was against a man who was really becoming feared at the weight. Chitalada was a champion at kickboxing in Thailand even before he took up boxing, a really tough, hard man. He had won the title the year before, after losing at his first attempt at a title in 1984 in his fifth fight! I knew I was going to be the underdog for this fight, and I knew it was a last chance, but I just wanted one more shot at the big time, and, even if I lost, at least it would be one more big night for me and my fans.

I gave it as good a go as I could on the night. When that bell went, I went out straight at Chitalada, and for two rounds I was hammering him with everything I had. I was really firing, and the crowd were coming to their feet. It didn't seem possible he could hang in there the shots I was hitting him with, but he was such a hard bloke. I gave Chitalada a bit of a boxing lesson in the first few rounds; I was really taking it to him, like I always did, trying to stamp on him in the first few rounds. I hit him with some really good hard shots in those first three rounds, and felt like I was doing really well. He took some real punishment to the body, but he never seemed to be hurt, though his corner said afterwards that he was hurt by the punches.

Trouble was, though, after that third round, the fight started to turn. Chitalada started to read my shots; he seemed to know where they were coming from and then he just turned up the heat. He was moving around the ring all the time and kept catching me with shots as I tried to catch him, and they were really painful accurate punches. He was a guy who could just punch non-stop once he got going, he didn't seem to get tired. I took a lot of shots in the fourth round, and I got cut near the end of the round, and I was starting to take a lot of punishment. Chitalada was so quick and he hit really hard as well, I couldn't seem to see the punches coming and he was really finding his range now.

After the fourth round, Terry and the doctors stopped the fight, because I had such a bad cut on my left eyelid which kept on opening up whenever I closed my eye. I think I could maybe have carried on a little bit longer, but Chitalada was really starting to get going, and I was feeling the pace, so it was for the best, I suppose, that it was stopped. The main thing was, as far as I was concerned, that I gave a good account of myself. There were a lot of fans there that night, the atmosphere was buzzing, and I gave everything I had to give, and that was good enough for me. At the end of the fight, I lifted Chitalada up for the crowd to cheer him, and they did; they realised what a good fighter he was, and it was good there was no booing. Chitalada did the same to me; he was a really nice geezer, he didn't speak any English, but it was a nice gesture by him to carry me around the ring.

Five years later, they did a big write-up on Chitalada, and he wrote in there that he'd boxed some good men during his career, but that the hardest shots he ever took were from me. He said I'd hurt him a few times, and I didn't even know at the time; that's how good he was, he didn't let on when he was hurt. I heard that Chitalada went blind in later life, but I don't know if it had anything to do with his boxing; it was sad to hear about anyway.

Chitalada was a great fighter, who went on to have a really incredible career. He went on to be a great champion, with two reigns at flyweight and nine defences in all. I'd have loved to have got in the ring with him when I was in my prime, rather than a few years past my best. I'm not saying the result would have been any different, but I would've loved to see how I got on.

I felt good after the fight; it was disappointing to lose, but I lost to a great fighter, and I knew that I made him work hard for the win, and that I gave everything I had to give in what turned out to be my last world-title shot. At the end of the day, if you've done your best on the night, you've got nothing to be ashamed of. It was great to have that one last big night in front of a massive crowd at the Alexandra Palace. That was all I'd wanted, to have one last big night in the spotlight, and give my fans something to cheer about.

CHAPTER 38

Last Knockings

Every fighter at some point in their career has to accept that the end has come, and, after the Chitalada fight, I knew I didn't have many fights left in me. I wasn't in love with the game any more, and, at 29, there weren't many opportunities going to come my way. I had been thinking about jacking it all in for a while, because I couldn't see where my career was going to go from there.

After losing to Chitalada, the only offer on the table for me was the rematch that my camp had agreed with Franco Cherchi, whose European title I'd taken on a cut. I'd actually given up the European title after beating him to take on Chitalada, and I went over there and I did him again, this time with no cut involved. I was in a nasty spiteful mood when I went over there, because I had to go and defend my title in his backyard, and because of the way the Italian fans had treated me last time out, and I took out all that anger on poor old Cherchi. It wasn't his fault, of course, he was just a fighter, but I wanted to make a point, and I did by stopping him in the second round after flooring him twice.

At the same time, things were really bad between me and Terry, who'd hardly spoken to me since the fight with Sot Chitalada, and the atmosphere when I walked in the gym was poisonous, all because I'd taken the opportunity that Frank Warren had put in front of me. But why shouldn't I have taken it? I hadn't betrayed anyone. Terry was still my manager, and I was happy for him to work with Frank to make the fight happen, but he wanted no part of it, because it broke up his little party with Mickey Duff and everyone else. As far as Terry was concerned now, I wasn't part of the gym, I was an outsider. After all those years training at the Royal Oak, all the titles I'd won for myself and for the gym, I didn't feel welcome any more. And all because I'd wanted to get a world-title shot that my manager said he couldn't get me. I felt it was all very unfair.

So I didn't even really train at the Royal Oak any more. I went there to check my weight and that, but really I was training down at a local gym above the Church Elm pub in Dagenham. It didn't even have any proper fighters there, and the only sparring I could get was against some local hard nut who fought on the unlicensed circuit as a light heavyweight! I had to just move and jab and keep him off me, because, no matter how good you are, a flyweight against a light heavyweight isn't a fair fight, even if they aren't much cop.

It was hardly ideal preparation to face a young up-and-coming flyweight who was hungry and gunning to get a big name on his record, but, with the atmosphere in the Royal Oak gym, I just didn't want to be there any more.

I wasn't really in a good state of mind any more. Boxing was making me unhappy, but I didn't know what else I was going to do for a living. I hadn't made enough money to retire comfortably, not by a long stretch. I had a bit of money tucked away, but not enough that I could just put my feet up, and the whole point of boxing, of doing something so dangerous as a career, is the idea that you can make enough money so that, when you retire, you don't have to graft for a living. I think a lot of people forget that when they look at fighters' careers. You're laying your bloody life on the line every single time you get in that ring; it could be your last day on earth, couldn't it? If that's the case, you want bloody well paying for it, don't you? Well, wouldn't you?

Now I was nearing retirement, I regretted all those years I'd waited for my title shot. The way I saw it, I should really have had a world title four years before I did. I was defending the European title over and over again, and I was right at my peak during those years, but the title shot came a bit too late for me. Flyweights have short careers; most of them are way past it by the age of 30, a lot earlier than that for some people, and I think I missed the boat a bit. I was at my best around the time I beat Laciar. I reckon at that point and just before I was at my absolute peak. By the time I got my title shot, I'd already slowed down a bit, and, of course, years of making weight had taken its toll on me as well. If I was boxing nowadays, I think that I would have moved up to super flyweight or even bantamweight. I'd beaten plenty of fighters who'd moved up to bantamweight, and I think I'd have had far better stamina as well, which was usually what gave me problems over the second half of fights as my work rate dropped off.

What people don't understand is that all those extra fights wear you out. You might think, 'Oh, I'm at Wembley, ain't that great.' But what if you get beaten? You're taking a chance every time you fight, and, when I was trying to defend my ranking with the WBC, the pressure was getting to me, because I was the kind of guy who worried about everything. I'd read the write-ups in the papers, and the comments like, 'He's got a glass jaw, he can't take a shot,' and I'd worry about that. I'd get in there thinking, 'I'm going to prove them wrong,' but I would let it get to me. I wished I had been boxing with the head I've got on my shoulders now, because I would have been able to take it much better, but, well, that's how it is.

So, I was European Champion again, but now what? After the Cherchi fight, I decided I'd find out what was going on, because normally I would always have a fight lined up, but, this time, nothing had been mentioned.

I came to the dressing room after the fight and said to Terry, 'So what's lined up for me?'

He said, 'There's not much out there for you.'

'But Cherchi had a world-title fight lined up. Why can't I have that fight?'

'No, it's WBA. Laciar's the champion.'

So, a fight that I'd wanted, and I'd signed with Terry to get in the first place, wasn't happening now, and there was sod all else on offer from what I could see.

I said to him, 'So what's in it for me now, Terry?'

'Well, Duke McKenzie's lined up to fight for the European title.'

'Why can't I fight for the world title?'

'No, you've got to fight Duke McKenzie.'

Now, Duke McKenzie was a young up-and-coming fighter, who was managed by Mickey Duff at the time. He was the British Champion, having won the vacant title the year before. Terry Lawless and Mickey Duff worked closely together, and Mickey Duff had Duke McKenzie; it looked like a nice little cushty arrangement for everyone concerned – except me, that is.

I thought, 'How much am I going to get for that?' It wasn't a big fight at all, and in the end it wasn't even a well-attended event, so it was all a bit sad really. I was being treated like an old horse, being put out to pasture, and it was a horrible feeling. McKenzie was the future, and I was the past, I guess that's how they saw it. It was a fight that wouldn't do my career much good. At the age of 30 I was looking for one last shot at the world title, but, instead, I felt like I was being fed to McKenzie as a good name for his record, and that I was there to make him look good.

I'll be honest about it, though, I think I underestimated McKenzie. Not that I was being cocky coming into the fight, but I didn't know that much about him, and, having mixed it at top level, and having been the best flyweight in the country for my whole amateur and professional career, I didn't really see him as much of a threat. I'd been the number-one fighter at the weight for so long that I guess I found it hard to imagine that another English fighter could beat me. He was the British Champion, but I was the European Champion, and I thought I would win. I couldn't understand what sense there was in me fighting Duke McKenzie, because it wasn't an opportunity for me, but it was a bloody good opportunity for him, a chance to add a former World Champion to his career. But, even if I didn't want the fight, the truth was that I badly needed the money at the time, as I'd a huge tax bill to pay.

During the build-up to the fight, I felt totally sick with it all. I don't think I really cared any more. I didn't want to lose, but I wasn't feeling good about the situation I was in. I had a manager who I believed wanted rid of me, and everyone was telling me to retire, and it didn't look like there were any other opportunities out there.

On the night, I came out for the first round like a bull at a gate. I knew that my best chance would be to stop him early; because he was the younger man, I wanted to take him out of his stride. I was on him from the first bell, but he was cute and he managed to slip or block a lot of them, trying to counter me where he could, but I definitely got through with a lot more shots and kept him running for the whole round, and I had him on the back foot the whole way.

I kept on it in the second, and managed to keep him on the ropes for long periods of time, but he managed to ride it out and stay tucked up for a lot of it. I was winning the rounds easily, but McKenzie hadn't come apart, and he seemed to be biding his time. He wanted to ride out the storm and get it to the later rounds. I didn't want to let him get there, but he was keeping himself together, even though I had him under the cosh.

I laid into him again in the third. I trapped him on the ropes at one point, and I really let him have it with big hooks under his guard and then up to the head; for a good 20 seconds I had him there, and I tried to get the finish, but he was a cool customer and he fought his way off the ropes. I hadn't been able to really hurt him yet, and, in the second half of that round, he found his own timing, and started to land some hard jabs and right crosses. I remember I could hear his corner screaming, 'Stay with him, stay with him, he's cracking.' They knew it was a matter of time.

I was leading, but it was still early and I hadn't made my mark yet, and he was beginning to get his timing going.

That fourth round was my last gasp, the last big effort of my career. I tried everything to turn the fight and end it right there, but it wasn't to be. McKenzie was fresh, young and strong, with his whole career ahead of him, and he wasn't going to just lie down and let me do what I wanted.

The fifth round would be the last of my career. I was taking hard shots, and he was pushing me back, landing his own shots. I knew that things were turning against me. Right then and there, I would rather have been anywhere than in that ring. I was in a fight I didn't want in the first place, against a young hungry opponent, and I felt like my own corner weren't even behind me. It felt like the end of everything. I was dropped, and barely made it up at nine. The towel came in from Terry Lawless, and the referee waved it over. I have no complaints about the towel coming in; nobody wants their career to end that way, but it was a fight I couldn't win, not at that stage of my career. I'd given it everything I had, but it wasn't enough, and the better, younger man won. I tried to turn back the clock, but you can't beat Father Time, as they say. Shots that I would have landed and hurt him with when I was a few years younger either missed him or didn't have the effect they would have done before. I landed some good shots on him, but I guess there wasn't that same sting in my punches. That and the fact that Duke McKenzie was a very talented fighter, who went on to win the WBC flyweight title, and then win WBO at bantam and super bantamweight. I'd given away height, reach and age and come unstuck, and that was all there was to it.

There was no shame in losing to McKenzie, looking back on it, especially when I think what he went on to do. He was a great little fighter just coming into his prime and I was past my peak by then; I was old for a flyweight, and coming to the end. I'd given it my best for four rounds, but I didn't have enough left to hang with him.

Duke McKenzie was the new kid and he went on and did well, didn't he? I was old news as far as Terry Lawless and Mickey Duff were concerned. I didn't make any announcement about whether I would retire after the fight; I just wanted to get out of there and get home, but, inside, in my heart, I think I knew that was it.

But, if I didn't then, what happened later in the dressing room made it clear to me.

CHAPTER 39

The Longest Round – Retirement

After the fight, Terry Lawless did something that I have never been able to forget or forgive him for. I'd just lost to McKenzie, and I felt like my career was over, and Terry waited with me in the dressing room until everyone had gone. Then he walked over to me, grabbed me by the face and shouted at me, 'Right, Charlie, you're going to have to just get off your arse and work for a living.'

Just like that! I was history. In other words, Terry wanted nothing more to do with me. I was 29 years old, and I was on the scrapheap. There was no long chat involved, no discussion about my career, no talk about where we went from here, just 'Thanks for everything, Charlie, now piss off.' OK, so he never said those words, but he might as well have done. I'd looked up to that man, I'd admired him and put all my trust in him to do right by me, to guide me through my career, and hearing him say that, well, I felt destroyed, betrayed. It was like being abandoned by your own family, a horrible, horrible feeling. I'd spent most of my adult life under the guidance of that man, and I'd given everything to boxing, heart and soul; nobody was more dedicated than I was to the sport.

As far as he was concerned, I was finished as a fighter. Just like that! I couldn't believe that this man, who I'd spent my whole professional career with, who I'd won British and world titles for, whose pockets I'd lined with my graft, and who I had once looked up to as a kind of father figure, could do that to me. I felt like I was lying on the floor, and he was stamping on my face. From that day to this, I've never spoken another word to that man and, as far as I was concerned, Terry Lawless no longer existed, and that's the way it has stayed. I doubt now that we will ever speak again.

The next morning, I got up really early. I didn't want anyone to disturb me, so I went out for a walk on my own. I'd never really been able to eat properly as a professional, and I was always cutting weight, so I used to walk around starving most of the time. I would have to eat or drink almost nothing at all during the period before the weigh-in. I was always living dangerously. So, the morning after the McKenzie fight, I went out for a walk and I went to a cafe and I had the biggest breakfast you've ever seen – eggs, bacon, sausage, fried bread, mushrooms, bubble, the works. I sat there stuffing my face with this massive big plate of food, loving every minute of it. I decided then and there that morning that I was finished with boxing. There didn't seem to be any point in carrying on; there aren't many options around for a 30-year-old flyweight, nobody was going to want to handle my career, and the truth was that there was only one way left to go, and that was down. So I made my mind up that morning that my career was over.

The next day, when I woke up, it was the weirdest feeling. It was like I'd gone to bed as one person, and woken up as another. The time seemed to just stop, like it was hanging in the air but not dropping. I felt like a man who has just been released from prison, after serving a long stretch, and suddenly realises that he can do whatever he wants. Suddenly I could eat what I wanted, drink what I wanted. I could sit around on my arse all day if I wanted to, or go and stay out until four in the morning every night if that's what I wanted to do. The truth of it was, though, I didn't want any of those things. I just wanted to be what I still was in my heart, a fighter, Charlie Magri the fighter.

I'm not ashamed to say this, because I'm sure that I'm not alone and that there's plenty of others in my shoes who have done the same thing. I can remember going for a walk the next day, and I cried my eyes out. I was walking alone in the streets early in the morning, the same time I would normally have been going for a run, and there were tears streaming right down my face, and, you know what, I didn't give a shit if anyone saw me. I'd lost my life, I'd lost everything. Without boxing, I didn't know who I was or what I was, or what I wanted to be any more. Boxing was my purpose, it was the reason I did everything. Everything I did and had done was geared towards winning at boxing and, without that, I didn't know what the point of Charlie Magri was. There was no fight coming up now, no training camp, no early-morning runs, no tactics, no kitbag, no corner men, no nothing – just me, and what was left of my life. I'd been in boxing since the age of 10, and now I was 30. I'd given 20 years of my life, all my adult life, to doing what I loved and now, suddenly, it was all over.

When you're still fighting, you never really think about the end; you don't want to think about it. You're always thinking about the next fight, about getting ready for the next bout, and then, suddenly, there ain't a next bout, there's nothing, and, I tell you what, it's the biggest punch you ever take.

Most people don't realise that it's a very lonely life as a professional fighter. People see you surrounded by people and crowds, but they don't realise what it's like to be there in that ring. You go out there on your own in your shorts and your gloves, and you're alone; you've got to be so single-minded to get in there and fight, and even more to win. That single-mindedness shuts out almost everything else in your life, at least if you want to get to the top, to be the best. When the end comes, you're not prepared for life after boxing, because you've not thought about it, because, if you spent time worrying about that, you'd never have got where you wanted to get in the first place.

After you've quit, it's funny sometimes what you remember from your career, little moments that nobody else probably even noticed, or if they did thought anything of. I can remember this one moment in a fight, I forget who against now, but it's the moment I remember, and it's strange how it stuck in my head. When you fight, you're in a packed arena, and there's loads of people screaming and shouting and all that, but you don't really hear any of it. It's like the place is silent, sometimes you swear you could hear a pin drop; you can hear the sound of your opponent breathing hard, and the sounds of the feet shuffling around the canvas, but the noise of the crowd doesn't really register with you, because you're so focused on what's happening. But, this one time, I could hear one voice in the crowd, out of all that noise, and it shouted out, 'Come on, Charlie, come on, get going!'

I can remember thinking to myself, 'Fuck you, mate, I'm in here and you're out there.'

You pick up on the strangest things out of all that noise, something odd which stands out that makes you notice it above all the rest of the noise. The atmosphere is so strange in the middle of the ring; people who sit at ringside don't realise just what it's like, you can't begin to imagine what a strange feeling it is. The weirdest things stand out in that strange silence you feel in the middle of a fight.

It takes a special kind of person to overcome everything surrounding the fight, all the pressure, the noise, the occasion. There are a lot of things that you have to be able to block out, and the ones who get to the top are the ones who don't get overwhelmed by it all. When you get in that ring, it's just you in there against your opponent, and, even when you're training, although there might be people all around you, you carry that feeling of loneliness that you feel in the ring around with you. The day of the weigh-in, there are loads of people everywhere, but you feel completely alone, alone with your thoughts and your worries. Your trainer and your people have some of those worries, but it's not the same, because you are the one who has to go in there, standing there in front of another man, ready to go to battle. It's the same as you make that journey towards the ring. Everything is geared towards that moment when you step in the ring, and your mind is on that all the time. Nobody can help you when you get in that ring; the corner can give you advice, but it's you that does the fighting. To be a champion, you have to have that single-mindedness to carry you through. I think that is why so many former champions you read about are divorced, or having other problems, because, when all that's over, and your career ends, that's your whole life over. Everything you identified as yourself is gone. You're not Charlie Magri the boxer, or Charlie Magri the World Champion, suddenly you're just Charlie Magri, and you have to start your life all over again; all those years of training, fighting and looking forward to the next challenge, that's all gone, all over. It's still you, but it's a different you, it's not the same person from before; there's something missing suddenly.

The other thing is time. Suddenly, you have to try to fill all this time on your hands that you never had to worry about. Time you used to fill with training and thinking about fighting has to be filled some other way. It must be worse for those fighters who never achieved what they wanted to achieve, but, even for those of us who did, retirement is the hardest fight of all. Most professional fighters can't accept life when they quit.

When I first retired, fucking hell, I just didn't know what to do with myself. I didn't have much education, because, when I was at school, all I thought about was boxing. I didn't have a trade, I didn't have anything to fall back on really. The only job I'd ever had was as a tailor's cutter, and that was only to support my boxing career. The one thing I had was a sports shop, although that was just a building, and I didn't control that really. And one thing I have to thank Terry Lawless for is that he advised me to take some of my money and put it in some pensions for when I retired.

But everything seemed completely pointless to me. Without boxing, what was the point of it all? Who was I?

At one point I considered a comeback fight. Frank Warren offered me a fight, he had an opponent and a venue lined up, and I went back into training. I went to the same rundown gym in Dagenham, the Church Elm, but in training I was getting whacked around by this unlicensed fighter. I realised then, that, if this guy was able to hit me, my heart wasn't in it any more, and I told Frank I wasn't interested. There was no point carrying on if I didn't care enough to let some big clumsy lump hit me.

One of the things I did soon after was get involved with the London Ex-Boxers Association, the LEBA. They'd only formed recently and they asked me if I would become one of the vice-presidents, along with the likes of John Conteh and Alan Minter. Although I was really only lending them my name as a fighter who had just retired and was a well-known London fighter, it was great to be asked to be involved in something like that, which would keep me close to boxing and to the people involved in it. It helped me a bit to know that I was still involved with boxing, but the question for me now was: what was I going to do with the rest of my life? You're not old at 30, and you've got plenty of bloody years ahead of you to think about what you might do, but I didn't really have a clue.

CHAPTER 40

The Training Game

One of the first things I tried my hand at after I quit boxing was training amateurs. I got involved with the Lion Club in Hoxton, and I worked with some of the kids down there. It gave me a good feeling to be involved with a new generation of fighters, and I'd always loved the atmosphere of the gym, so I felt right at home there. I was training amateurs for about a year after I retired, and I really enjoyed it. One of the problems I had, though, was that I could never find fighters who would train as hard as I used to do. I think that's one of the reasons that some of the best trainers out there are people who didn't have long or successful careers. I think that, when you've been at the very top of your game, you expect people to work at it as hard as you did, and when they don't it's a big disappointment to you. Some of the amateurs I worked with used to ask me advice about turning professional, and so, one way and another from working with amateurs, I got my manager's and trainer's licence and I started with professional fighters. I ended up working with Barry Hearns who offered me a contract for a year to train fighters that he was promoting. I'd only been out of boxing for a couple of years by this point, and I ended up working with one of my old mates from the Royal Oak, Jimmy McDonnell.

It was November 1989, and Jimmy was scheduled to fight Azumah Nelson, a Don King fighter, on a Barry Hearn bill at the Royal Albert Hall. I've known Jimmy for years and, let me tell you something, Jimmy is the sort of bloke who never made any excuses about anything. He probably won't thank me for telling you this, but the truth's the truth, and I feel I should tell people the way it was.

Jimmy was having a few problems during the build-up to his world-title challenge to Azumah Nelson. He got into a bit of a row with his management and his trainer, which I won't go into, but let's just say that everything wasn't great between Jimmy and his camp at that time. The bottom line was that he had to fight Azumah Nelson and, with the problems he had, he felt like he needed a bit of a boost, so he gave me a call and asked if I'd be in his corner just to give him a bit of help and advice. Jimmy knew I'd been there and done it before, and, although I wasn't his official trainer, I guess he felt a bit more secure knowing I was in that corner with him, a bit of moral support and that. And I was only too glad to.

At the time, Azumah Nelson was 31 and, while that would be over the hill for a lot of fighters, Nelson was so good that he was considered pretty much unbeatable. He hadn't lost in eight years, and that was as a last-minute replacement against the great Salvador Sanchez! Nelson was an absolute monster, who few people wanted to fight, and a lot of people figured it was a good job for Barry McGuigan that the two of them never met, because, at featherweight, Nelson was the absolute guv'nor.

Nelson had moved up to super featherweight now; he'd been the champion since 1988, and he'd already defended it three times.

Jimmy had just scored a big upset in his last fight, stopping Barry McGuigan's comeback on cuts, against all predictions. He'd handled Barry pretty well, and he was really confident going into the fight against Nelson. He had just scored the best win of his career, he was younger than Nelson and he felt he was stronger. Nelson was a tough, tough man, though, and, although there'd been a couple of close ones in his recent fights, he was still bowling them over. He had just stopped Mario Martinez the fight before, a guy who had given him a close match before. Nelson was an all-time great, simple as that, one of the best featherweights of all time.

Now, the day before the fight, we got Jimmy on the scales to do the weight check, to see how he was going, and we got a bit of a shock. Jimmy was bang on the weight, which was a big surprise, because normally Jimmy would be a few pounds over the weight, maybe two or three the day before, and he'd work his way down to the weight by training during the day, and sweating it off overnight, eating a lemon and going to bed with loads of clothes on. During the night, he'd sweat buckets, avoid having much to drink before the weigh-in, and then come in bang on the weight. Only this time, strangely, he was already on the weight. Jimmy was really shocked, because he never weighed in so light, but I told him that it was probably just all the nervous energy before the day of the big fight making him sweat loads at night and stuff, and that he'd probably lost more water than normal in the run-up to the fight. Knowing that he'd have no trouble at the weigh-in, Jimmy took it easy that day with a bit of light training, and ate and drank normally. That's what we thought anyway. The day of the weigh-in, at the Albert Hall, we got a right bloody shock! Jimmy got on the scales, and they called out his weight: 'McDonnell, 134!' That was four pounds over the bloody limit! It was an absolute disaster.

I said, 'What?! You can't be, Jimmy; you were bang on the weight yesterday!'

It was a very strange situation, Jimmy had never weighed in that light in his whole career, and then had gained three pounds overnight, so I'll always wonder about those scales. But to cut a long story short, we had to get the weight off for the fight. So I took Jim up to the boiler room of the Royal Albert Hall, and I got him to imagine that he was skipping, because he didn't even have any of his gear with him and I had to lend him some sweat gear. He did an hour of running on the spot. When he finished, he was bang on the weight, but he should never have been doing that to make weight before fighting someone like Azumah Nelson. Jimmy was the sort of feller who never wanted to mention that, even though I told him he should have done. The fact is, though, even with that, Jimmy put up one hell of a fight that night; it was one of the fights of the year and, even though he got stopped in the end, he really gave it to Nelson, and let him know he was in for a rough night.

Another fighter I trained early on while I was working with Barry Hearn, training some of his stable of fighters, was Bradley Stone. Bradley was another fighter whose name is connected with a tragedy in boxing. He died after his British-title fight with Richie Wenton in 1994. Bradley walked away from that fight apparently fine, but collapsed an hour later and never regained consciousness. It was very sad, because Bradley was a kid who had had it really hard. He was from a really tough background, his brother had died of an overdose, and he'd had a really hard time with his family growing up. He was a lovely kid, though; he just couldn't control that temper of his.

I was with him one day when he was training down at the Peacock gym, and there was this big wrestler bloke there who was using the gym for his training. Bradley walked past him and brushed into him by accident, so he said to the bloke, who was at least 16 stone, 'Sorry, mate.'

The wrestler went, 'You'd better be, mate.'

Bradley got the right hump, and said to him, 'Oh, yeah, mate, why's that then? What you going to do if I'm not?'

Bradley was all of nine stone in weight, so he was giving him at least five or six stone.

The bloke went right into his face: 'I said YOU'D BETTER BE!'

That was it, Bradley went completely berserk, and started whacking the geezer, he didn't care how big he was; he had to be pulled off him. Bradley was climbing all over this great big man mountain of a bloke, and the geezer didn't know what had hit him.

When Bradley was with Barry Hearn, I used to train him there, and there was this kid there who was a bit better than him. So, I said to Bradley, 'If he goes hard, you go hard, mate.'

Well, that was like a red rag to a bull for a kid like Bradley. As soon as the kid went for him, that was it, Bradley went completely bananas; he ended up on the floor all over the kid. Bradley was like a firework, he just couldn't be controlled, or at least I couldn't control him.

It was such a sad story what happened to him; his tough background made him what he was. What was even more sad was that, when he got the British-title shot against Richie Wenton, Bradley had recently got married and things seemed to be going well for him. Bradley was stopped in the 10th round of the fight, but seemed to be fine and left the arena looking OK. He collapsed a couple of hours later, and, two days after that, died in hospital. He was only 23 years old.

Sometimes it's hard to follow boxing when things like this happen, but sadly it's all a part of the game.

Dean Pithie was another guy I worked with as his trainer and manager; he'd been a top amateur, but, when it came to the professional fight game, I couldn't get him to spar with people. He never wanted to spar with anyone even a few pounds bigger than him. When I was fighting at flyweight, I used to spar with lightweights, light welterweights, anyone really, and they would go hard on you sometimes, and you'd have to protect yourself. To me, the fighters I was training often seemed soft, pampered. I thought it was the only way to learn the game; going in there with bigger boys taught you to defend yourself and use your speed and skills.

But I couldn't get Dean to spar with anyone who outweighed him by even a few pounds.

So, Peter Harrison phoned me up once, and he told me that he wanted to get some sparring for his son Scott who was turning pro in the near future with Frank Maloney. For once, I'd got Dean some sparring with someone smaller than himself, because Scott was a featherweight and Dean was a super featherweight. Well, let me tell you, when Scott got his gear on and started loosening up and shadow boxing, he looked like a million dollars. He was totally quiet when he came in; he never said a word to anyone, just looked dead ahead.

I said to Dean, 'Take your time, Dean, this kid looks good, watch yourself in there.'

'Nah! He don't look like nothing,' Dean said. 'He's nothing special.'

Let me tell you, that kid absolutely took Dean apart. He had absolutely everything, did everything right, and he looked world class right then and there. He was pounding him with the jab, and this was just a young guy who hadn't even turned professional yet. I went over and shook his hand after the sparring session, and said to his dad, 'I think that's a fantastic fighter you've got there.'

I remember Dean getting the right hump, but I had to be honest, Harrison looked absolutely amazing.

Sadly, Scott doesn't seem to have lived up to that potential, but, my God, he couldn't half fight! He was absolute class and Dean couldn't even get anywhere near him. As an 18-year-old, Scott Harrison looked like one of the best fighters I'd ever seen. I thought he was one fighter who was going to go to the top and stay there, but the wheels just fell off.

One of the last guys I ever worked with was Matthew Barney. I trained and managed him. He was a raw novice when I first got hold of him, but he was a fighter through and through; it was in his blood. He was from a family of travellers, and those travellers have got a reputation as being right hard men, and, let me tell you,

Matthew lived up to that. He wasn't scared of anyone; Matthew would get in the ring with absolutely anyone, he didn't care who they were.

Matthew had very little amateur background, and had only had something like 13 amateur fights. I remember I got him a sparring session against Adrian Dodson, a big-punching middleweight, who at the time was a highly regarded fighter, but he was known for going really hard in sparring, and because of that they had trouble getting him sparring partners, as nobody fancied being bashed up by him.

I told Adrian's handlers, 'I've got this kid, he's hard as nails, and he's got a punch on him like a mule kick.'

I knew what Adrian was like, and so I told Matthew, 'Listen, don't take any prisoners, mate. This Dodson bloke, he's come here to knock you out, mate, so don't let him take the piss out of you.'

Matthew winked at me as he went out for the first round, and, as soon as the bell went, he grabbed hold of Adrian and started pulling him around all over the ring, and got him on the ropes and started bashing him up. He was really roughing him up. Next thing you know, Adrian Dodson got out of the ring and said, 'That's it, I've had enough of this, I'm off. He's going too hard!'

Matthew could really handle himself, despite not having a lot of amateur experience. His only problem was that a lot of his fights weren't exactly fun to watch. He had a style which made watching his fights hard work for the punters even when he won. He had some good results in his career, though, going to Germany and getting the draw against Thomas Ulrich, a genuine world-class fighter who still has the European title at light heavyweight; in my opinion, he got shafted in that fight, as I think he beat Ulrich fair and square. Then he moved up to light heavyweight and beat Toney Oakey. Matthew had a great jab, but what people didn't know was that he could really punch as well. When I took him on the pads, he used to have a great right cross; it was a really hard stiff punch. I've seen him knock people over in sparring with it, but he would never use it when it came to a real fight, I could never work it out! He got a long way with just that jab of his, but, if he'd ever shown what he had in the gym in the ring, he'd have been a great fighter; he had all the ability, but just didn't make the most of it, and to this day I don't know why. Matthew is still going now, he's fighting at cruiserweight and doing OK. I wish him well, because he was a pleasure to work with.

One character who I remember with a smile from those days is Ernie Fossey, Frank Warren's old matchmaker, who passed away in 2003. He was a really good man, a boxing man through and through, who loved the game and brought a lot to it. Having said that, he was a tough man to deal with, and could be right miserable sometimes. He was a quiet bloke and he talked through his nose because of all the fights he'd had when he was younger. Ernie used to phone me up when I was managing some fighters after I retired, asking me if I had a middleweight, a lightweight, a welterweight, whatever it was that Frank Warren needed at that time for his bill.

One time I got a call from him, he wanted to know whether or not I had a middleweight for a show that was coming up. Now he knew bloody well that I had a middleweight, because I was managing Matthew Barney at the time. I asked him, 'Who is this for?'

'I've got this kid,' he said. 'Can't punch his way out of a paper bag, Paul Bowen his name is. He's Nigel Benn's cousin. He's had nine fights and won them all, but, to be honest with you, he's no good really.'

'How many knockouts has he got?'

'Eight.'

'Eight! You're telling me this Paul Bowen's had nine fights, he's knocked eight of them out, and you expect me to believe he can't fucking punch and he's no fucking good? Who's he been fighting? Blind boxers?'

'Come on now, Charlie, stop pissing around, will you, mate? I'm being serious here, he's no good, I'm telling you. It's an eight-round fight, and we'll give you two grand for it.'

Now the truth was, a couple of thousand for an eight-rounder wasn't bad money, it wasn't that bad a purse, but I wanted more for my fighter than that.

'Now listen, Ernie, I'm telling you, I wouldn't take this fight for ten grand, mate. You want me to put my man in with someone with eight knockouts from nine fights on short notice. He's only been a professional for a year, and you want me to take a risk like that for two grand, Ernie? I'm not being funny, mate, but you can stuff your fight right up your arse.'

'I tell you what, I'll give you two-and-a-half thousand for it, Charlie, final offer.'

'I don't think my man is good enough to take this bloke on. Let me see what my bloke's looking like in training first, and I'll give you a ring back.'

Bear in mind this was the Wednesday night, and the fight was on the Saturday in Cardiff, so he'd only got a few days to train up for it. Matthew Barney, though, was the sort of bloke who was always sparring because he loved a tear-up.

I went along to Matthew's gym and asked him, 'How'd you fancy fighting Paul Bowen for a couple of grand, son?'

He went, 'Yeah! Why not?'

That's the sort of bloke that Matthew Barney was, he would really fight anyone anywhere. He would have fought King Kong on the moon if you'd paid him to do it!

Anyway, on the Thursday, I found out a little bit of information that gave me a bit of leverage. So, when Ernie phoned me back, I said to him, 'Ernie, yeah, I've thought about it, mate, and I don't reckon it's a goer! I've just found out something, Ernie. This boy of yours Paul Bowen, he's Southern Area Champion, isn't he?'

'Yeah, he is, but he's been out injured for a few months, Charlie. This is his comeback fight.'

'And you want to get him a nice easy tune-up fight, do you? No way, Ernie, no way, mate. Either this is for the Southern Area title or the deal's off.'

'You must be bloody joking, Charlie, you're taking the piss! There's no way I can get a Southern Area title fight accepted by the Board at this short notice!'

'Well, you'd better see what you can do!' I said and put the phone down on Ernie, with him still screaming in my ear.

A few hours later, he phoned me back. 'I've spoken to Frank, and he's called the Board. Apparently, they're willing to make it for Bowen's Southern Area title. You've got what you wanted, Charlie, so have we got a deal or not?'

'Well, we're talking money now then, aren't we, Ernie?'

'Awww no!' Ernie went. He wasn't happy at all.

'I want four-and-a-half grand now, Ernie, otherwise it's not happening. That's my final offer.'

'You're having a fucking laugh! I can't give you that sort of money at this notice. You're taking the right piss now, Charlie.'

'Better see what you can do then, Ernie, or we're off again.'

Matthew Barney was laughing his head off listening to Ernie going mental on the other end of the phone.

'You're up for this, aren't you, Matt?' I asked him.

'Yeah, Charlie, I'm well up for it.'

Matthew was the easiest kid to manage ever. He was only a couple of pounds overweight because, even though he didn't have a fight coming up, he was always training, always sparring, he just loved to fight, and he'd spar against heavyweights, cruiserweights, monsters, anyone. He really couldn't care less who he fought as long as he was getting paid.

Ernie phoned me back after a while. 'All right, Charlie, it's Ernie here, now this is the last time I'm calling you. You've got your Southern Area title fight, and I'm offering you £4,000. Take it or leave it.'

'OK, Ernie. What I want you to do is bring the contracts to the gym tomorrow, and we'll sign them right there. There's no way I'm getting tucked up here.'

So, when Ernie got there, I signed the contracts, and I said, 'Right, Ernie, I want you to do one last thing for me.'

'Oh no, Charlie, come on now! What is it now?'

'I just want you to split the purse into two bits; I want one bit in a cheque and the other in cash.'

Anyway, the night of the fight came, and in truth it was an awful fight, lots of grabbing, holding and the two of them throwing each other around the ring; it was a silly fight really, but I thought Matthew Barney did enough to win it. As it happened, though, it was given as a draw, which sometimes you've got to accept when you're taking on the house fighter, which Paul Bowen was. Bowen was badly marked up, he was battered and bruised all over, and my guy was hardly marked at all.

Anyway, when I came to give Matthew the money, he didn't even know about the £4,000 that I'd got him. I told him after the fight to bring his dad over to talk to me and I'd sort the money out. I showed him the cheque for £2,000, which was in my name, and gave that to him to hold, and his dad said, 'I thought it was two-and-a-half thousand, that's what you said before.'

'Well, yeah, it was, but, remember, I got this for a Southern Area title.'

'Right ...'

'Well, I got a bit more, didn't I?' With that, I showed him the £2,000 in cash.

His dad was over the moon, and he said, 'Charlie, take your 25 per cent, and take a bit more.'

The truth is, I don't think I was hard enough for the management game personally; having been a fighter myself, I didn't really like taking money from my fighters, something that other managers certainly weren't shy about in my day. I used to get tucked up by some of my fighters. One fighter, whose name I won't mention, tucked me up good and proper. I was stupid enough to get the cheques made in his name, and I got a fight for £20,000; now that was a bloody good payday, and the sod never paid me a penny. I was owed 25 per cent for getting him that fight, and I never saw a penny of it.

I wish I'd known the ropes a bit better to make a better go of management, but the truth is I found it very stressful. If I'd had some backing, a bit of money to start off with, then maybe I'd have been able to make a better go of it, but, if you haven't got the money, then you're starting off with novice fighters all the time. What you want is to have a stable of successful fighters, because that's what brings you the interest, the excitement and the joy of it all, seeing your fighters do well. When you're starting from scratch, it's bloody difficult. You don't want to have fighters who are always turning up as the opponents all the time, fighters who are expected to get beaten and are up against it. If I was going to be a manager, I wanted to be the best, but it was different to when I was fighting, when I could get in there and do the business, and decide who came out on top. As a manager, I was a little fish in a big pond, trying to make my way, and there were plenty of other bigger fish out there who wanted to keep it that way.

In the end, I just turned it all in. It was more grief than it was worth as far as I could see. Part of the reason was that, by this time, I was starting to go through a very bad patch with my ex-wife, and it all seemed too much to handle. I had two kids with her, but the marriage was right on the rocks. It had got to the point where we hardly saw or talked to each other, even though we were still together. She seemed to always be with her family, and I seemed to spend all my time on my own with my dogs. It was a horrible situation to be in, and the stress of managing fighters, and having to deal with the shark-infested waters of boxing, well, it was too much for me to handle. It's just as well too, I reckon, because in the end, I went through a really messy divorce, and there was no way I could have coped with both at the same time. I thought I was going mental just dealing with that on its own!

So, one day, I phoned up all the fighters I was managing and told them that I was turning it in. Most of them were pretty upset, and they tried to talk me in to staying on as their manager, but that was it for me. Justin Newton, Matthew Leonard, Paul Bowen and Matthew Barney; sometimes they still ask me for little bits of advice, and I'm happy to give it to them. I don't regret turning it all in, as I don't think I was ruthless enough to have really made a go of it. I did the best for my fighters, but I don't think I would ever have got rich as a manager.

One opportunity I do regret missing out on was a contract to work with Ian Darke on the Sky TV shows; I did the very first Sky show with *Matchroom*, and I did two or three shows after that, but then I turned it down because I had fighters to train. I felt I couldn't look after the interests of my fighters if I had to be in the studio while they were getting ready for a fight on the same bill, and so in the end I told Sky that I would have to back out of it. I look back on it now and wish I'd stuck with the commentary, because I think I could have made a go of that, but, well, that's life, isn't it? You make your choices in life and you've got to live with them. I might have missed out in the end by making that choice, but at the time it seemed like the right thing to do, and I felt I owed it to the fighters I was working with.

CHAPTER 41

The Queen Victoria

After my divorce in 1999, I guess you could say that the next big thing that happened to me was getting the Queen Victoria pub in Mile End. The years since retirement hadn't been great for me at all, and I had to battle against the slump that leaving boxing and a nasty divorce had put me through. I needed to find a new direction, and it kind of fell into my lap. I'd tried my hand at training and managing fighters, but it hadn't worked out and, after the break-up of my marriage, I just couldn't handle the pressure of it all any more. I needed a change. Trouble was, aside from the money I'd invested in pensions, and little bits here and there, I didn't have any money coming in, so I needed to do something fast, and what could make more sense than a pub run by an East End bloke in the East End called the Queen Vic?

It came about when I was doing a bit of demolition work, just to bring some money in. It wasn't the sort of work I wanted to be doing, but, well, you've got to earn a living, haven't you? I was at work one day, sitting down eating my sandwiches at lunchtime and I got a call from my brother Georgie, who told me that a mate of his, Kenny Bush, was looking at taking on the leases for a few boozers around the East End of London, and he'd told Kenny that I could maybe run one of them for him.

To be honest with you, I was in dire straits at the time. Money wasn't easy to come by, I was in arrears on my mortgage and I just needed a job to tide me over. The geezer said he had a couple of boozers that he had the leases for, and that he might need some help running them. I'd already run this pub called the Dundee before for a while in Bethnal Green, and so I knew it was something I could do.

So I arranged to go and meet him one day at King's Cross Station, and we came down to Mile End to have a coffee and a little chat and a look around at a couple of pubs. He showed me the Wentworth, which Kenny wanted me to take, but it was too small and I didn't know what I could do with it. So we went and looked at the pub I run now, the Victoria, in Grove Road. It was completely dead and rundown and everything, but it was a nice big boozer, with plenty of scope to be done up. So I said, 'I'll take this one.'

Kenny said, 'How the hell are you going to fill that place, mate? It's too big for you.'

'I tell you what, mate, if I can fill Wembley Arena, I reckon I fill this bloody pub up.'

My first day here, the opening night, we had no beers or anything, and I thought to myself, 'Christ, what are we going to do? I'm going to look a right wally when everyone turns up.'

I got on the blower to the geezer, and I said, 'Look, we haven't got anywhere near enough drinks in here, we need to get some in.'

He said, 'What are you going to need on the night?'

I told him we were going to need tons of stuff, as, once I knew I was taking over the pub, I phoned absolutely everyone. I had John Conteh, John H Stracey, Alan Minter, Dave Boy Green – absolutely everyone was there for my opening night. I think we did about 20 barrels of beer that night, and there were well over 200 people in the pub. It was packed to the bloody rafters! The whole garden was packed, everything.

On the opening night, I had a very special guest as well. Francis Ampfofo, who had been a bantamweight who fought around the Bethnal Green area in the 90s, called my mobile before we opened up and said, 'Charlie, it's Francis, guess who I'm driving about at the moment?

I said, 'Who's that then?'

'Azumah Nelson!'

'Shut up, mate, you're having a laugh, aren't you? How on earth would you be driving Azumah Nelson about, mate?'

'I picked him up at the airport, Charlie, he's going to the York Hall because there's a fighter down there he wants to watch tonight, so I'm bringing him down, and then he wants to come down your pub.'

'Do me a favour, Francis, go away, will you, mate? Leave me alone, mate, you're winding me up, now go away.'

With that, I put the phone down on him. I didn't believe a word of it. I told my brother Joey what Francis had said, and he said, 'Go away, will you, Charlie, as if Azumah Nelson's coming down your pub!'

So I left it at that, and later in the evening I'm standing there with Terry Marsh, when all of a sudden everyone started parting in the room, moving out of the way, and this figure strode through the crowd in a big long black leather coat, looking really smart. I looked over and bloody hell! It *is* Azumah Nelson, all the way from Ghana!

I couldn't believe my eyes. Azumah Nelson was one fighter who I thought was the absolute business; he was absolutely brilliant, one of the best Featherweight Champions ever. Nobody with any sense wanted to fight that man, and, when he was in his prime, hardly anyone was good enough to beat him. Most people reckoned Barry McGuigan avoided him for years, even with Nelson calling him all sorts, calling him a woman with a handbag and all that. He was only a little bloke, but, when I walked over and touched him on the shoulder to say hello, he was absolutely rock solid!

What a nice person he was. He came over to me and said, 'Charlie, I think you're great!'

I couldn't believe it! I said to him, '*Me* great! What about *you*, mate!?'

Azumah's so big in Ghana he's even got his own beer named after him over there called Zum-Zum or something like that. Now, to be honest with you, I was amazed that Azumah Nelson even knew who I was. I mean, I know he was a boxer and all that, but he was from Ghana, and I wondered when he'd ever seen any of my fights during his career. What I didn't realise during my career, but found out later, was that Mickey Duff used to sell the rights to my fights all over the world, for a few grand here, a few grand there. I didn't know that Azumah Nelson had been sitting home in Accra watching me fight! He was even selling them in Ghana! That's what you call good business!

Nelson is a legend in his own country, a very important man. He used to travel all over the world fighting, and when he came back, he would give money to people back home; he looked after all his people back home, he'd give his money away, it was just the sort of person he was. It was a real pleasure to meet the man, and I can honestly say what a nice bloke he was.

And what a fighter Nelson was! To show how good he was, when he was a young fighter, only a novice really, he came in as a late substitute against the great Mexican Salvador Sanchez, who was Featherweight Champion at the time. Sanchez had won the title from Wilfredo Gomez who was another Mexican legend. Sanchez died at only 24 in a car crash. He was a great fighter, and Nelson came in at a few weeks' notice and only got knocked out in the 15th round, as a young professional. Nelson gave him a right hard fight; he was the sort of fighter who was always training and so was ready, and he really made a name for himself that night. He travelled all over the world. I remember he went to Australia to fight Jeff Fenech twice, knocking him out in their rematch.

Eventually, in 2006, I took over the Victoria completely with my cousin Bernard and I've had it since then.

I have to be honest that it's not all been a smooth ride running a pub, there are a lot of things that come along with running a boozer in this day and age. You've got to contend with local drug dealers coming in and trying to set up shop in your boozer, something I had problems with, having to get rid of a whole crowd of people who are going to bring you nothing but trouble. Of course, where you've got a boozer, you've also got drunks and, where you've got drunks, you're bound to get fights from time to time; it comes with the territory, and it can be really stressful. I'm not a big drinker, never have been, and, to be honest, I don't really drink at all these days, and I don't like to hang around with people who are drinking a lot. You can't be a pisshead and run a pub; otherwise, you'll be dead before you know it. The temptation is too much. You've got to have your head screwed on, otherwise you're in trouble. When I was first running the pub, I had to work behind the bar as well, which I didn't like, because I had to listen to all the banter and people taking the piss a lot, which wasn't really my cup of tea. Nowadays, I'm not around it most of the time. Part of me would like to have a normal job where, once I close the door, it's over and I don't have to deal with anything. When you run a pub, you've got all the noise that comes with it, but having the pub allows me to put on some evenings with my pals from boxing, like Jimmy Batten and John H Stracey, John Conteh, Alan Minter, Dave Boy Green, Colin Jones and all those people. I put on little events inviting former fighters down to give talks and stuff. It's nice to be able to put those nights on and bring some of my old mates and people I know from boxing to the boozer.

I used to like doing some of the other after-dinner shows, where you'd hire a big venue and put on a big show. We had some big names down there, people like Thomas Hearns, but things didn't work out with the person I was working with, and I lost out on a lot of money I should have earned. I've always been a little bit soft, I guess, a bit too trustworthy for my own good and, as a result, people have taken the piss. After my divorce there were a few people – and they know who they are – who took advantage of me at a vulnerable time in my life, and made money off my back. I don't talk to any of them any more and I've learned my lesson.

Now, like I said, owning a pub and being a well-known boxer don't necessarily go together. As you can imagine, the combination of a bar, a bloke who used to be a professional fighter and pissed people wanting to prove something can be a bad one, and, as a result, I've had a few people trying to take liberties while I've been here.

There was this one night when two people came in when I was working behind the bar; these two big lumps were in there, and I overheard the more pissed one saying from the other side of the bar, 'I reckon I could knock him out. Look at him, he's only little, ain't he? I could give him a clump and put him over.'

His mate, who seemed like the guv'nor of the two and was less pissed than his mate, turned to him and said, 'Shut up, will you, you idiot, just shut up!'

The pissed idiot said, 'Nah, wait a minute, mate, I can knock him out.'

His mate said to me, 'I'm sorry about this, mate. Do you want me to shut him up for you?'

I said, 'Do what you like, mate, he's your mate. I'm not going to do anything.'

That was it, he turned round, clumped his mate and knocked him spark out on the floor! You don't half get some idiots sometimes when you're well known.

I've had to have a few fights in the pub because of it, because of people playing up. It's not that I wanted to, but some people just won't leave it alone. They get in your face, and they won't leave it.

One night, this fat bloke came in, bit bigger than me, with a big bald head, and he was with this Thai girl, who was much younger than him. When she went home, the bloke was there with this old Irish bloke, and he started being rude and obnoxious to people in the pub, so I was keeping an eye on him from behind the bar.

He came walking over to the bar, and he ordered a double vodka and a Smirnoff Ice, and he knocked both of them back. It was my birthday, as it happens, my 48th, I think it was, and I wasn't working that night, because I was getting ready to go for a meal. So he was leaning up beside the bar, and he started abusing this old geezer and his missus who were minding their own business at the bar. The old guy who was a regular customer came over to me and said, 'Do us a favour, Charlie, will ya, this geezer's interrupting us all the time. Have a word, will you?'

So I went over to the bloke and I said, 'I tell you what, mate, do yourself a favour, take your drinks and go and sit down over there and shut up. Don't talk to him like that, he's a good customer of mine, so, go on, do one!'

He went, 'Listen here, you little shit, don't underestimate me, 'cos I'll have you.'

I told him straight, 'Don't you underestimate *me*, mate, because I'll do you right now, no problem, mate.'

He came right up to my face, and he said, 'Oh, yeah, you reckon you can do me, mate, do you? Come on then, let's have it.'

That was it, I'd completely gone, my eyes had gone, and I said to him, 'Right, mate, you've been warned, that's it. Come on then, we'll go outside and sort this right now.'

My mate Lee was there, a big bloke about six-foot-two, and he asked me what was going on because he could see I was all steamed up, and the geezer tried to hide behind him as I was trying to get a hold of him. While he was doing that, I noticed his head was sticking out behind Lee's shoulder, so I leaned to the side and bosh! I clumped him with a left hook and knocked him out.

I called a taxi firm, and told them, 'It's Charlie Magri here at the

Victoria, we need a cab, mate, there's some bloke lying here chewing the carpet. Come and take him home.'

Lee picked the bloke up off the floor, and as he was escorting him to the cab, with his mouth all bleeding, he turned to me and said, 'Charlie … am I barred, mate?'

I said, 'Listen, mate, you're welcome back, if you want a return match, just show up next week!'

There was another geezer came in the pub once when I first took it over. I'd only been there a couple of days, it was 12 o'clock and there was nobody in the place. He walked straight over to me and said, 'Allo, mate, is Charlie about?'

I thought, 'This is a bit bloody weird,' because, well, I'm Charlie, aren't I? I was standing right there in front of the geezer, and I thought, 'How can he not recognise me?' So I said, 'Nah, mate, sorry. Charlie's not about at the moment.'

'Oh, that's a shame. What's he like to work for anyway?'

'Oh, he's all right. He has a bit of a moan and groan now and then.'

'Nah, get away! He's not like that, is he? Tell you what, mate, I'll have a word with him next time I see him. I'll give him a clump for you next time I see him and sort him out.'

'Oh, yeah? So you know Charlie well, do you, mate? Where do you know him from then?'

'Oh, I go way back. Yeah I know his mum, his brothers, his sisters; I know the whole family I do. I tell you what, when he comes back, ask him about me, and tell him Barry popped in here.'

I'd never seen this geezer before in my life, didn't know him from Adam, and here he was telling me to pass a message on to myself! He went round the pub looking at all the photographs in there, pointing at them, talking about all these times he spent with me in nightclubs, going on about how I could pull a bird, how he used to go clubbing with me and all this rubbish, and there I was stood right there beside him!

The phone went behind the bar, so I walked over to the bar and answered it, and it was one of the barmaids, telling me that she was going to be late. But I told the bloke that it was Charlie, saying he wasn't going to be down today, and the geezer made his excuses and left, and, as he left, he said, 'Remember, Barry.'

To this day I've not got a clue who that geezer was!

Another time, this geezer came in the pub one night when I was working, walked over to me and said, 'Allo there, Charlie, cor, I've seen all your fights I have, tremendous stuff!'

I said, 'Oh yeah, mate, which ones? York Hall, Albert Hall, Wembley?'

'No!' he said. 'All in here, mate, I've seen the lot of 'em.'

I couldn't stop laughing, but the thing was, he meant it! There are some silly people around.

CHAPTER 42
Looking Back

Sometimes, when I've got a moment to myself, I go to a room in the house above the pub which is full of boxing memorabilia. In there, I've got all the cases with my boxing stuff in. Like most boxers, I guess, I'm pretty sentimental about that sort of thing, all the little trophies you won as a young schoolboy amateur, the programmes that you kept from all those club shows and stuff. Every single one of those things is full of memories, it means something to you, it's part of your life that's gone now, but it stays with you forever; it made you what you were, what you are. Sometimes, I get the cases out, and I sit and I look at all those things, all those memories, and especially the belts I won as a fighter. The Lonsdale belt, which is absolutely lovely, the European belt and my WBC title belt.

Looking at those title belts I won during my career gives me a special feeling, each belt, each trophy, they're like a little moment in time. I can remember where I was and the moment when they put a belt around my waist or handed me a trophy. All fighters are proud of everything they've won, even the little trophies they would have won as a schoolboy boxer. All of those things are something to mark what you did as a fighter, whether it's at amateur or professional level, something you can actually touch and hold which is a reminder of your life in boxing; moments in your career which you can never forget, when your arm was raised above your head, when you were a winner, a champion, when you were on top. Life outside the ring can be a lot harder, a lot more complicated, and you can't always make things turn your way, but, in the ring, when you were on top, you were the guv'nor, when it was all in your hands. In a way, I suppose, life's a lot simpler in the boxing ring than out of it.

The Lonsdale belt, in particular, well, that is something really special. You ask any boxer, at least in this country, and they will tell you that it's the most beautiful boxing belt in the world. Unlike any other belt out there, you only get to keep the Lonsdale belt if you defend your title. If you win a world title, you get to keep the belt. With the Lonsdale belt, you used to have to defend it twice, but now it's three times before you get to keep it. It's made from gold and porcelain, and it costs a bomb to make, and when they put it around your waist it weighs a ton, and feels really solid; it's a beautiful thing.

I got to keep one, but, funnily enough, I never got to defend my title, but I still got to keep it. It wasn't my fault; the problem was that I never really had any worthy challengers at my weight, because I was too good for the British flyweights out there. I'd cleaned them out as an amateur, and as a professional I didn't really have any competition. And so, after defending the European title all those times, they just gave me the Lonsdale belt outright, as I'd not had a chance to defend it against anyone. I was at that time the only fighter, as far as I know, to be given the belt outright without ever having to defend it.

Another item in my collection which is a bit special to me is the WBC ring I got after winning the world title. I think they stopped doing them after I was presented with mine. It's really big and made of gold, with loads of yellow and green jewels in it. Funnily enough, one day there was a massive punch-up that broke out in my pub, and the police came round and said to me, 'We know it's you, Magri.'

I said, 'It weren't me, and there's no bloody way you can prove it either.'

'Oh, yeah, Magri, well, how come that one of the geezers who got a clump has got "WBC" printed backwards on his head?'

Actually, I made that bit up! But I tell you what, it would've left a right dent on someone's face if you were wearing it when you clumped them one!

I waited quite a while to get that ring. Not long after I won the world title, the WBC had their annual convention in Seville in Spain. They invited a few of us British Champions over – John Conteh, Ken Buchanan and myself, as we were all either former or current WBC Champions.

While I was there, I happened to get talking to the president of the WBC, Jose Sulaiman, who is still the president now all these years later. Jose came over to me, and he said, 'Did you know, Charlie, that you were the last person we gave that ring to when you won your title?'

I said, 'What ring?'

'The ring, Charlie, the WBC ring that we used to give to all our champions.'

'I never got no ring, Jose.'

Now I don't know where that ring went, but, if it was given over by the WBC, I have my suspicions that someone's had it away, because I never got it.

I said to Jose, 'I don't know what's happened to this ring you're on about, Jose, but I'm telling you now that I never received it, and, if someone's had it away with it, then I think that's bang out of order. Because that's part of what I'm owed.'

So, in the end, I had to go back and forward, sending faxes to the WBC, asking for this ring I was owed. It went on for months and months, and in the end Mickey Vann was on a title-fight assignment in Mexico, and Jose Sulaiman arranged to have a WBC official meet Mickey at the fight, and hand the ring to him. Then, at a show some time later, Mickey presented it to me in the ring.

It's been a funny experience for me, sitting down and thinking about my own life, and writing this book. It has made me look back on my life in boxing, and really, for me, a lot of my life was boxing. I was someone who lived for boxing so much that I think really it made me a bit of a loner. Boxing suited me, because I was someone who thrived on the challenge, and wanted to do it alone. All those long days in the gyms, and long sleepless nights, running in the middle of the night because I couldn't sleep, it was an obsession, something which totally overtook every aspect of my life. Everything else almost didn't exist for me. I didn't realise it at the time, but now I can see, from a distance, that I really was too obsessed with it in a way to really enjoy it. I'm older and wiser now, and there's a lot of things I'd like to have done differently, but, well, I guess we can all say that, and what's done is done. I've got no regrets really.

Looking back over my career, I'd have to say that boxing really is a hard old life, there's a lot of knockbacks and disappointments, a lot of things which you wish had gone differently. I've also got to say, though, that, as well as being a hard life, it's an interesting one. Yeah, there are loads of sad moments, but there are also loads of good moments, the roar of the people in the crowd chanting my name over and over again: 'Charl-eee, Charl-eee, Charl-eee' is something I'll never forget, I can still hear it now. Being known was a buzz; it was lovely that people knew who I was, and followed my career, it made me feel like a superstar in my own way, and who wouldn't like to have that feeling?

One of the big downsides with boxing, for me anyway, was that you never knew what was going on. I was always kept in the dark about the business end of things. I don't know whether it was like that for everyone, but I think it was probably the way things were in that era: fighters fought, managers managed, and promoters promoted. You got in the ring and did the business, but the business, so to speak, was left to your manager and your promoter. You didn't have a say in things; on who, when and where you fought, or on how much you were earning. The problem with that is that, when your career is all over, and you look at what you're left with from the money you earned, you end up feeling like you've been used.

I wish I had the head on me then that I have now, because I would have stood up for myself a lot more. I was too much of a soft touch, I think, too ready to let other people run my career. I could have left Terry Lawless when I was unhappy, but I stayed out of loyalty and because I'd spent so long with him. There were so many times that I can remember before a fight, when I'd be training, and I would think to myself, 'How much am I going to get for the fight?' I'd wander over near the office and hang around by the door, and I'd think, 'I'm going to find out what I'm getting for this next fight.'

Then Terry would look over and say, 'Is there a problem, son?'

I'd say, 'Nah, nah, no problem, Terry.'

The truth was I was scared to ask! I was scared of asking the man. I had no reason to be scared of him; after all, he should have been working for me. I should have taken the attitude that he was there to do things for me, not the other way around. Today fighters are cottoning on to the fact that their managers and promoters are there to make the most money for them, not the other way around.

I used to keep looking over while I was training and I'd think over and over again, 'I should go and ask him,' but I never did. It used to really cut me up inside that I was fighting but I had no control over anything at all. I'd get in the ring and have a right hard fight, get all bumped and bruised up, and, over the years, it built up, until, by the end of it, I hated the whole business. When I finally quit boxing, I was disgusted with the whole thing.

On the rare occasion that Terry would tell me what I was getting, I never seemed to get the money I was promised. Truth was, I'd have loved that man if he'd told me the truth. I felt that was naughty, and it messed my brain up. Terry was like a second dad to me and I totally relied on him and trusted him, but, at the end of the day, you come out of it feeling like you've been tucked up. But that's the boxing game for you. Jimmy Graham had warned me all those years ago about that, and the truth is he was right.

The simple fact is that, whatever managers or promoters might say, without fighters they can't get the money; they can't get big fights without you. It's sad because you don't have a say, just 'Do as you're told, and get on with it.'

At the end of the day, I did my best. I won everything as an amateur that I wanted to win, except for the Olympics. I won the British title, the European and the WBC world title, and not a lot of fighters get to say that. My head was filled with loads of ideas, but, at the end of the day, I felt I never made as much money as I should have, considering the career I had and how many tickets I sold. Not enough to show for all that hard work and punches in the ring. All I wanted to do was fight and win; money didn't bother me, but it should have. I can remember my pal Sylvester Mittee asking me how much I got for my first fight. Jimmy Batten was fighting for the British title; I was second top of the bill, in an eight-rounder, and Sylvester had fought on the bill in a six-rounder, but me and Sylvester got the same money for that bill!

I will say this for Terry, though, he did give me some good advice that stood me in good stead later on. He always advised me to bank money and put it into pensions, which is something that more fighters should have done. I had money put away that I couldn't spend. It didn't mean I was rich when I retired, but I wasn't left with nothing like so many boxers are. Look at someone like Mike Tyson, who earned more money than any other boxer in history, and he's bankrupt! You wonder how that could happen to someone who has earned over $100,000,000, but when you're not in control of your money, or yourself, it can happen. Being a fighter, you always think there's another payday around the corner, and you're used to getting big lumps of money, but then, one day, all of a sudden, it's all gone.

I look at someone like Audley Harrison, who has made a packet off the back of his Olympic gold. I know that Audley Harrison won an Olympic gold, but I won the ABAs six times, I went to the Olympics and I won 28 times as an international. I did this and did that, but Audley made more money in his career, just off the back of that gold medal, than I did in 10 years as a top-level fighter. I was British, European and World Champion! In fact, Audley made more from his first deal with the BBC, when he got a cheque for a million pounds, than I did in my entire career, including three world-title fights, seven defences of the European title, the British title and countless top-of-the-bill appearances at the biggest venues in the country. I reckon I probably earned about £200,000 in my career, which might sound a lot, but, when you consider that's over nearly 10 years, and how many big shows I sold out, then, even for those times, £200,000 doesn't seem that much money to me. I reckon, even with the difference in the value of money between now and then, he still out-earned me!

Audley has taken a lot of flak for the way his career has gone, but, you know what, as a former fighter myself, I think, 'Good luck to him.' You might not expect me to say that, but I know better than anyone that you have to get what you can from this sport, because there are no guarantees and you never know when it's all going to be over. At 30, most people would think of themselves as a young man, but, for me, I was an ex-boxer with no trade and, as far as I could see, no future. That's a hard thing to take. I look at people like Frank Bruno, who has had a really hard time since he left boxing behind. Audley might be taking the knocks from people now, but he's a smart man who made a lot of money out of boxing and I respect anyone who can make a good living from boxing, because it's a nasty, vicious business where you're either in control, or you get the thin end of things.

I'm so glad I'm sitting back now and looking back at it like I am. I've been blessed really in many ways. I've got my health, and I've still got all my marbles, so I've got a lot to be thankful for. Especially when I think of people I came up with who weren't so fortunate, people like poor old Johnny Owen who paid the ultimate price, or Bradley Stone who died so young when he had so much to look forward to and a young wife. Plenty of other former fighters from my era or fighters I've worked with have either suffered terrible injuries or died. Rod Douglas who came up with me as an amateur, Michael Watson, Paul Ingle, Spencer Oliver. I'm one of the lucky ones.

Some of the other guys I came up with aren't in such good health any more and it's sad to see, and a reminder of just how dangerous the fight game is, and how lucky I've been to come out of it intact. Many others have wound up without much to show for their careers, and, while I'm not a rich man, I've managed to get by OK after boxing. I've got a name that I've been able to trade on, which has allowed me to make money from after-dinner speaking and other events, and I've got my reputation and my career to look back on, which nobody can take away from me, nobody.

I'll tell you honestly, there were times during my career when I used to hate boxing, hate fighting, hate training. Other times I loved it, but the endless grind of being in the gym I guess got to me after a while. When I was fighting, I think a lot of the time I used to feel so miserable. People would talk to me and they must have thought, 'What a miserable sod that Charlie Magri is.' It's not you really, you're a nice person, but the life of a fighter can make you really mean-spirited. I guess the whole regime around boxing makes you feel like that, all the training and the weeks and weeks of waiting around. The whole thing is geared towards making you feel mean and spiteful, because you've got to have that spiteful streak in you in the ring, otherwise you aren't going to come out on top.

To be honest with you, I realise now that part of the reason boxing suited me was that I was a bit of a loner. I wasn't the sort to really hang out in nightclubs or go around living it up. I think that really I didn't have many proper friends; there were plenty of people I was friendly with in boxing, but I was always distant from people deep down. My only friends back then were my family, because those were the people I could trust. I guess I was a bit antisocial in some ways. I had my boxing and that was such a big part of my life that I didn't worry about a lot else; I pushed other things to one side. There were loads of hangers-on around in those days, people who wanted to be around you because you were Charlie Magri, the British, European and World Champion, who were there when the good times were rolling. When I was struggling, though, when I needed people around me, they weren't there. I couldn't even name half of them now, I don't even remember who most of them were, and they're long gone, gone with my career and all the publicity I got back then.

One of my biggest regrets that I always carry with me, one thing I can never forget, is that, during my career, I pushed my father away. My dad wanted to look out for me; he used to ask me to let him get involved in negotiations with Terry Lawless, and, at the time I felt slightly embarrassed; my dad's English wasn't that great, and he had a bit of an accent, and I didn't think he would understand the business. I'm ashamed to say I was a little embarrassed. It must have hurt him that his own son didn't want him involved in his career in any way, and I realise now that he was giving me good advice, that I needed someone there with me to help make deals with my management to make sure I got the best out of it. I was young, though, and I thought that everything would work out for the best. How I wish now that I'd let my dad get involved in it. I hurt his feelings badly, I think, because he was a proud man, and he was just trying to do his best for me. My dad was the sort of bloke who spoke his mind, and didn't take any shit from anyone. The truth of the matter is he would have spoken up for me in a way that I didn't speak up for myself, whether he understood the business or not.

With other people in the gym, it was a different matter, because they were grown men who knew more about the business side of things. Jim Watt, for instance, had his head screwed on. Terry Lawless and Mickey Duff worked for him, not the other way around. Jim would pretty much run his own ship up in Scotland, where most of his fights were, and Terry and Mickey would take their cut. I know a lot of promoters and managers would disagree with this, but this is the way it should be. The fighter is the one doing the business in there after all, and they are the ones who should be in control of things. The trouble is that a lot of fighters aren't from the kind of backgrounds where they are well educated and know about the world of business, and so, in a lot of cases, it's easy for people to take advantage of them. That's not to say that promoters or managers are all bad, but I sometimes felt like I didn't get what I was due.

Despite everything I might have said against boxing, I still love the game, and I still follow the sport. My hero when I was a young amateur starting out was Ruben Olivares, and of today's fighters my favourites are probably Ricky Hatton and Manny Pacquiao. Pacquiao for me has got to be the best fighter in the world. It's not just that he's won a lot of big fights; it's the way he's done it. He goes out there to take his opponents apart and I like to see that in a fighter, because that's what I always wanted to do in the ring, get in there and do the business.

I like fighters who go out there and challenge the world, who want to go out there and prove themselves. I think today Ricky Hatton is the kind of fighter who thinks like that, who wants a challenge. He's got the right attitude. It's taken a while, but now, as I write this, he's getting ready to challenge Floyd Mayweather. Who knows how that's going to turn out? Personally, I think

Floyd's arse is going to go when he feels how strong and relentless Ricky is in there. I don't think he will have ever faced anything like it, but the point is we'll find out one way or the other, because Ricky has gone looking for the fight; it won't be one of those 'Oh I wonder what would have happened if they fought?'

The only thing that worries me about Ricky is the way he lets himself go between fights. I wish him all the best, I really do, but I know just how hard this business is, and bloating up like that and losing weight is bad for your body, and, if you're drying out every time to make weight, the chances are that one day it'll catch up to you.

Ricky, though, unlike me, had the bottle to change manager to get what he wanted, which in his case was more money; he wanted to get the most that was on offer, and fair play to him, you're a long time retired, and you'd better get what you can while you're fighting. I didn't have that sort of bottle. I didn't want to leave Terry Lawless. I always felt that Terry and his partners, like Mickey Duff, could have helped me a bit more. Of course, you need good promoters and managers in the boxing business to get to the top, but it's you in there doing the fighting and taking the punches, and people should remember that when they think about fighters. It's not them who walks away with a black eye and cut mouth, or pissing blood in the middle of the night; it's you who gets hurt.

To any young fighter today out there who is fighting as an amateur, and who thinks they're good, I would say, Good luck to you. If you think you're good, go out there and do your best and prove it; don't listen to what anyone else says, and, if you can walk the walk and make the best of it, make as much money as you can from the game. Get some bloody good advice, get yourself an accountant and someone to advise you on money matters if you start making some good coin, because, believe me, the money won't always be there, and you never know when it's going to come to an end.

When I've thought about it, writing this book, I realise now that my happiest times in boxing were as that young amateur, on his way to his first titles, winning the NABC title, then the Junior ABA, and getting picked to represent England for the first time. I realise now that those times were magical, something you could never replace, because it was all just one big adventure, something you did for the love of it all, for the love of competing and winning, nothing more. I didn't have to worry about anything else but the boxing, no commitments, no business side of things to ruin it.

Looking back, the more I think about it, I think I've been bloody lucky to have done what I've done with my career and, despite all the hard knocks, with my life. I've been to so many places and done so many things that most people can only dream about, and, let's be honest, how many people get to be good enough to do something they love doing and make a living at it? Not many, and I was lucky enough, and good enough of course, to do that. It's all been one big rollercoaster ride, for this young lad who came over on a boat to the East End of London at 18 months, and, for a little while, for one moment, got to be king of the world.

CHAPTER 43

Seconds Out – The Next Round

So, that's me, Charlie Magri, and that's the story so far, but, of course, it's not the end of my story. I'm 51 years old now, and my boxing career is long behind me, but my life's not over, not by a long chalk. There's plenty of life left in this old dog.

It's only in the last few years that I think I've finally accepted life after boxing. I've done everything I wanted to do in boxing, and, now, there's a new door opening up to me, a new life. It's taken a long time, but I can look forward now instead of backwards. I couldn't accept my life without boxing; I didn't like my life any more. Suddenly I was off in the world on my own. I retired from boxing and then I got divorced, and I was just drifting along. A big door opens up in front of you, and you don't know what's on the other side, and it's frightening. I guess some of that determination that made me a successful fighter helped me to find the strength to carry on and find a new way in life. It's all down to you; nobody can do it for you. As soon as you finish boxing, you find out the hard way who your friends are.

I'd be lying if I said it hasn't been a long hard journey to find a purpose to life after boxing, as it's been a real hard slog to be honest, but it's the same for all us ex-fighters, and the more successful you've been, in some ways, the harder it is to live life after boxing. Then again, I wonder what it's like for those fighters who never got where they wanted to go in their career; it must hurt, because I know how badly I wanted to win all the time, and I'm sure it's the same for all of us.

I've got a lot to look back on to be happy about, and I take comfort from that. When I started out, I would never have dreamed that I would have been a British Champion, let alone European and World Champion. I always felt I was good enough to do everything I tried for, but you don't know how things are going to work out, do you?

I struggled really badly for many years after boxing. I didn't know who or what I was any more. Before I'd been Charlie Magri the boxer, Charlie Magri the British and World Champion, now, I was just Charlie Magri, and that's a hard thing to accept. All the buzz goes out of life when you leave boxing, and it takes a strong man to find something to replace that buzz. I've been lucky, I've been able to find something which kind of replaces it, in doing boxing events and giving talks, bringing other fighters into it, people I came up with, like Alan Minter, John Conteh, Dave Boy Green, Jimmy Batten, John L Gardner, Jimmy McDonnell, all those people; it sort of makes it feel a bit like the old days. It's a bit like reaching out and touching it all again.

Of course, it's not the same; nothing compares to that feeling of being up there in the ring and listening to the roar and noise, to that feeling of sickness in the stomach, the excitement and the adrenalin that rushes through you as you climb the steps to the ring, but it's a reminder of those days. Even now I get little touches, little things that happen which remind me of my career and what I did. People still stop me in the street sometimes, and say, 'You're Charlie Magri!' It's a nice feeling to be remembered, that people saw or heard about what you did, a lovely feeling.

I've been through some horrible things in recent times. A nasty divorce, which spoiled things between me and my children, Emma and Charlie Junior, which has really been hard on me, something I've not really talked about here, and is best left as it is, a private matter. And I don't want to badmouth anyone or sling any dirt around. I had to deal with the death of my mum and dad, God bless them. Dad died in 1986, and Mum died in 2005, she was 78 years old, and she was buried in the cemetery at St Patrick's Church in Leyton. I was lucky that neither of them really suffered much; there was no long illness so they didn't have to be in pain for ages or anything like that, but, of course, it hurts when your parents pass away. Mum was always praying for me, God bless her, and I know that Dad was really proud of me and what I did, and they both did a good job in raising such a big family. All in all, it's been a lot to deal with, but luckily I've had a big family to fall back on to help me through these times, and I'm grateful for that.

Another sad event for me was the death of Jimmy Graham, my old amateur gaffer, who really, in all honesty, taught me most of what I learned about fighting. I owe almost everything I learned to Jimmy who, I think, was the unsung hero of my career.

I'd heard that Jimmy was seriously ill, and I went to visit him at Bart's Hospital. It was very sad, as he was dying, and he knew it, and he was lying there on his deathbed when I went to see him. I tell you what, he was in a very bad way, and in a hell of a lot of pain. I walked in there and said to him, 'Hello. Jimmy.'

He said, 'Hello, Charlie. Cor, it ain't half good to see you.'

He smiled when he saw me, despite the pain he was in. He started going back over all the old times, remembering all these different things from when I was 13 and 14 years old and we talked about the years when he was training me as an amateur. I could see it made him feel better, for a moment anyway, to go over those old times, and it was lovely talking about those days, because they were some of the best times of my life.

I sat and talked to him for about an hour, and then I had to go upstairs, because, as it happens, I was ill myself and I had to go into hospital to be treated. I never spoke to him after that, because he died that same night, but I was so glad I'd got to see him before he died, because that man was the one who really took an interest in my career and turned me into a champion. It was him who saw that spark in me and wanted to make sure that my talent came through. Funnily enough, that night I finally found out a secret about Jimmy, something that all of us at the Arbour Youth used to wonder about. We never could tell just how old he was. For some reason, he'd always kept his age a secret around the boys at the club, and nobody knew how old he was. When I was in the hospital sitting beside him at his bedside, I caught a glimpse of his wristband, which of course had his date of birth on it. He was 85 when he died. He was a great bloke Jimmy Graham, a very kind man who meant the world to me as a young man learning his trade in the sport. I owe an awful lot to him, because he made me the fighter I was, and allowed me to achieve all the things I did, and see all the things I got to see as a result. Looking back, I can see now why Jimmy Graham was against the professional fight game, because it is such a hard world, and it can leave a bitter taste in your mouth.

Like they always say, though, where there's life there's hope, and you never know what's around the corner. About a year-and-a-half ago now, something happened quite out of the blue that I would never have expected, which was meeting my partner Tina.

I suppose you could say it's a little bit like something out of a film what happened with me and Tina, a bit of a love story if you like. Believe it or not, I'd known Tina since we both went to the same primary school as young kids. Not only that, we grew up in the same area, and our families even knew one another. My mum knew her mum from the church, and Tina's mum worked with my auntie at the hospital. We were friends all through school, and I can remember having a bit of a crush on her, to be honest with you, but, well, when you're a young kid, you forget about that later in life. We always got along well, but our lives went in different directions. We went our separate ways, though, and kind of lost touch. I'd gone on and got married and Tina had been married as well.

Years and years later, probably 15 years ago, I was at some Krays-organised dinner show I'd been invited to, and I ran into Tina. We hadn't seen each other in years, and we said hello to each other and had a little chat, and that was that really, we didn't see each other again. The years passed, and me and Tina lost touch again, and I never thought much about it after that. In the meantime, I got divorced from my wife, and I took over the Victoria. Then, one day, out of the blue, I got a phone call from Tina. She was calling me from her house in Canvey Island, and she was feeling upset and needed someone to talk to, and, well, I'd known her all those years and I was glad to talk to her. It turned out that Tina's husband had died in the years since, and like me she was on her own. She'd been seeing someone a couple of years after her husband died, and that hadn't worked out and she was going through a rough patch. I told Tina we should meet up and have a chat, as we hadn't seen each other for years, and we arranged to meet the next day. So we had a drink and a chat, and, what do you know, one thing led to another, and we're together now. We were both lonely, I suppose, when we met, and we'd both been through hard times in recent years.

It was so unexpected, and yet I suppose in a way, it's not that surprising, is it? Me and Tina, we've known each other forever really, and she knows me about as well as anyone, and, well, we always got on like a house on fire. It all seemed so easy when we were in each other's company. I know I can trust Tina because we've known each other since we were just little kids. It's nice after all the trouble I've had over the last few years to meet someone I can be with and be happy with, someone who understands me. Nobody wants to be alone, do they? Especially as you get older, you really appreciate how important it is to be around someone who makes you feel good about life. I've been lucky to find that when I least expected it. Me, Tina and my dog Sonny, we're a happy little family.

Another thing happened recently to me which made me really happy. I went along to a fundraiser recently at the Birmingham International Centre for the British Boxing Hall of Fame, set up by a guy called Ray Caulfield, who heads the LEBA. As I'm one of the vice-presidents of the LEBA, he asked me to come along. What a great day that was! It was terrific standing with all these other fantastic British fighters from the past – Henry Cooper, Dave Boy Green, Jimmy Batten, Ken Buchanan, John Conteh, John H Stracey, Clinton McKenzie, Duke McKenzie, Pat Clinton, Floyd Havard, James Cook, you name it, they were there! There were loads and loads of British fighters there, former British, European and World Champions, more than I could even hope to remember. There were over 1,000 people there, and it was reckoned to be the biggest gathering of British ex-boxers ever anywhere, and it was a cracking night. What a lovely feeling it was to be a part of that, to be a part of boxing, and of this country. When you've been a fighter, things like that mean a lot to you. What I did may be a long time ago now, but I guess your reputation and what you achieved lives forever, doesn't it?

The tickets were a couple of hundred quid each so you can bet that a tidy sum was raised on the night.

It's great to be involved with something like that, and hopefully one day I can stand there in the British Boxing Hall of Fame, and maybe even see myself in there. It'll be good anyway to give something back to boxing, because, whatever I've said, I know boxing gave me a hell of a lot. I still love boxing and I always will. It's about time we had our own boxing hall of fame in this bloody country; I'm amazed nobody got around to doing it before. I can't wait to be involved in it all.

So there's still plenty left for Charlie Magri to do. I ain't finished yet, not by a long chalk, and I've come to terms with looking life after boxing straight in the eye. I've got that spring back in my step again, and I'm looking forward to life. The main thing for me is that now, finally, I can wake up in the morning and look straight in the mirror and be happy being who I am, Charlie Magri.

Charlie Magri
Professional Boxing Career Record

1977	Oct 25 Nov 15 Dec 6	Neil McLaughlin Bryn Griffiths David Smith (*Wins British Flyweight Title*)	Kensington, England KO 2 Bethnal, England KO 2 Kensington, England KO 7
1978	Feb 21 Apr 4 Apr 25 Sep 12 Oct 24 Dec 5	Nessim Zebelini Dominique Cesari Manuel Carrasco Sabatino De Filippo Claudio Tanda Mariano Garcia	Kensington, England KO 3 Kensington, England KO 4 Kensington, England W 8 London, England KO 7 Kensington, England KO 1 Kensington, England KO 3
1979	Jan 23 Feb 20 May1 May 29 Sep 25 Oct 23 Dec 4	Filippo Belvedere Mike Stuart Franco Udella (*Wins European Flyweight Title*) Fred Gonzalez Ray Pacheco Candelario Iglesias Manuel Carrasco (*Retains European Flyweight Title*)	Kensington, England KO 1 Kensington, England KO 3 Wembley, England W 12 Kensington, England KO 3 London KO 6 London KO 3 London W12
1980	Jan 22 Jun 28 Sep 16 Oct 14 Dec 8	Aniceto Vargas Giovannai Camputaro (*Retains European Flyweight Title*) Alfonso Lopez Enrique Castro Santos Laciar	Kensington, England KO 3 London KO 3 London W10 London KO 1 London W 10
1981	Feb 24 Jun 20 Oct 13	Enrique Rodriquez Cal (*Retains European Flyweight Title*) Jose Herrera Juan Diaz	London KO 2 London KO 1 Kensington, England KO by 6
1982	Mar 2 Apr 20 May 4 Sep 18 Nov 23	Cipriano Arreola Ron Cisneros Jose Torres Enrique Rodriquez Cal (*Retains European Flyweight Title*) Jose Torres (*Retains European Flyweight Title*)	Kensington, England W 10 Kensington, England KO 3 Wembley, England KO by 9 Aviles, Spain KO 2 Wembley, England W 10
1983 1984	Mar 15 Sep 27 Aug 24	Eleoncio Mercedes (*Wins WBG and World Flyweight Title*) *Relinquishes European Flyweight Title* Frank Cedeno (*Loses World Flyweight Title*) Franco Cherchi (*Regains European Flyweight Title*)	London KO 7 London KO by 6 Cagliari, Italy KO 1
1985	 Feb 20 Oct 30	*Relinquishes European Flyweight Title* Sot Chitalada (*For WBC and World Flyweight Titles*) Franco Cherchi (*Regains European Flyweight Title*)	 London KO by 5 Allesandria, Italy KO 2
1986	May 20	Duke McKenzie (*For British Flyweight Title,* *loses European Flyweight Title*)	Wembley, England KO by 5